Strategies for
Closing the
LEARNING GAP

WEEK LOAN

Mike Hughes
with Andy Vass

First Published by
Network Educational Press Ltd
PO Box 635
Stafford ST16 1BF
www.networkpress.co.uk

First published 2001
Reprinted 2003, 2005
© Mike Hughes 2001

ISBN-13: 978 1 85539 075 1
ISBN-10:   1 85539 075 2

Edited by Gina Walker
Design & layout by Neil Hawkins, Network Educational Press Ltd.
Illustrations by Barking Dog Art, Stroud, Glos.

Printed in Great Britain by MPG Books Ltd., Bodmin, Cornwall

Acknowledgements

There are many people who have contributed directly and indirectly to the writing of this book. Not least, the countless teachers and even more students who, over many years, have both challenged and shaped my thinking, influencing my personal approach in the classroom and the collection of strategies that can be found in this book.

In particular, I wish to thank:

- Andy Vass for agreeing to contribute to the section on state. His insight and expertise have added a different dimension to the book and I am sure that teachers will find his ideas and strategies as useful and effective in the classroom as I did. You know that something is making a difference, when a 4 year old says, '*maybe* it is time to go to bed Dad, *and* I'll be up just as soon as Thunderbirds finishes!' (see page 111);

- Clayton Hughes, Mike Davis, Jane Steer & David Grikis for sharing their strategies and allowing me to reproduce them;

- Chris Dickenson, Jim Houghton, Paul Bordeux and David Potter for their personal and professional support during the last few years;

- My ex geography teacher, who taught me so much;

- The Davids, Stephanies, Adams and Gregs who have helped make the last 18 years so rewarding;

- Gina Walker and Debbie Pullinger for their professional advice and personal encouragement during the editing stage;

- Rachel, Ben and Sam for once again putting up with so much.

The author and publisher gratefully acknowledge the following for permission to reproduce material: the results of the Action Research project (page 140) and French song (page 256) by permission of Clayton Hughes at Denbigh High School, Milton Keynes.

Foreword

A teacher's task is much more ambitious than it used to be and demands a focus on the subtleties of teaching and learning and on the emerging knowledge of school improvement.

Teaching can be a very lonely activity. The time-honoured practice of a single teacher working alone in the classroom is still the norm; yet to operate alone is, in the end, to become isolated and impoverished. This book addresses two issues – the need to focus on practical and useful ideas connected with teaching and learning and the wish thereby to provide some sort of an antidote to the loneliness of the long distance teacher who is daily berated by an anxious society.

Teachers flourish best when, in key stage teams or departments (or more rarely whole schools), their talk is predominantly about teaching and learning and where, unconnected with appraisal, they are privileged to observe each other teach; to plan and review their work together; and to practise the habit of learning from each other new teaching techniques. But how does this state of affairs arise? Is it to do with the way staffrooms are physically organized so that the walls bear testimony to interesting articles and in the corner there is a dedicated computer tuned to 'conferences' about SEN, school improvement, the teaching of English, and so on, and whether, in consequence, the teacher leaning over the shoulder of the enthusiastic IT colleagues sees the promise of interesting practice elsewhere? Has the primary school cracked it when it organizes successive staff meetings in different classrooms and invites the 'host' teacher to start the meeting with a 15-minute exposition of their classroom organization and management? Or is it the same staff sharing, on a rota basis, a slot on successive staff meeting agendas when each in turn reviews a new book they have used with their class? And what of the whole school which now uses 'active' and 'passive' concerts of carefully chosen music as part of their accelerated learning techniques?

It is of course well understood that even excellent teachers feel threatened when first they are observed. Hence the epidemic of trauma associated with Ofsted. The constant observation of the teacher in training seems like that of the learner driver. Once you have passed your test and can drive unaccompanied, you do. You often make lots of mistakes and sometimes get into bad habits. Woe betide, however, the back seat driver who tells you so. In the same way the new teacher quickly loses the habit of observing others and being observed. So how do we get a confident, mutual observation debate going? One school I know found a simple and therefore brilliant solution. The Head of the History Department asked that a young colleague plan lessons for her – the Head of Department – to teach. This lesson she then taught and was observed by the young colleague. The subsequent discussion, in which the young teacher asked,

> *"Why did you divert the question and answer session I had planned?"*
and was answered by,
> *"Because I could see that I needed to arrest the attention of the group by the window with some hands on role play, and so on."*

lasted an hour and led to a once-a-term repeat discussion which, in the end, was adopted by the whole school. The whole school subsequently changed the pattern of its meetings to consolidate extended debate about teaching and learning. The two teachers claimed that because one planned and the other taught both were implicated but neither alone was responsible or felt 'got at'.

So there are practices which are both practical and more likely to make teaching a rewarding and successful activity. They can, as it were, increase the likelihood of a teacher surprising the pupils into understanding or doing something they did not think they could do rather than simply entertaining them or worse still occupying them. There are ways of helping teachers judge the best method of getting pupil expectation just ahead of self-esteem.

This book focuses on straightforward interventions which individual schools and teachers use to make life more rewarding for themselves and those they teach. Teachers deserve nothing less for they are the architects of tomorrow's society and society's ambition for what they achieve increases as each year passes.

Professor Tim Brighouse

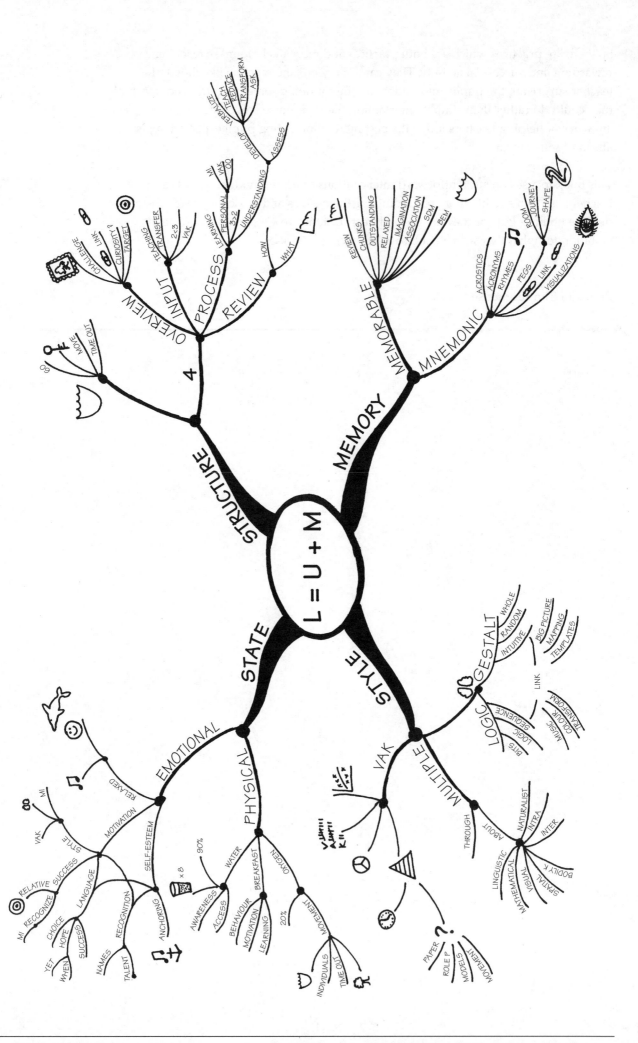

Contents

The tools are here. The time is now. The script is yours to write – or dance, or sing, or play, or act, or draw, or orchestrate. Welcome to tomorrow.

Gordon Dryden and Jeannette Vos
The Learning Revolution

Introduction

I had a dream recently in which I was a doctor telling a patient that there was nothing more that could be done for him. He was astounded when I told him that in fact there were techniques and strategies that could help him a great deal but that no one in the profession used them, most doctors simply prescribing leeches. I confirmed that, in normal circumstances, if the leeches were not having any effect then more leeches would be prescribed.

I went on to explain to him that as our understanding of the human body had developed and techniques and strategies had evolved to build upon this new knowledge, there was a fear that any advances in methodology and the abandonment of the leech would lead to a decline in standards. I went on to explain that doctors were being placed under increasing pressure to achieve results, with ever more outrageous targets being imposed upon them and that, in the opinion of the Chief Medical Inspector at least, the best way to achieve them was to prescribe more and more leeches. I defended my position by explaining that the motive for such a strategy, as it always had been, was to reduce suffering and prolong human life. Strangely, this failed to appease him.

In a second, separate, yet strangely related dream, I was a teacher telling a young child that there was nothing more that could be done to help him. He too was astounded when I told him that there were techniques and approaches that could help him a great deal, by accelerating and deepening his learning, but that few in the profession used them, most teachers sticking to tried and trusted traditional methods. I confirmed that if these approaches were failing to help him learn then we would suggest he spend more time on them – a few more hours after school or even a few weeks of his summer holiday.

I went on to explain to him that, although the rapid advances in our understanding of the human brain had enabled us to develop learning strategies that are compatible with the way in which the brain works, and so considerably enhance learning, there was a fear that the abandonment of traditional methods would lead to a decline in standards. I replied to his question, confirming that the methods that I was referring to were indeed the same ones that had failed so many and limited the attainment of countless others.

I was determined, however, not to be sidetracked and went on to explain that teachers were being placed under increasing pressure to achieve results, with evermore outrageous targets being imposed upon them and that, in the opinion of many politicians at least, the best way to achieve them was to 'prescribe more leeches'. I defended my position by assuring him that the motive behind such a policy, as it always had been, was to achieve the highest possible standards. Strangely, this failed to appease him.

Sadly, there is a considerable danger that the situation described in the second conversation becomes a recurring reality as we cling, leech-like, to the status quo, blindly equating traditional methodology with high standards. For in much the same way that increased understanding of the human body leads to medical advancement, is it not inevitable that increased understanding of the human brain will lead to developments in the way in which we help people learn? The objective may remain the same but the pedagogy will surely evolve.

There are no guarantees;
no magic wands – we are
simply suggesting
strategies that make it
more likely that students
will learn effectively.

Our understanding of the brain and the learning process is greater than ever before, with dramatic advances in the last few decades. Equally as dramatic, however, are the enormous learning gains that have resulted from learning programmes and approaches that have been based upon this new knowledge and designed with the brain in mind. As we further unlock the complexities of the human mind, so our approaches to teaching and learning will continue to evolve. It is as inevitable as the disappearance of the leech from medical practice.

Certainly we should be cautious as a profession – as cautious as our medical counterparts – with new approaches, rigourously evaluating and researching the new methodology prior to embracing it. There is, however, a considerable difference between treating scientific advancement with caution and dismissing it out of hand. We are on the verge of a 'Learning Revolution'. The motives may be the same, but now we have the methodology to achieve them.

Brain-based learning

These methodologies are often referred to as 'brain-based', 'accelerated' or 'super' learning and, although not particularly new, have generated much interest in recent years. However, the extent to which these techniques are having an impact in the classroom, despite the range of books and the extensive training opportunities, is debatable. Indeed, my considerable excitement at the rapid advances in our understanding of the learning process and the subsequent developments in pedagogy is matched only by my frustration that these developments have, as yet, failed to become established in the majority of schools.

'Brain-based learning' and 'accelerated learning' are simply umbrella terms that encompass approaches to learning that are compatible with the way in which the brain operates and learns most effectively. They have been warmly and enthusiastically embraced by some but rejected as gimmicky and dismissed as the latest fad by others. They are neither a gimmick nor a fad, but effective, common-sense learning strategies. Those that dismiss them often fail to understand them, tarring them with the progressive, 'find out for yourself' brush and struggling to see beyond the perceived jargon of the label.

I was once asked during a training session, how OFSTED would view a lesson taught along accelerated learning lines. I replied that if an OFSTED inspector observed a group of highly motivated pupils thoroughly engaged in their learning – making sense out of the information that was presented to them and making obvious and significant learning gains during the course of a lesson – they would be suitably impressed. At least I hope they would! OFSTED, like the rest of us, simply want to see pupils learning and making progress. They might use a slightly different language; referring to teachers *sharing the learning objectives with pupils at the start of a lesson*, as opposed to *providing pupils with the Big Picture*, but the meaning is the same.

There are numerous reasons why so many teachers have failed to adopt what may be loosely termed the 'accelerated learning' methodologies. A curriculum that remains horrendously overcrowded and a suffocating climate of accountability being just two of the factors that have deterred teachers from straying too far from a track that they have individually and collectively trod since the days when they were the ones being taught.

Translating the research into practical strategies that are effective, even within the constraints of the classroom, is the key to enhancing learning and raising attainment. That is the focus of this book.

However, the overwhelming obstacle preventing teachers from incorporating brain-based learning into their teaching repertoire is the uncertainty of precisely what it 'looks like' in the classroom. There are many teachers who are receptive, even enthused by the concept that learning can be enhanced by making lessons 'brain compatible', but who lack the confidence and understanding to apply these learning principles in the classroom. Translating the research into practical strategies that are effective, even within the constraints of the classroom, is the key to enhancing learning and raising attainment. *That* is the focus of this book.

This book attempts to:

- highlight some of the key issues emerging from the latest discoveries in how the human brain works and the developments in brain-based learning
- simplify them
- offer proven, practical strategies and suggestions for how to apply this new research in the classroom.

This is essentially a practical manual written in response to the countless requests that I have received from teachers for strategies that work in the classroom. These strategies are extensions of the ideas contained in my earlier publications, *Lessons are for Learning* and *Closing the Learning Gap,* and are based upon the principles and philosophy outlined in these books. It is highly recommended that *Strategies for Closing the Learning Gap* is read in conjunction with them.

They are not the answer; there is no claim that these activities and this approach represent the 'Holy Grail' of the classroom. Indeed, it is recognized that teachers and schools operate in their own unique contexts and strategies that work for one teacher in a particular school may not always be as effective in a different curriculum area or different environment. Consequently many of the strategies outlined will have to be adapted to suit a particular set of circumstances.

Strategies to Close the Learning Gap has been written by a teacher, for teachers and all of the ideas in this book have two things in common: they have been devised with the brain in mind and have been successfully implemented and refined in the classroom. All have proved effective in increasing motivation, improving learning and raising attainment. I very much hope that every teacher will find at least one strategy that they can adopt or adapt that will help make their teaching more effective and so raise the attainment of their pupils.

Structure of this book

Section One: Learning

This section looks at the significance of learning in the classroom and explores four key ideas:

- closing the learning gap
- lessons are for learning
- Learning = Understanding + Memory
- state, style, structure.

Section Two: State

If students are going to learn effectively, they have to be in the correct state to learn. In particular, they need:

- water and oxygen
- to be relaxed, yet alert
- to feel confident
- to be motivated
- to be well behaved.

Section Three: Style

People learn best in different ways. This section explores the importance of giving students the opportunity to learn in their preferred style and suggests a range of strategies to cater for different types of learner.

Section Four: Structure

Learning requires the learner to go through a series of distinct phases. This section recommends a four-phase approach to planning and structuring lessons:

Phase one   link the lesson
             provide the Big Picture
             describe learning objectives and outcomes
             set goals
             ask questions.

Phase two	input/exposition
	new information
	use strategies to engage visual, auditory and kinaesthetic learners.

Phase three	making personal sense of the information
	tasks and activities that engage the learner and challenge them to think
	immediate use of learning
	demonstrate understanding.

It is during phase three that understanding is fully developed. A comprehensive range of strategies, designed to challenge students to think and so deepen understanding, are suggested.

Phase four	review and recap
	achievement of goals
	recognition of success.

This section also explores how to use the four-phase lesson plan to identify which specific aspects of classroom practice could be tweaked to effect the maximum difference to students' learning.

Section Five: Memory

Learning involves memory. Section Five looks at the way in which teachers can make it more likely that what they teach is remembered. It is organized into three subsections:

- teach students memory strategies
- make your lessons memorable
- how will you remember this forever?

The style of this book

This book has been deliberately written in an easy-to-read style and adopts the left page/right page approach of *Closing the Learning Gap*. It is hoped that this will encourage teachers to browse through it during the lunch hour or a non-contact period.

The 'Learning Gap' is the difference between what we know about the brain and the learning process and what is happening in the classroom.

Identifying and closing the Learning Gap is central to genuine and sustainable school improvement.

Section One: Learning

Closing the Learning Gap

The 'Learning Gap' is the difference between what we know about the brain and the learning process and what is happening in the classroom.

All teachers, however effective, will have a Learning Gap. It is the discrepancy between the way in which the brain learns and the way children are taught, that occurs when, for example, kinesthetic learners are compelled to spend large parts of the school day reading, writing and listening, or when natural and highly efficient contextual memory systems are ignored and overloaded with vast amounts of content which the human brain is simply not designed to absorb.

Identifying and closing the Learning Gap is all about improving the quality of learning. As such it is central to genuine and sustainable school improvement.

Much has been made in recent years of the drive to improve standards and raise attainment and we have heard much of national initiatives, LEA development plans and school improvement. But teachers know that the difference is really made not at the macro level, but in the classroom. It is teachers and the way they teach that is the major influence upon how effectively children learn.

This view is endorsed by the findings of a great many OFSTED inspections; the quality of teaching being a significantly high correlate with good and very good schools. It is a relationship that is widely recognized, with Professor David Reynolds suggesting that teachers and what he refers to as 'the learning level', make between three and four times the difference to attainment than the school itself.

If that is so, it is the quality of teaching that holds the key to improving learning and raising attainment and that must therefore provide the focus for improvement programmes. However, as anyone who has ever held responsibility for improving the quality of teaching within an institution will confirm, encouraging teachers to critically reflect upon their practice is far from easy. The reluctance of some colleagues to engage in a professional improvement programme is partly due to the isolated nature of the profession (exacerbated by the constant carping and criticism of politicians and the media), which has made many teachers defensive and introspective. It is human nature to respond to perceived attack with aggressive defence.

Tweaking your teaching

We are not looking for a radical overhaul –
just a few tweaks and a bit of polish.
In order to do this, we need to:

- be *specific* and accurately identify
  precisely which aspects of our
  performance need tweaking

- identify *strategies* that will enable us
  to do the tweaking.

In other words, having identified what to
tweak, we need to be clear about how to
tweak it.

Strategies for Closing the Learning Gap

It is also true that the vast majority of teachers are highly skilled and experienced professionals who are already doing an excellent job in the classroom, thus leaving relatively little scope for improvement. If you suddenly took up running as a way of keeping fit, running a little farther and a little faster every day, you would notice a dramatic improvement in a short space of time. However, as you became fitter, the capacity to improve would reduce until any improvements were relatively small – a few seconds rather than a few minutes trimmed off your time – and only gained through a large amount of effort.

So too in teaching, with entrants to the profession learning quickly during training and the early years how to survive in the classroom and the strategies that are effective in helping children learn. Teachers with a few years experience have learned their lessons, refined their practice and are not in a position to make such dramatic improvements in their teaching.

Nevertheless, the fact that most teachers are doing an excellent job does not detract from our professional and moral responsibility to seek constant improvement in our practice, however small. Runners have a mentality of constantly seeking to improve their 'personal best' and that is precisely the attitude that we must adopt in order to raise the attainment of our pupils. However well we are doing currently, there is always scope for improvement.

Improving your golf

Suppose an average amateur golfer wants to reduce their score for a round by a couple of shots. They go to a professional for some coaching. It is likely that the professional would suggest a number of *minor alterations* to their swing, possibly widening their stance, twisting their shoulders very slightly or making a minor adjustment to their grip. These seemingly minor adjustments may well add up to an improved swing, longer and straighter driving and a significant improvement in scoring; the overall impact being significantly greater than the sum of the parts. It is highly unlikely that they would suggest anything as dramatic as holding the club the other way round! They wouldn't need to, because most amateur golfers have mastered the basics and are competent at hitting the golf ball. What we are looking to do by seeking expert coaching is to identify the relatively minor, but *specific* improvements that we can make, that together will enable us to hit the golf ball more effectively.

Improving your teaching

The same is true of most teachers. The basics have been mastered and they are doing a perfectly competent job in the classroom. *The challenge for them is to identify the specific and relatively minor adjustments that they can make to their teaching, that together will add up to a significant improvement in the way in which their pupils learn.*

Seemingly minor changes in the way we teach – a bit of polish applied in the right place or a slight change in emphasis and approach – can lead to dramatic improvements in learning, with a total impact far greater than the sum of the parts. To parody Neil Armstrong's famous line: *'one small step for the teacher, one giant leap for the learner'*! Even if a slight change in approach enables just one pupil in the class to learn more effectively, then we are making progress – and that is what school improvement is all about.

Where are you now?

● Before you read on, pause for a while and reflect upon the quality of the lessons that you currently teach. How do you judge your current performance – what mark out of ten would you award yourself for the quality of your teaching?

● Whatever mark you awarded yourself, you will remain at that level until you do something different.

● This book is about raising your score by at least one mark. It doesn't matter what score you awarded yourself – the key question is how are you going to improve it? If you scored 4/10 (remember that you awarded the mark) how will you make it 5/10? If you scored 8/10 how will you make it 9/10?

In much the same way as the exhortation to 'hit it further' or 'improve your putting' is unlikely to make you a better golfer, a simple desire or even a requirement to become a better teacher is unlikely to make much of a difference. In order to improve, two things are required:

- We must be *specific* and accurately identify the aspects of our teaching that we need to polish in order to enhance learning. 'Improving our teaching' is much too vague; we need to know precisely which bits of our lessons we need to work on to make the difference. In short, we have to know which bit we need to tweak before we can tweak it!

- We must also know how to tweak it and this involves *strategies*. Whenever I read about the need for teachers to improve or how we need to provide greater opportunities for kinesthetic learners during our lessons, I hear a little voice that simply says, '*how*?' over and over again. Teachers do not need to be told to teach more effectively, nor do they need abstract theory, however interesting. Teachers need proven and practical strategies that will work in the classroom – even with 9B on a wet Friday afternoon. We know the what, we are seeking the *how*.

Keep learning high-profile

Put this on every teacher's desk.

- What have they learned?
- How do you know?
- How is this activity helping them learn?

Put this on every classroom door – so it is the last thing that students will see as they leave the classroom.

What have you learned today?

Lessons are for learning

> Let me nail my colours to the mast: lessons are for learning...
>
> Children should leave the classroom at the end of the lesson knowing, understanding and being able to do more than when they came in. If we achieve that, then we are doing our job. Consequently, both as a reminder and an instantaneous, if somewhat simplistic, self-evaluation, 'WHAT HAVE THEY LEARNED?' is the question that should be on every teacher's lips at the end of every lesson.
>
> It is a crude analysis, but if I am guilty of stating the obvious and oversimplifying the issue, I offer no apology as I can think of no more appropriate gauge for how effective a lesson has been, if only as a rule of thumb. It is also precisely the simple, unambiguous benchmark that is required as a salutary reminder that lessons should be all about learning...

Mike Hughes, Lessons are for Learning

It seems simple enough; lessons are for learning. Few, if any, will disagree. Of course lessons are for learning, it is almost self-evident. Yet, I observe many lessons in which children learn very little. Sometimes – too often – children fail to learn anything at all.

For learning is not the same thing as being occupied, sitting quietly or producing copious notes. Learning involves memory and understanding. Students may leave the classroom with more notes than when they entered and with exercises successfully completed, but if they do not understand and do not remember, then they haven't learned.

And if they haven't learned anything, they haven't made progress and that, according to OFSTED, is now unsatisfactory. In 1997, I expressed my concern that lessons that involved little more than a transfer of information and the odd low-level comprehension exercise, could all too easily delude teachers and OFSTED alike and pass as acceptable. Well, not any more; the new OFSTED framework, that came into effect in January 2000, clearly states that '*a lesson cannot be satisfactory if pupils are not making progress*'. It is one of a number of significant changes in the new framework.

The emphasis is now clearly upon learning. '*How is this helping them learn?*' must be at the front of every teacher's mind at the beginning of, and throughout, every lesson that they teach. When all is done, teachers must be clear about what has been learned and – as the lesson ends – what children know, understand and can do, that they couldn't do at the beginning.

Keep the focus on learning. Provide constant and highly visible reminders to teachers and students alike that learning is the core business of a school. Prepare and place labels for every classroom in the school. Some suggestions are shown opposite.

$$L = U + M$$

Strategies for Closing the Learning Gap

Learning = Understanding + Memory

> *Understanding is a precious commodity – the Holy Grail of the classroom, to be pursued, nurtured and cherished – because without it, there can be no genuine learning.*

Mike Hughes, *Closing the Learning Gap*

Learning involves understanding *and* memory. It is not an either/or situation; both are essential components of learning. If we do not understand, we cannot claim to have learned. The same is true if we cannot remember.

Understanding is central to learning and, if lessons are for learning, promoting understanding must be our conscious goal. Yet there are too many classrooms where understanding is an infrequent and incidental visitor, sacrificed in the drive to cover the curriculum and transfer information. 'Cover the curriculum' is a horrible phrase: cover the curriculum and we transfer information; explore the curriculum and we cognitively grapple with it, and only then do we begin to make sense of it.

For making sense – personal sense – of something lies at the heart of understanding and is the very essence of learning. It is the moment when the fog clears, everything clicks and the brain silently exclaims 'ah ha!' It is the point at which things start to become easy. Learning is done *by* people, not *to* them; for understanding is the product of doing rather than receiving. When students receive information, it is merely information; when they are required to do something with it – explore it, manipulate it, think about it – there is a greater chance that it will be understood.

Beware the impostor though, because much can masquerade as understanding. Pages of notes, particularly when they are written neatly, can be a convincing disguise. But if they are not understood, they have not been learned and if they have not been learned, no progress has been made and we do not need OFSTED to tell us that this cannot be satisfactory.

Let's not forget memory. Although understanding something significantly increases our chances of remembering, it does not guarantee it. Understanding and memory are separate processes – inextricably linked, undeniably, but nonetheless distinct entities. To ensure that our students learn, we must nurture and develop both.

As a teacher, few things are as frustrating as starting a lesson with the question, '*Now then, who can remember what we did last lesson?*' only to be met with silence and a classroom of blank faces. Yet, it should come as no surprise because we know that people will forget as much of 80 per cent of the information that they encounter within 24 hours. This is not the result of inattention; it is the natural process of forgetting and simply reflects the fact that the brain is not designed to absorb the sort of content that it encounters in the classroom.

If that is the bad news, the good news is that there are strategies and techniques that we can use to combat the natural forgetting process and to help make learning stick. They are techniques that all teachers should master and employ for, without them, information is no more than a temporary visitor to our short-term memory. It may be information that has been understood, but if isn't remembered, it hasn't been learned.

Three keys to effective learning

State

People learn best when they are in an appropriate physical and emotional state. Learning is optimized when the brain is nourished and students are relaxed, confident and motivated.

Style

People learn best in different ways. For maximum progress, people must have frequent opportunities to work in their preferred learning style.

Structure

Mature, successful learners progress through discrete phases of learning quite naturally. Lessons should be structured to reflect these stages, in order to guide immature learners through the learning process.

State, style and structure

State, style and structure are the keys to effective learning and are the foundations of any brain-based or accelerated techniques. For it is only when people are in an appropriate state – physically and emotionally – to learn, when they are able to work in their preferred style and when they systematically progress through the key phases of the learning process, that learning will be optimized.

Physically, the brain needs fuel. Water, oxygen and glucose are required for the brain to operate efficiently. It means that students who come to school without having breakfast are disadvantaged before lessons even begin. Similarly, as students spend the day sitting in a classroom, their heart rate decreases and less and less oxygen reaches the brain. Combine this effect with a lack of water (do the majority of your students drink coke or fresh water?) and it is apparent that the brain will become increasingly inefficient as the day progresses.

When the brain is denied the amount of oxygen and water that it needs to function efficiently, attitude, behaviour and motivation are all affected. Learning is, at best, impaired and often prohibited simply because the brain is not in an appropriate state to operate.

Learners must also believe that they *can* learn – and succeed. Expectations inform outcomes; don't be surprised when students who say, *'I'm no good at maths'*, struggle. Conversely, students who believe themselves to be talented and capable will go on to achieve. It is a self-fulfilling prophecy. Learning is also heavily dependent upon desire. There is a massive difference between a student who wants to learn or, better still, is desperate to learn, and a student who cannot see the personal relevance of their work and has a 'couldn't care less' approach.

When students are in an appropriate *state* to learn, they have a chance of learning; a chance that will be significantly enhanced if they are able to learn in a manner that is compatible with their own preferred learning *style*. We each have a preferred way of learning. This does not mean that it is the only way in which we can learn, simply the way we learn best – and when we have regular opportunities to work in this way, learning, not to mention motivation, is enhanced. Indeed, many would argue that a mismatch between a student's preferred learning style and the teacher's typical teaching approach is a major source of underachievement.

As learners, we all progress through a number of distinct phases when we learn. We first gain an overview of a topic and determine how and why we are going to learn about it. Then we seek detailed information, thinking carefully about it in order to understand it and make personal sense of the material that we have encountered. Finally, to cement the information and to demonstrate our new-found understanding, we review what we have learned.

Successful, mature learners move through these phases naturally and often subconsciously. Students however, as immature learners, need to be guided through these learning phases – phases that correlate with discrete and distinct parts of a lesson.

Strategies for Closing the Learning Gap

27

The self-belief and the desire of the student is undoubtedly the hardest thing for a teacher to influence.

However, a positive influence on the emotional state of the learner will have the greatest impact upon learning.

When lessons are *structured* around these key phases in the learning process – an overview, encountering new information, activities to develop understanding and a review – learning is enhanced.

Of the three – state, style and structure – the most difficult for teachers to influence is, without question, the state of their students. However, positively influencing the outlook of the student will have the greatest impact on learning. For being in an appropriate state to learn is a prerequisite for effective learning. A student who, emotionally and/or physically is not ready to learn, quite simply will not – irrespective of opportunities to work in their preferred style or through distinct, key phases of the learning process.

For anyone, adult or child, confidence and motivation are two vital factors in successful learning. Take either away and learning suffers. It means that, arguably, the emotional state of the learner – the self-belief and the inner drive – holds the key to the extent to which they will learn. For self-belief and inner drive are the foundations on which learning activities are built. If these foundations are shaky, even the best teacher, with a wealth of resources and the most effective learning strategies, will struggle to make an impact.

As educators therefore, our first conscious task is to ensure that our students are feeling positive about themselves and their work. It is too important an issue to be left to chance. Yet how many schools have a motivation policy or Head of Self-esteem? It is a serious question. Surely, if these two aspects hold the key to improving learning, schools should adopt a consistent and concerted approach?

No one claims that it is an easy thing to do. On the contrary, the emotional state of our students is the hardest thing to change. We cannot change it, simply because we do not control it. Self-esteem and motivation belong to the individual and are moulded by a great many factors. All that we can do as schools and teachers is influence it. And we do. Everything that we do and say will have a subtle influence upon the way each student regards him or herself. As teachers we must be aware of our influence and ensure that all our interactions with our students have a positive impact on their state of mind. Even teachers who do this naturally and intuitively will benefit from consciously employing the strategies outlined in Section Two.

The fact that it seems we are relatively powerless to influence students who show not the slightest interest in their studies must not deter us. These are precisely the students who need our intervention the most. Similarly, we must not be overwhelmed by the external influences upon our students and the fact that the strategies at our disposal appear to be little more than 'drops in the ocean'. It was Mother Theresa who responded to the claim that her work with the sick and the poor in Calcutta was '*a drop in the ocean*', with the retort that it was '*a drop in the right ocean*'.

For, 'enough drops in the right ocean', will begin to make a difference. We may not turn the hardened school cynic, forged by years of negative messages, into the keenest scholar, but we can make a difference. And if we can make a difference to the attitude of our students – even one of them – we have taken a significant step towards improving the quality of learning in our classroom.

If a teacher's job is to help students learn, then the first task of the teacher must be to ensure that students are in an appropriate state to learn.

Section Two: State

In this section we will see that for students to learn effectively, they must first be in an appropriate physical and emotional state to learn. For when learners are not receptive and focused upon the task in hand, no wonder-resource or teaching strategy – however imaginative – can compensate.

In particular, students should be:

➡ *in an appropriate physical state to learn. The brain needs water, oxygen and glucose to function efficiently;*

➡ *relaxed yet alert;*

➡ *confident – believing that they can do something;*

➡ *motivated – wanting to do something;*

➡ *well behaved – focused upon learning.*

There will be those who will no doubt struggle to recognize the highly motivated, confident and alert learner and it is acknowledged that there are many teachers who grapple every day with children who are in anything but an appropriate state to learn. Let us not pretend otherwise.

However, it is equally important to be aware of the optimum state for learning and to aim for it. It is our goal, not our current reality. The closer the match between this ideal state for learning and the actual state of our students, the more effectively they will learn.

In many respects, getting students in the right state to learn is the key to success in the classroom. For of all of the variables that impact upon learning – the environment, the resources, the quality of the teaching – it is the attitude and state of the students themselves that has the greatest bearing upon how much is learned. All teachers would agree that there is a massive difference between teaching students who want to learn and believe that they can succeed, and struggling with students who show little or no interest in their work.

Unfortunately, the state and attitude of the students lie outside the teacher's direct control, and are therefore the hardest things to change in the classroom. Indeed, it is tempting to take the view that, given the overwhelming negative influences on a child's state of mind, teachers are powerless to make any difference. Low levels of expectation, lack of parental support, peer pressure and prior experiences will all have a significant bearing upon the motivation and self-image of the individual. Similarly, lack of sleep, poor nutrition and lack of exercise will adversely affect a student's physical state.

We have no control over
the state in which
students arrive at our
lesson.
We have total control
over our response.

However, it is the children who have skipped breakfast, are dehydrated and bring a 'couldn't care less, I'm no good at maths' attitude to the lesson that particularly need to have their state altered before the learning can begin. It is also precisely because teachers have so little *control* in this area, that we must seize every opportunity, however small, to exert a positive *influence* over the physical and emotional state of our students.

Ah but, we have no control

We may not have control over the state of our students, but we do have an influence.

Let us accept that so many of the factors – parental attitudes, sleep patterns and eating habits – that can negatively affect the student are beyond our control. On a more immediate level, we have no control over what happened during the previous lesson or what was said in the playground. While all these are rightly areas of *concern*, it is important, not least for our own sanity, to maximize the positive support that we *can* provide, and to target our professional energies at our areas of *influence*.

For everything that we do and say in the classroom will have an influence upon the students and how they regard themselves as learners. This influence may be positive or negative, conscious or inadvertent. However, in the same way as *we cannot not communicate* (see page 69), *we cannot not influence*. We must therefore be aware of the impact of our words and deeds and deliberately talk and act in a manner that will support and enhance the self-concept of our students.

Simply smiling and greeting a student as they arrive at the lesson is a major contribution to their ability to *change state*; to turn the frustration of a negative experience into something more optimistic. Many teachers do this instinctively and intuitively. However, some do not. More accurately, some do not smile at the students who they regard as difficult, surly and unco-operative. Ironically, these are the students who arrive at the lesson in a totally inappropriate state to learn and who we need to influence the most!

There are two particular areas where we have little or no control: the state in which students arrive, and what we are required to teach.

If we have no control over the state in which students arrive at our lesson, we have total control over the choice of our response. When students arrive at our lesson and, through no fault of ours, are clearly not in the mood to learn, we have two choices:

1 be frustrated and get annoyed – the consequence is quite probably a bad lesson
2 positively influence the students.

Consider David. David was an angry young man who frequently found himself in trouble during his school days. He would often arrive at a lesson feeling aggressive, perhaps as a result of an incident that had taken place at home, or during break or even during the previous lesson. His state upon arrival prevented him, and frequently others, from learning. When teachers saw David arriving at their lessons in one of these moods, they no doubt began to hear that voice in their head, telling them that they were in for a bad lesson. Many responded to David by challenging him, usually aggressively, on his appearance or punctuality. Their approach and tone were as a red rag to David who, more often than not, ended up in the head's office having reacted to the teacher's manner with an inappropriate outburst.

A drop in the ocean

We are simply seeking to put enough drops in the right ocean to make a difference.

A drop   Lots of drops

Contrast this with the approach chosen by David's English teacher. She would recognize David's fragile mood and respond to it with a smile and an enquiry about David's motorbike. She knew that his bike was his pride and joy and that by engaging him in conversation about it would significantly change his attitude and mood. It was a conscious strategy and a deliberate attempt to change David's state so that he could learn. David left school with a GCSE pass in English – his only qualification.

A second area in which teachers lack any substantial control, is over what they are required to teach. Anyone who has taught, even for a few weeks, will have been faced with students demanding to know, *'What are we doing this for?'* or *'How will this help me when I leave school?'* and will have heard that, *'This is boring'*.

I once asked a Year 8 class what they wanted to know about the North Sea. *'If I'm honest Sir'*, came the reply from a girl at the back, who was no doubt voicing what many were thinking, *'absolutely nothing'*. When students fail to see the relevance – personal relevance – they are unlikely to be motivated or sufficiently interested to work at their best.

It is a source of frustration to many teachers that as a profession, we have very little control over *what* we are required to teach. In this respect, teachers could claim that they have not been dealt a particularly good hand. It makes our choice over *how* we go about teaching it even more important as this is the only area that teachers have any control. The fact that we may not have been dealt many cards, makes it even more important that we play the ones that we have got wisely.

A drop in the ocean?

Our actions and the strategies at our disposal may seem inconsequential compared with the significant negative influences at work on our students. Nevertheless it is important that we use whatever techniques that we can to have a positive impact upon the confidence and motivation of the children we teach. The fact that so much remains outside of our control makes it even more important to fully utilize the strategies at our disposal.

In Section One, I quoted Mother Theresa's famous comment that her work was a *'drop in the right ocean'*. Putting drops in the right ocean is precisely what we are trying to do as we seek to influence the state of our students. We are not seeking miracles and accept that we cannot conjure up confident, motivated and focused students at the click of our fingers. We are simply seeking to put enough drops in the right ocean to make a difference.

It is also significant that Mother Theresa choose to put her 'ocean drops' into Calcutta – a place where a difference, however small, was particularly needed. The same is true of our students; it is easy to smile at well-behaved, highly motivated students who turn up for our lessons eager to please and ready to learn. However, the students who will most benefit from our intervention and who desperately need a positive influence on their emotional and physical state, are the students who arrive at our lessons devoid of hope, ambition or drive.

Lots of little drops make large oceans and by consistently and congruently employing a range of techniques, such as the ones outlined in this section, we can begin to make a difference to a student's frame of mind.

I've come to the frightening conclusion that
I am the decisive element in the classroom.

It's my personal approach that creates the
climate.

It's my daily mood that makes the weather.

As a teacher, I possess a tremendous power
to make a child's life miserable or joyous.

I can be a tool of torture, or an instrument of
inspiration.

I can humiliate or humour, hurt or heal.

In all situations, it is my response that
decides whether a crises will be escalated or
de-escalated, and a child humanized or de-
humanized.

Haim Ginott
from *Teacher and Child* (Macmillan, 1972)

Congruence is the key

Many experts claim that very little communication is done through the words that we use. The subtle clues of the tone of our voice and our body language are much more important, with over 50 per cent of communication being done through body language.

There is a little point, therefore, in starting a lesson by welcoming a group if your body language does not confirm that you are indeed pleased to be there. Students of any age will quickly pick up any contradiction between what they hear and see. Everything that we do and say – or don't say – is communication. Everything that we do and say in the classroom must therefore be congruent and put children at their ease.

This is unlikely to happen if we say, *'it's nice to see you'*, whilst simultaneously thinking, *'I hate teaching you lot!'* The key for us as teachers is to establish congruence in our inner beliefs as it is they, and our deeply held values, that drive our external behaviour. *The most effective teachers have an unconditional belief and a deep conviction, that:*

- the only thing they control in the class is themselves
- students are more than the sum of their problems
- all students can be winners in one context or another
- dignity and respect are fundamental even (especially) when angry
- protecting self-esteem is a primary goal
- certain basic and mutual rights are non-negotiable
- successful teaching is founded upon high-quality human transactions rather than the delivery of a curriculum.

Teachers create the climate of the classroom

We cannot get students in the right state to learn if we are not in an appropriate state ourselves.

Don't expect the students to be relaxed if you, the teacher, are uptight. Do not be surprised if your students lack motivation if you are giving the distinct impression that you are not enjoying yourself. There is nothing new in this. Wise old teachers in the corner of the staffroom have always smiled and said, *'quiet teachers equal quiet classrooms'*.

It is, however, easy to forget that everything we say and do influences each and every student and contributes to the *climate of the classroom*. It is also all too easy, particularly in a highly charged, emotive situation, to act – or more accurately, react – in a manner that makes the situation worse rather than better. The fact that a comment or look was inadvertent fails to compensate for the lasting damage it can have on an individual student or the atmosphere of the classroom.

To a certain extent, we can avoid this situation if we enter the classroom equipped with a range of strategies and techniques that are consciously designed to have a positive impact upon the state of the students and the climate of the classroom.

Everything we do and say will have an influence over the students in our classroom.

We must therefore:

- ensure that our words and actions have a positive influence

- take every opportunity to exert a positive influence.

It is more likely that we will have a positive impact upon students if:

- we are aware of the many ways in which our words and deeds influence students

- we consciously employ a range of previously identified strategies to complement and reinforce the things we say and do intuitively.

Conscious strategy

Many of the things that teachers say and do instinctively and intuitively have a positive impact upon students. However, this is too important an issue to be left to chance and the work of even the best teacher will be enhanced if the range of strategies at their disposal are extended.

The strategies in this section are based upon the convictions outlined on page 37. By using them consciously to complement rather than replace existing approaches, we are seeking to do two things:

- to ensure that everything we do and say has a positive influence upon individual students and the atmosphere of the classroom

- to fully exploit the opportunity that we, as teachers, have to influence the attitude of our students.

The strategies that follow are grouped under broad headings but the groups are by no means unrelated. Strategies that relax, for example, may affect motivation. Similarly, it is recognized that many of the techniques that teachers can use to motivate students will also have a positive impact upon their self-esteem. The headings are simply for convenience.

The categories reflect the optimum state for learning that is our conscious goal, namely:

- appropriate physical state
- relaxed–alert
- confident
- motivated
- focused.

Let us accept that some children *will* move during a lesson.

The issue then becomes:

do they move on their terms or yours?

Our conscious strategy must be to influence the state of students by creating and managing opportunities for them to move during lessons.

Appropriate physical state

The brain needs fuel. In particular, it requires oxygen, water, rest and glucose to function efficiently and when it is deprived of them, learning is inevitably impaired. Sadly, many students do not enjoy either the diet or the rest that their brain requires for optimum learning – in effect, their brains are running on 'empty'.

Oxygen

In oxygen terms, the brain is the greediest organ in the body, using around 20% of our oxygen intake. As students sit during a lesson, their heart rate slows, thus reducing the amount of oxygenated blood flowing to the brain. In short, the brain is becoming increasingly inefficient as the lesson progresses!

As teachers, we need to compensate for this by *consciously including opportunities for children to stand up and move around during a teaching session*. Teachers can often be wary about allowing, never mind encouraging, students to leave their seats during a lesson, equating movement with potential for disruption and misbehaviour. They are right to be cautious; it is unlikely that very much productive learning will take place unless a calm and orderly atmosphere is maintained. However, far from increasing the likelihood of poor behaviour, allowing students to move around the classroom can significantly reduce disruption and enhance learning – *provided that it is done in a controlled manner*.

The following strategies are designed to allow the teacher to influence the physical state of students by creating opportunities for students to move and 'break state'. They can be mixed and matched and adapted to take account of the particular context, for example – the nature of the students, their age, the size of the group and so on. Use them to 'chunk' the lesson into smaller pieces (see page 259) and to ensure that students are not required to concentrate for longer than their natural concentration span (see page 183) without a physical and mental break.

Break state

For teachers who are reluctant to allow students to stand up and move during lessons or in circumstances when such a strategy would threaten the teacher's classroom control, the students can simply be asked to stop what they are doing in order to 'break their state'. For example, if students are engaged in a written activity, ask them to stop and get out their homework diaries or last week's homework. The action involved in bending down and rummaging around in their bags will change the state that they are in, give their brains a break from learning and will provide a degree of stretching and moving that will be particularly welcomed by the 'fidgeters'.

Spread out resources and materials

Strategically place the materials and resources that students require around the room so that they have to leave their seat and move at regular intervals. Rather than students collecting the necessary resources at the beginning of the lesson and then spending the remainder of the time in their seats, try to build into your lesson-planning the need for students to collect a new resource midway through. Manage movement around the room by directing students to collect resources a group at a time.

The benefits of time-outs

- Students break state.

- Students can stand and so increase the amount of oxygen to the brain.

- Students who 'need' to move around can do so.

- The brain has some 'down time', important for subconsciously processing information.

- Students have an opportunity to discuss their work with each other and so help their understanding.

- Students are not required to be 'on task' for longer than their natural concentration span.

- The lesson is divided into 'chunks'. This creates a number of 'beginnings' – the time when concentration and the capacity to remember are greatest – in the lesson.

- Students can ask questions without fear of embarrassment.

Strategies for Closing the Learning Gap

Time-outs

Call a two-minute time-out after approximately 30 minutes of activity. During a time-out, students are allowed to do anything they wish (within reason!), including standing up and moving around. The benefits of this simple, but extremely effective strategy are shown on the opposite page.

Let them in on the secret!

Tell students about the importance of getting oxygen to the brain. Ask them to stand, walk slowly around the room and return to their seats.

'Target' individual students

All teachers recognize the 'fidgeter'! Some children appear to need to fidget and move around more than others and these students in particular will benefit from the opportunity to stand and move. Identify these students and consciously select them to give out resources, collect in homework or pop to a neighbouring classroom on an errand. Indeed, even if you do not need the set of text books next door, asking a particular student who has a great need for physical movement to go and get them does no harm. On the contrary, it is a deliberate strategy, designed to break state, enhance concentration and improve the atmosphere in the classroom.

Brain Buttons

By gently massaging the hollows that lie just below the collar bone on either side of the sternum, we can stimulate the flow of freshly oxygenated blood to the brain. These hollows, known as 'Brain Buttons' in Brain Gym®, are key acupressure points and lie directly above the carotid arteries that carry blood to the brain. Try it next time you are weary or feel a headache coming on.

Use movement in your lesson

Build in learning activities and tasks that require students to move during a lesson. These will help all students, by 'breaking their state' and increasing the amount of oxygen that is flowing to their brains. Kinesthetic learners will benefit particularly as they are given the opportunity to learn in their preferred style. A range of suggested learning strategies can be found in Section Three.

Trees

Whenever the arms are raised above the head the heart rate quickens slightly and more oxygen will flow to the brain. I used to work with a colleague who regularly required his students to stand up midway through a lesson, raise their arms and sway gently, pretending they were trees! Interestingly, his students were all aware that this rather unorthodox classroom activity signalled the end of one learning experience and the beginning of another (see page 182). They also knew that the teacher would use each new beginning to introduce a key point and would consequently pay particular attention at these moments. By using state breaks such as 'trees', teachers not only increase oxygen flow to the brain; they can *signpost the lesson*, giving clear messages to alert students to when the really important bits are coming.

Cross Crawling

March slowly on the spot, bringing your left knee up to meet your right wrist (and vice versa).
Motor movements that involve both sides of the body in this way, simultaneously engage both hemispheres of the neo-cortex and stimulate communication between the two sides of the brain via the corpus callosum. Use as a warm-up or 'state break' activity before and during lessons.

Brain Buttons

Gently massage the small hollows that can be found between the first and second ribs on either side of the sternum. These points lie directly above the carotid arteries that carry oxygenated blood to the brain. Experts believe that gentle massage stimulates blood flow and so increases the amount of oxygen flowing to the brain. Useful for students to give themselves a boost during a lesson or in an exam and for teachers to stay alert during meetings!

Warm up the body and the brain

Borrow an idea from Brain Gym® to prepare students for learning, by simultaneously warming up the brain and the body. 'Cross crawling' (see opposite) involves marching on the spot, touching the left knee with the right wrist and the right knee with the left wrist.

Motor movement in the left-hand side of the body is controlled by the right hemisphere of the neo-cortex, whilst the left hemisphere is responsible for movement down the right-hand side. This 'cross over' activity involves both sides of the brain, stimulating communication between the two hemispheres of the cortex via the corpus callosum. In effect, this neural activity warms up the brain and prepares it for learning.

By cross crawling for 30–60 seconds prior to learning, the heart rate is raised slightly and the flow of oxygen to the brain is increased.

For more information on Brain Gym® see:

- *Making the Brain Body Connection* by Sharon Promislow (General Distributing, 1998)
- *Brain Gym* by Paul and Gail Dennison (Edu-Kinesthetics, 1989)

Restructure the school day

Reflect on the structure of your school day. Are students required to spend long periods of time in lessons without a break? Would it be possible to restructure the day so that students have regular oxygen breaks? Two short breaks in the morning will do more good than one longer one as it will increase the opportunities for students – and teachers – to get oxygen to their brains and so improve their physical state for learning.

Water

The brain, which is 90 per cent water, requires water to function properly. Water conducts the tiny electrical currents that drive the brain, removes waste and toxins from the body and allows significantly more oxygen to bind to the blood. When we are dehydrated, learning is impaired as mood and concentration deteriorate.

Experts suggest that we need between five and eight large glasses of water a day; more if we drink alcohol or coffee, are under stress or are working with electrical machines. It is best taken in small quantities at regular intervals. This means that the vast majority of students, and teachers, are permanently dehydrated to some degree. Vast amounts of money are spent on training and resources, seeking to enhance the quality of learning, and yet much of the sought-after improvement might simply be achived by drinking more water!

Sharon Promislow describes water as *'an instant brain boost'*, claiming that it:

- heightens energy
- improves concentration
- improves mental and physical co-ordination
- enhances academic skills.

Two breakfast scenarios

EITHER

The student comes to school in a bad mood. They have had little sleep and, as usual, came to school without having breakfast.

They arrive at the first lesson without any equipment. The teacher challenges them for their failure to bring a pen. The student responds by being rude. They are chastised and issued with a minus slip. The student scowls and sulks throughout the lesson. Not only do they fail to learn anything, they also miss the instructions for the next homework, ensuring that the beginning of the next lesson will be every bit as unsuccessful as this one.

It is the worst possible start to the day – a start from which the student is unlikely to recover.

OR

The student is met at the breakfast bar by their LSW. As they have a drink, a piece of toast and a banana, the LSW, recognizing their depressed and somewhat angry mood, engages them in conversation. The focus is positive, the conversation dwelling on the successes – in and out of lessons- of recent days. A joke is shared, the LSW's smile and cheery manner slowly being matched by the student.

As breakfast draws to a close, the LSW checks the student's equipment and, discovering they have none, lends them a pen: 'We don't want you getting into trouble now, do we?'

The student arrives at the start of the lesson in a totally different and wholly more appropriate mood.
It is the best possible start to the day.

Water is so important in optimizing learning, yet few students drink anything like sufficient. Although we have no control over what young people put into their bodies, there are three ways in which we can have a positive influence over a student's water intake:

- *Increase the awareness* of teachers, students and their parents as to the importance of regular and sufficient water intake. Take every opportunity to remind people that water helps the brain and the body function efficiently.

- *Increase access*. How easy is it for students and staff to get a drink of water? Make bottled water and/or water dispensers easily available around the school.

- *Increase opportunity*. Are students *allowed* to drink water during a lesson? Are they encouraged to do so? In many schools, students have traditionally not been permitted to drink during lessons. Ironically, allowing them to sip water would improve their state and enhance their learning. It may be time for schools to review their policy on water!

Breakfast

There are numerous studies that link poor diet with discipline and learning problems. When children arrive in school without having a proper breakfast – and a great many do – concentration and behaviour is impaired and learning will inevitably suffer. By educating parents and students about the importance of diet and providing a breakfast-bar service, schools can do something to ensure that increasing numbers of students arrive in lessons in an appropriate state to learn.

Breakfast clubs can be self-financing and catering contractors are often looking for ways to increase turnover and to maintain staffing and profit levels. In many schools, the breakfast club provides the first socializing opportunity of the day. 'Setting up activities' can be arranged for troubled students, including semi-formal contact with a learning support worker. During this time, we can increase the likelihood of the day getting off to a good start by ensuring that the student has the correct equipment and so on and, if necessary, begin to change their emotional state.

Teachers, students and parents, be aware – the brain needs fuel!

Under negative stress, the brain will not learn effectively.

Under stress emotion and instinct override logical, rational thinking. The brain goes into survival orientated, 'flight or fight' mode which, in the classroom, can often manifest itself as discipline issues. When students 'panic' in this way, learning will be inevitably impaired, and in extreme cases, prohibited.

Relaxed–alert

The brain will not learn effectively when it is placed under negative stress. Although a small degree of stress can heighten concentration and actually improve learning, when stress becomes too great, learning is significantly impaired. Under stress, brain activity defaults to the emotional and instinctive centres of the brain and rational, logical thought is prevented. It is an automatic, physiological response that we cannot control.

When the brain encounters stress – and each individual will have different stress triggers – the brain goes into 'fight or flight' survival mode as emotion overrides logical, rational thinking. The brain reacts to stress by preparing the body to survive. Blood is diverted from the digestive system to the skeletal muscles of the limbs – this is what enables human beings to perform extraordinary feats of strength when under threat – the eyes go into peripheral vision (a significant disadvantage if we are trying to read!) – and the ears filter out sound as they listen for signs of an attack.

When a student encounters stress in the classroom, the automatic and inevitable response will be the same; an emotional instinctive response will replace logical and rational thought. *Learning will inevitably be impaired and in extreme cases prevented.* Survival behaviour in the classroom often manifests itself as discipline issues, as, in their attempt to 'survive' a stressful situation, students divert attention away from the task or the question that was generating their stress.

People learn best when they are relaxed and focused upon what they are learning. Many people refer to this ideal state as *'relaxed–alert'* and it is the state that we must strive for in the classroom. This state corresponds to brain waves in the alpha band and is achieved when the brain slows down a little.

The brain operates on four different wavelengths:

1 *Beta* – 13–25 cycles per second. It is the state of the awake brain. You are attentive and alert – your mind is 'buzzing'.
2 *Alpha* – 8–12 cycles per second. At this reduced rate the brain is more relaxed and reflective. It is the brain wavelength associated with daydreaming, when your imagination is most active.
3 *Theta* – between 4–7 cycles per second. This is the state of the brain in deep meditation and light sleep. It is the prevailing wave length while you are dreaming.
4 *Delta* – 0.5–3 cycles per second. These are the brain waves of deep sleep.

Both beta and alpha brain waves are useful for learning. Many experts suggest that when you are problem solving or grappling with new information, you will benefit from being in the beta state. *However, it is also suggested that for much of the learning that students are required to do in schools, they would benefit from the slower, more reflective state associated with alpha brain waves.* Dominic O'Brien, the world memory champion, goes a stage further and suggests that memory is enhanced when the brain is in the twilight world of theta rhythms (see page 247), the brain waves Diana Beaver refers to in *NLP for Lazy Learning* as the *'brainwaves of inspiration'*.

Manage your state

- Sip water frequently during the day.
- Keep energy levels up by snacking on fruit, barley sugar and so on.
- Play music that you like between lessons or at breaks.
- Place pictures of things which make you feel good around the room.
- Have pictures of your children, partners or loved ones on your planner or diary.
- Breathe deeply – breathing out for double the time you breathe in is a rapid de-stressor (only do this a few times in a row!).
- Open windows or doors to get some fresh air.
- Imagine how good it will feel to hug the kids, pat the dog and so on when you get home.
- Grab an opportunity to stretch, move or jig around between classes.
- Use Brain Buttons (see page 44).
- Remember a joke or funny incident to get you smiling.
- Keep a Victory Log of things you have done well (however small) and flick through it.
- Deliberately notice the students who smile, bring books, respond well and so on – and take the credit!
- Go in your mind to a time when you were relaxed and happy. See what you saw, hear what you heard and feel what you felt then and now experience it all over again.

Strategies for Closing the Learning Gap

What about you?

In simple terms, our goal in the classroom must be to *relax students and create a stress-free learning environment*. However, it is highly unlikely that you will create relaxed students who are in the correct frame of mind to learn if you are not in this state yourself! We use language (verbal and non-verbal) strategies and rapport-building skills to create or elicit states in other people in a variety of contexts, whether it's in a classroom or explaining how good a film was. *The key to doing this successfully is first to go into the state that you wish to create in others.*

However, this may be easier said than done. How do you begin to create this state when you are tired, under pressure, being given a hard time by certain students, may have issues outside teaching that play on your mind and so on?

There is no suggestion that it is easy or that there is one magic answer. We are simply seeking to identify a range of strategies that people can employ to make it more likely that they will be able to create the desired state. These strategies have a common theme: they rely on the individual to do something. Our emotional state is our personal responsibility and requires that we are proactive in managing and influencing our mood. One of the things that separates us from other animals is the ability to make a choice between the moment of receiving a stimulus and that of making a response. It is these choices, or the way we frame current experience, that directly affect our state.

Having relaxed ourselves it is more likely that we will be able to relax students. The following strategies may be useful.

Smile!

The simplest and yet one of the most effective strategies of them all! Smiles are reciprocated and trigger the release of endorphins – the 'feel good' chemicals – into the body. Greeting students in the corridor as they arrive for your lesson, making eye contact, addressing each in turn using their first name, but above all, smiling, is the ideal way to start a lesson. Students are more likely to enter the room feeling welcomed, valued, relaxed and ready to learn.

Tell students why smiling is so important and encourage them to smile at each other. Don't let them sit down until they have smiled. A Year 7 class that I taught recently used to begin every lesson with the 'smiling ritual' and as they smiled, used to say, '*That's right Sir, let those dolphins go!*'

Identify students 'at risk'

Although many students feel comfortable in the school environment, there are a great many children who spend their school days in an almost permanent state of nervous apprehension. These are the children who have a low self-image and who dread the thought of being made to look foolish in the classroom. Entering a learning situation in a state of worry, that for some borders on panic, is hardly an ideal learning state. Identify these students and go out of your way to reassure them. A smile goes a long way for these children!

Music in learning

- Relax students. Play baroque music at approximately 60 beats per minute to relax students and induce the alpha brain waves.

- Do a 'mental warm-up'. Listen to Mozart before learning. This 'mental warm-up' has been shown to improve test scores. Neurons are stimulated and primed for learning. Maths is a subject area that particularly benefits from this so-called 'Mozart effect'.

- Improve recall. Information is more likely to be recalled while someone is listening to the music that they could hear while they first received the information (see page 255).

- Trigger a feeling. Help students to feel confident and relaxed by associating the feeling with a piece of music (see page 73).

- Set a time limit. 'You have 3 minutes 46 seconds to complete your challenge, GO!' You can time it exactly as 3.46 is the length of the track that you play while the class is working. Different pieces of music, with varying tempos, played at different volumes, will be appropriate for different challenges. (The theme from *Mission Impossible* is particularly appropriate for setting a time challenge!)

- Use music to occupy the 'right brain'. A number of experts talk about the need to occupy the right hemisphere of the neo-cortex to allow the left hemisphere to concentrate upon the detail of learning. This is particularly important for students who have a dominant right hemisphere. By listening to music, the right brain is occupied processing the sound and so does not 'wander', distracting the left brain from the learning activity.

Welcome!

Use a 'welcome' sign and/or symbols (such as a smiley face) on your door, to let students know that you are pleased to see them. Include a subject-specific dimension on your sign.

Teachers who enjoy the best relationships with students are the ones who convince the students that they like and value them. When students sense that the teacher is expecting problems and would rather not be teaching them, they act accordingly – the teacher becomes increasingly irritated and a vicious cycle is put in motion. The cycle needs to be broken – don't expect the students to do it. If you want better relationships, welcome every class – *particularly the ones that you dread* – as if it were your favourite group.

Use music

Music is a powerful and effective way of influencing state; it can be used to *excite, energize, relax or focus*. Use gentle background music to help calm students down as they enter a room. Many schools are also using music in the dining room, where they claim significant reduction in noise levels.

Music can do more than just calm students down. Baroque music, which has roughly 60 beats per minute (approximately the same as a resting heart), can be used in the classroom to induce alpha brain waves and put students into an appropriate and receptive state to learn. Suitable pieces of music include: *The Four Seasons* by Vivaldi, the *Water Music* by Handel and the *Brandenburg Concertos* by J.S. Bach.

Do not worry if you are a non-musician. It is possible to buy pre-prepared CDs with music specifically selected to relax, focus or energize. More information about suitable pieces of music and the use of music can be found on page 283.

Using music to influence and alter state is a skilful business and teachers should experiment with various tracks upon themselves before using it in the classroom. Alter your state using the 'Iso principle': first select music that matches your existing mood (for example, if you are excited; select music that is loud with a fast beat). After a few moments change the music, gradually reducing both the volume and the tempo. As the music changes, so will your state, the reduction in tempo being matched by a gradual reduction in heart rate and blood pressure.

There is growing interest in the use of music to prime the brain for learning – the so-called 'Mozart effect'. Research conducted at the University of California in 1993, found that students performed better in intelligence tests after listening to Mozart's Sonata for Two Pianos in D Major for ten minutes. Scans show that when people listen to Mozart, neurons are activated, or 'fired' over large areas of the brain, in a similar pattern and location to those that are fired by high-order thinking and spatial tasks. By listening to Mozart before the tasks, the brain is primed – in effect, the stimulation from the music acts as mental warm-up.

Asking questions is fundamental to developing understanding.

Asking questions without fear of embarrassment is crucial to protecting self-esteem.

Therefore, the more strategies that we employ that enable children to seek clarification without fear of ridicule, the more likely it is that they will learn effectively.

Although the effect of the music was temporary, there is growing interest in the role that music can play in shaping the young, developing brain and in preparation for cognitive activity. Maths is a subject that would seem to particularly benefit from a musical warm-up.

For more information on the part that music can play in learning, see:

- *Tune your Brain* by Elizabeth Miles (Berkley, 1997)
- *Learn with the Classics* by Ole Anderson, Marcy Marsh and Arthur Harvey (LIND Institute, 1999)

Avoid putting people on the spot

Teachers can inadvertently cause stress. When I was young, many lessons started with the teacher firing out questions, each directed at a particular pupil. Even if I wasn't selected, the stress generated by the thought that I might be, was sufficient to send me into stress mode. Indeed, such was my vigilance in avoiding a question (avoid eye contact at all costs, never sit on the end of a group – strategies that I still employ today), I rarely relaxed enough to learn anything.

Enable students to ask questions without embarrassment

Don't kid yourself – however kind and reassuring you are, there will still be students who are reluctant to admit to gaps in understanding in front of their peers. Providing students with a 'safe' and discreet way of asking questions – and doing so on a regular basis – is a key strategy in reducing student stress. For example:

Use a question box. Students write down any questions they have and drop them in a question box. It can be used informally, with questions being dropped in as and when they arise. To avoid embarrassment, students can drop them in as they leave the room or come back in at break and use the box. A variation is to require *all* students to put a question in the box after a learning experience. For example, everyone in the class writes down a question after watching a video. It enables the teacher to check for any misunderstandings and encourages curiosity among students (see pages 217–219).

Generate group questions. Students work in small groups to generate three questions that a student who had not understood the work might ask. Subtle, but effective! A variation on the theme is to establish 'Learning Groups'. Seat students so that when they turn to a pair sitting behind them, there is a range of reading and conceptual ability. (An alternative is to organize groups so that there are students with different preferred learning styles.) The groups then identify two or three questions that they need answering in order to understand the topic in more detail. After a few minutes the spokesperson will ask the questions on behalf of the group. '*Our group would like to know…*', is very different to, '*I don't understand…*'.

An alternative to a test

- Use a noughts and crosses framework.
- Ask nine questions - students write the answer in the appropriate space.
- Award a 0 for a correct answer; X for incorrect.

The aim for all students is to get a row, column or diagnal of Os

¹ O	² X	³ X
⁴ O	⁵	⁶
⁷ O	⁸	⁹

- By making questions 1, 4 and 7 within the capability of the weakest students of the group, everyone can achieve the aim of a row, column or diagonal of Os.
- This technique offers an opportunity to review work first done approximately one month earlier (see page 221).

There is a massive difference between 3/9 or 33% and achieving three Os in a row.

Time-outs (see page 43)

A time-out is a two-minute break in a lesson, during which time students are free to do anything (within reason!). Some will talk about the work and ask their friends for clarification. When the group discover none of them know the answer, they are much more likely to seek help, than are isolated individuals. Again, it is much easier to say, *'Excuse me, **we** don't understand'*, or *'Could you help **us**'*, than it is to say, *'**I** don't get it'*.

Be proactive during time-outs – hover around the group that you know are the most likely to have misunderstood. By smiling, making eye contact and using a very subtle invitation to ask a question, you provide the students with an easy way in to the conversation.

Traffic lights

Some schools use red and green cards – or a red and green cover on the homework diary – so that students can indicate whether they have understood something (green) or if they need further explanation (red).

There are, of course, some children who will still be reluctant to admit to a gap in understanding. Extend the red and green cards into a *traffic lights* system; green indicating *full* understanding, amber *some* understanding and red *no* understanding. Children who are reluctant to admit to no understanding are often prepared to admit to only having some understanding. With many children, and the class teacher will know who, an amber card is a request for extra help.

A variation on the theme, is to ask for a show of fingers – five fingers indicates full understanding, while no fingers indicates a total lack of understanding. Again, teachers can use their knowledge of a particular group; for some students, three or four fingers may well mean they have some understanding; for others, it is a plea for help. (Most teachers will know perfectly well what two fingers mean: it is a good idea to establish the ground rules early – palms facing the front!)

Keep people informed

Not knowing what is going to happen can be a major source of stress. Your inevitable frustration at being caught in a traffic jam would be significantly reduced if you had been informed how long it was going to be before you would be moving freely again. Make sure you tell the group at the beginning of the lesson exactly what to expect: what they are going to study, what the activities are going to be and how long they will last (see page 185).

Use positive, stress-free language

Nothing has greater potential to create stress among students than the word *TEST!* This stress will be intensified if there is a requirement to achieve at least 7/10 or to redo the test at lunchtime. Replace the word *test* with an *opportunity to show me what you can do*. Remember how you felt when you had a test when you were a child. Compare that feeling to how you would feel if the teacher had begun the lesson by saying:

Relax!

Play suitable relaxing music.

Focus on various parts of the body in turn:

- Close your eyes.
- Focus on your feet. Consciously relax them. Allow them to sink into the floor.
- Now concentrate on your legs. Allow them to become loose and relaxed.
- As you focus on each part of the body in turn, notice how deep and slow your breathing has become.
- Dwell a little longer on your shoulders and the back of your neck. It is important that these areas are properly relaxed.
- Open your eyes. You will feel relaxed, refreshed and ready to learn.

> *Good morning everyone. I'm really looking forward to this lesson and I know you will be too when you hear what we are going to do. Today, I'm going to give you an opportunity to show yourself how much progress you have made during this module. I'm excited because you've all produced such excellent work and I know you will be dying to show it off.*

Try a simple experiment: substitute the word *quiz* for *test* and notice the difference.

Provide students with choice

A major source of stress is the feeling of not being in control. Consider the students in the classroom; they have very little control over their destiny – invariably they are told what they are going to learn and how they are going to learn it. Combat this considerable source of stress by providing students with choice – at least perceived choice – at every opportunity.

For example:

- *Do you want to do exercise A or exercise B? Your choice.*
- *Would you like to write a short paragraph to explain that, or draw a labelled diagram? You decide.*
- *We have an important assessment activity to do today. Would you like to do it at the beginning or the end of the lesson? It's up to you.*

There is no question that the students are going to do an exercise. The choice does not extend to whether they wish to participate or not! It doesn't even matter if exercise A and B are the same – what matters is the *perceived choice* and *feeling of control* enjoyed by each student.

The reply sends an important message to the subconscious brain: '**I want to** *do exercise A/B*'; '**I want to** *draw a diagram*', and so on. How often do you hear students say '**I want to...**' ?!

Relax your students

How many teachers would not be interested in a simple technique that could boost their examination results by 25 per cent? During research carried out at Stanford University, a group of students who had been taught relaxation techniques outperformed a group of students who had not, by 25 per cent. It shouldn't come as any surprise; the brain needs to be in a relaxed state in order to think and perform higher-order skills efficiently.

The easiest way to relax students is to encourage them to focus on their breathing – see page 247. An alternative is to focus on various parts of the body in turn (see opposite).

The whole exercise takes only three or four minutes. Before you say to yourself, '*I couldn't possibly do that*', consider this: what would you say to a colleague who said, '*I couldn't possibly use a technique that will improve test scores by up to 25 per cent*'?

For more information regarding simple relaxation techniques, see:
- *The Learning Adventure* by Eva Hoffman and Zdzistaw Bartkowicz (*Learn to Learn*, 1999)

Neurovascular holding points

Place your fingertips on your forehead (roughly halfway up your forehead at the midpoint of each eyebrow) using gentle pressure to push the skin slightly upwards. The energy in your fingertips will attract blood to the frontal lobe and help you think through a stressful situation in a rational way.

Provide high-challenge, low-stress environments

Do not confuse stress with challenge. High-challenge, low-stress activities must be our goal. Students, particularly boys, respond positively to a challenge. Use the phrase, 'I bet you can't', and watch them go!

- *I bet you can't think of three reasons.*
- *I bet you can't ask me a question about this that is so hard, I can't answer it.*
- *Last time you got seven, I bet you can't beat that!*

One of the key differences between a challenge and a stressful situation is the feeling that the mental resources to complete the task are possessed. In other words, the task – although hard – can be done. Whether an individual can complete a task or not is less significant than the belief that they can. However, as teachers we must beware: although there is a massive difference between stress and challenge, there is only a thin dividing line, with every child drawing it in a different place.

Hold your neurovascular holding points

The neurovascular holding points – also known as 'positive points' in Brain Gym® – are located on your forehead, just above your eyebrows. Place your fingertips on these points and pull up gently on the skin. Sharon Promislow explains the effects:

> *The energy in your hands is enough to keep blood and warmth in your front brain, and stop the classic stress response (flow of blood from front brain to back survival centres).*

This is an effective strategy (for teachers as well as students!) whenever a stressful situation is being faced. By holding our positive points while we think through the problem, we enable the brain to deal with a stressful situation in a logical and rational, as opposed to an emotional, manner.

For more information on this, and other Brain Gym® techniques, see:
- *Making the Brain/Body Connection* by Sharon Promislow (General Distributing, 1998)
- *Brain Gym* by Paul and Gail Dennison (Edu-Kinaesthetics, 1989)

Mental rehearsal (visualizing success)

Certain situations are likely to create stress. For students it may be an exam or a presentation to the rest of the group; for a teacher it may be an interview, taking their first assembly or teaching a group they dread on a Friday afternoon. It is a feeling that is often exacerbated when the situation is being faced for the first time.

Thinking through the situation, before the stressful event, can be comforting and provide the reassurance associated with rehearsal and thorough preparation. Having first imagined yourself succeeding, it is more likely that you will.

When the students are in a relaxed state – it may help to hold the neurovascular holding points – simply think through the event, step by step. At each stage, encourage students

Many children who behave badly in school are those whose self-esteem is threatened by failure. They see academic work as unwinnable. They soon realise that the best way to avoid losing in such a competition is not to enter it.

Elton Report

to visualize themselves feeling relaxed, confident and succeeding at whatever they are doing. Help students to concentrate upon what they can see, what they can hear and how they feel during the event.

Mental rehearsal is common among sportsmen and women and can be equally effective in the classroom. It works at a variety of scales, from drawing a graph to sitting GCSEs.

See Picture it! on page 261 and Anchoring on page 73.

Confident

> *Great learning is such a fragile flower*

Professor Stephen Heppell

A little while ago, I was talking to Stephanie, who was a student in Year 9. Steph had experienced her fair share of problems during her early years at secondary school, a pattern that, by all accounts had been established during the primary years. As we chatted, the conversation turned to maths and I asked her how she was getting on. Immediately, almost as an involuntary response, Steph informed me that she was *'no good at maths'*. When I asked her who told her that she was no good at maths, she replied, *'my Dad'*. She went on to explain that her Dad had told her she was 'useless' at maths when she was very young. In fact, she told me, it had happened so long ago that she couldn't remember a time when she wasn't useless at maths.

For years, she had been walking in to maths lessons, 'knowing' that she was going to fail. Not surprisingly, she hated the subject. Not surprisingly, she messed about. Not surprisingly, she made little progress.

I can relate to Stephanie. To this day, I will tell you that I'm 'no good at maths'. I 'know' this to be true, because my maths teacher told me. He didn't actually say the words, *'you're useless'*. He didn't have to. His body language, the way he ignored me, his response to my questions – I soon stopped asking them – told me all that I needed to know. The horrible realization that I was useless at maths dawned on me during my second year of secondary school – when I had a different teacher. From that moment on, I walked into maths lessons, 'knowing' that I was going to fail. Not surprisingly, I hated the subject. Not surprisingly, I made little progress.

And yet, as a young child I enjoyed maths and considered myself quite good at it. Indeed, reading my old school reports recently, I discovered that during my first year at secondary school, I was in set one for maths and, amazingly, finished 18th out of 35 pupils in the end of year exam! I was interested to note that in the same report, my geography teacher – I went on to get a degree in the subject – had written, ' *I have every confidence in your ability in this subject'*. I probably already suspected that I was quite good at geography but, from that point on, it was official!

Teachers do more than teach – they touch lives.

For, whether it is called self-concept or self-esteem or given any other label, believing that you can succeed, believing that you are a capable learner, is the foundation of successful learning. It is, therefore, of huge concern when a number of research studies have revealed that although most children enter primary school with a positive self-image (most studies put the figure at 80 per cent or more) there is a huge decline in the number of students who feel good about themselves (on average, less than 20 per cent, with some studies placing the figure as low as 5 per cent) when they leave formal education.

Self-esteem belongs to the individual. We cannot build it for people; we can only create the climate and provide the experiences in which it is most likely to develop. Many factors help shape self-concept and our beliefs about our ability as a learner, including our parents, our environment and our peers. However, we should not underestimate the influence that we as teachers have over the way students feel about themselves and their ability to learn.

As is the case with most things, it is easier to destroy than create. There is, I believe, a Chinese proverb which reads, *'the good work of a hundred years can be destroyed in a second'*. So too, the fragile flower of great learning. It takes time and painstaking effort to nurture the self-belief necessary to be a truly successful learner; it takes one comment or one look, to destroy it.

Motivation

> *The three most important factors in learning are motivation, motivation and motivation*
>
> Sir Christopher Ball

There are very few teachers who would disagree with Sir Christopher Ball. In countless training sessions with colleagues from every phase of education, teachers consistently identify motivation as one of, if not the single most significant influence upon learning and attainment.

People, never mind children, learn better when they want to learn. Better still, when they need to learn. I started having a few driving lessons when I was 17, but was never really that bothered about learning properly and had still not sat my test when I was 22. When I got my first teaching post, some 12 miles away from my accommodation, I realised that I faced a very awkward and inconvenient journey into work every day on public transport. Within weeks I had passed my driving test.

Working with motivated children is like teaching in a different world: such is the significance of motivation and the contribution that it makes to effective learning. If they are motivated, the battle has largely been won. I refer to this as the 'O' factor: it is the difference between students saying, even subconsciously, *'Oh good, it's maths today'*, and, *'Oh God, it's maths today'*. One little 'O' makes the world of difference.

For if they arrive at the lesson feeling positive and motivated, they will work that little bit harder and have a greater chance of succeeding and receiving praise, which in turn will add to their enjoyment and boost their motivation. It is a self-perpetuating upward

Think about someone you have met who has made a positive difference to your life. Maybe they inspired you or were there for you when you needed someone most. Perhaps they valued what you offered to them. Possibly they recognized there was more to you than any difficulty you experienced and saw more of the real you. Maybe they just made you feel special in some way.
Now...

- How were they able to do that?

- What was it about the things they said and the way they said them that made the difference for you?

- What did they do that communicated their confidence in you so powerfully?

- What kind of beliefs must they have held that allowed them to do and say these things in ways that still have this effect on you?

spiral that we must do all in our power to create. Conversely, the downward spiral that results when demotivated students struggle, fail and are chastized, is a situation we must strive to avoid at all costs.

The feelings of confidence and motivation that we seek are actually a combination of chemicals – that is what emotions are – that when released, create a *physical* feeling. These physical sensations which we associate with the words and behaviours of motivation and confidence result not from what happens to us, but rather from our interpretation of that reality. In most cases this interpretation takes the form of internal dialogue or 'self-talk'.

Self-talk applies to teachers as well as students. Imagine walking out of the staffroom towards a class who are challenging and you are not looking forward to teaching. What sort of self-talk is going through your head? What types of behaviour do you choose when you get to the classroom? Contrast this with walking towards your favourite class. How are your thoughts, feelings and, consequently, your behaviours different? The 'O' factor applies to us as well! There is a massive difference between thinking, '*Oh good, it's 9B*', and '*Oh God it's 9B*'.

Two things are of use at this point. Firstly, imagine that the worst class that you teach are your best class. As you approach the classroom convince yourself that you are really looking forward to the experience. Try it for a few weeks and notice the difference. Secondly, imagine that your students are 'wired up' in the same way as you! What kind of self-talk is going on in their heads as they walk in to your classroom? In what ways would this knowledge be useful to you?

Teachers do more than teach – they touch lives. It is a privileged position, but it carries an awesome responsibility. If a child thinks for one moment that we think they can't, they will almost certainly fail. Yet if we believe in them and we convince them they can, they almost certainly will. If there is a more important part of the teacher's role than believing in children and letting them know that we believe in them, then I cannot think of it.

We have a collective and individual responsibility to immerse children in optimism and to surround them in self-belief, knowing that our attitude towards them will have a powerful influence upon their attitude towards themselves. This is not the road to Damascus. We are not looking for, nor should we be expecting, miracles. Children who believe that they are useless and have little interest in learning are unlikely to become your most confident and switched-on students overnight. We must chip away however, as everything we do and say will influence their concept of themselves as learners in some way.

To a large extent, motivation and conviction are dependent upon a sense of hope and the perception that progress is being, and can be, made.

Imagine waiting in a long cinema queue. Although you are waiting you rarely stand still – you shuffle slowly forwards. What would happen if you stayed still while the queue in front cleared and only then you walked into the theatre? Well, first, you would irritate the people behind you! Second, it wouldn't make your entrance to the cinema any speedier. However, *shuffling makes it feel better*.

Use the language of possibility

Student:	*I can't do this. It's boring.*	The student is actually saying, *'I don't **believe** I can be successful with this and therefore don't want to take the risk'.* NB It may or may not be 'boring'.
Teacher:	*Of course you can. Just keep trying and put a bit more effort in and you'll get it.*	Inadvertently, we have denied the validity of the student's feelings. Exhorting her to 'keep trying' is not motivating if she believes the task is beyond her. Asking her to put a bit more effort in presupposes she isn't trying hard enough and it's her fault. Again – not motivating.

A simple shift in language may have the desired effect.

Student:	*I can't do this. It's boring.*	By initially agreeing with the student, we are validating how she is actually feeling, which will **always** (*sic*) be correct. This is a start to gaining rapport and therefore effective communication. However, by reframing the problem as 'a little tricky at the moment', we have also diluted the severity of the problem and made it a temporary stage.
Teacher:	*OK, it's a little tricky **at the moment**. Which **bit** can't you do **yet?***	*'Which bit can't you do yet?'* repeats the student's words (can't), which she will accept, and also lessens the difficulty by presupposing it's only 'a bit.' The inclusion of the word 'yet' serves to emphasize the temporary nature of the difficulty and retains a connection to the possibility of things improving.

The strategies that we are describing here are a deliberate and conscious intent to use feedback that connects students to a sense of possibility and hope that they can 'keep shuffling'.

The use of language

Richard Bandler (the co-founder of the discipline known as Neuro-Linguistic Programming (NLP)) once said that it's impossible not to communicate. It is important for teachers to recognize that words can inadvertently wound and contribute to negative self-esteem, but they can also help build healthy self-esteem and confidence, reduce stress and encourage the risk-taking so vital to effective learning.

Positively affect student motivation and confidence by consciously considering the language patterns that you use on a daily basis. Even teachers who instinctively use language effectively can enhance the impact of their words by considering the language patterns below.

Use the language of success

Tell students at every opportunity that you believe in them and that you have confidence in their ability. Use phrases such as, '*I **know** you can*'..., and, '***when** you have completed...*' They are messages that convey expectation and confidence and are so much more powerful than, '*I **think** you can...*', or, '***if** you complete...*'

Use the language of hope

Ban the phrase, '*I can't do this*', from your classroom. Replace it with, '*I can do this but I'm going to need a little help*', or, '*I can do this, but not yet*'. Display the phrase on the wall. Draw attention to it whenever you feel a student is going into the 'I can't do' mode. '*I can do this, but not yet*', is a very different way of looking at a situation to, '*I can't do this*'.

Use the language of possibility

Students get in 'stuck states' at times. These occur when they have developed a belief about some aspect of their character or their capability as learners that limits the choices they feel able to make and 'disconnects' them from the possibility of change. It also inhibits their motivation to move into an area of risk and try something which is challenging.

Our use of language and the choices we make about how we engage children in stuck states will often determine whether they stay in them or take those first tentative steps towards change.

Students' language will often give us clues as to their limiting beliefs. Words such as,

> *always   never   everybody   totally   all the time*

imply a fixed state that never changes and it is important to challenge or reframe these beliefs in a way that doesn't create either blame or conflict.

Useful words and phrases for the classroom

- *When* you finish
- I *know* you can
- Which part didn't *I* explain well enough?
- I'm sorry, *I* should have made it clearer
- What do *we* need to *remember* here?
- OK, so you haven't *quite* mastered it *yet*
- *Up to now*, this bit has proved a little tricky
- Today you have a fantastic *opportunity* to show *yourself* how much you've remembered from the last module

- Quiz
- Rehearsal
- You *will* remember
- Your choice / it's up to you / you decide
- Maybe... and...
- That's right, isn't it?
- I can do this and I'd really benefit from a little extra help!

Reframing them by using words such as,

sometimes   occasionally   recently   so far   yet   up to this point

- dilutes the problem because it acknowledges there are times when it doesn't occur
- implies that any difficulties are part of a process rather than fixed
- keeps students 'shuffling' (see page 67).

An example of how this might work in a conversation is given on page 68.

Remember, it's not just students who need to reframe their language. Get in the habit of talking sense to yourself too. A colleague recently declared that he was '*totally and utterly depressed*' about work. When another teacher responded, '*So **some** things have been **getting you down a little lately**'*, the colleague sighed and agreed that this was indeed the case. He went on to suggest some of the strategies he was going to try so that '*things will get better*' (his words).

Remember that:

- *sometimes* I make poor choices in class
- *so far*, I haven't created the climate I want in 9B
- *a lot / many / some* students I teach are pleasant and co-operative
- *up until now*, I haven't managed to stay as calm as I would like to in class
- *most* of the time I am well organized and prepared for classes
- *at some point* during each day I make a positive difference to a child's life.

Remove the language of failure

Remove the word and the feeling of failure from your classroom. Replace failure with *rehearsal* or *experiment*. Making mistakes, is a vital part of the learning process. However, when getting something wrong is seen a failure, it is demotivating and damaging to the self-concept of the learner. Encourage all students to regard mistakes as a rehearsal and a step towards successful completion of the task.

'*Great rehearsal! You're now a step nearer getting the right answer*', is a very different message and will have a very different impact to, '*You're wrong.*'

Use 'no blame' language

'*Which bit haven't **I** explained well enough?*' and '*What do **we** need to remember here*', are very different messages to, *What don't **you** understand?*' and '*What have **you forgotten**?*'

Affirmations

'I can do this.'

'Dream it. Believe it. Do it.'

'Whatever you can do or dream you can, begin it. Boldness has genius, power and magic in it. Begin it now!'

Goethe

'If you think you can or you think you can't, you're right.'

Henry Ford

'Nothing great was ever achieved without enthusiasm.'

Ralph Waldo Emerson

'If you can dream it, you can do it.'

Walt Disney

'By a consistent effort of will it is possible to change your whole life.'

Emil Zatopek

'Man's mind, once stretched by a new idea, never regains its original dimension.'

Oliver Wendell Holmes

Use affirmations

Do not underestimate the power of positive affirmations. There is widespread agreement that a significant proportion – some would claim as much as 99 per cent – of learning is non-conscious. Ensure that students are surrounded by positive, 'can do' messages by displaying positive affirmations in each and every classroom in the school. Look at it another way: what would be the impact of negative messages around the school?

- *You're a lousy teacher.*
- *This is a dreadful place to work.*
- *I hate teaching.*

Imagine how would you feel if you faced these constant negative reminders all day. Fairly quickly you would begin to feel negative and eventually you would become negative. Affirmations are influential. Make sure that the subconscious messages received by the brain are positive and remind the student that he or she can achieved. Some suggestions can be found on page 72.

Anchoring

'Anchoring' is a term used in Neuro-Linguistic Programming (NLP) – it simply means using a trigger to influence the state of an individual. We can use these triggers or 'anchors' on ourselves or we can use them with our students. The principle behind them is simple and is similar to the way in which something can trigger a memory – the sound of a particular piece of music reminds you of the time you met your partner, or the smell of a particular food reminds you of your childhood. The subtle difference is that we are triggering the memory of a particular feeling or state and as we remember it, we begin to actually feel it. In effect, we are recapturing good experiences and feelings at will.

For example any mother, when watching the birth of a baby on television, will experience the same feelings of love (and pain!) and the strong maternal instincts that were present during the birth of her children. Similarly, any rugby player will react to the smell of 'Deep Heat' in a changing room: a physical change will take place as adrenalin is released into the body in anticipation of the game to come. By using these feelings and consciously associating a trigger with them, we can change people's state on demand, simply by activating the trigger. In effect, we are bottling the feeling and the emotion and using it when it is most appropriate.

As is so often the case, the best way to illustrate how an anchor can work, is with an example. Laura and Charlotte were Year 11 students who felt very nervous about the impending GCSE exams. They frequently told me how worried they were, and that they were, 'no good at exams' – a sentiment confirmed by their negative body language. Their firmly held belief that they were no good at exams was preventing them doing justice to the ability that they possessed.

The first time that I worked with them, I asked them what they were good at. They both replied, *'nothing'*! I explained that I didn't mean just school work; I was looking for anything that they were proud of and felt that they could do well. For some students it might be sporting prowess or the ability to play a musical instrument or it could simply

A step-by-step guide to triggering a 'state'

This can be done with individuals or with groups of students. It is a technique that can recapture feelings of confidence. Alternatively, it can be used to relax students and/or help them feel safe and secure.

1   Relax the students.
2   Ask them to think of something that they do well (or makes them feel relaxed and so on). It may well be something that has nothing to do with school!
3   Encourage them to be as precise as possible. What do they see, hear and feel?
4   Intensify the feeling. Use phrases such as, *'I bet that makes you feel terrific'*. Pay attention to the way in which you say it.
5   Help students consciously associate something with this feeling. It could be a piece of music or a physical act such as clenching the fist. (It needs to be something they can 'activate' in an exam.)
6   Encourage them to associate the feeling and the trigger when the feeling of confidence or relaxation is greatest.
7   Next time they need to feel confident, they activate the trigger (listen to the music, clench the fist and so on).
8   The more times they associate the emotion with the trigger, the stronger the connection will become.

For more information, see:
* *Introducing Neuro-Linguistic Programming* by Joseph O'Connor and John Seymour (Mandala, 1990)

* *In Your Hands – NLP in ELT* by Jane Revell and Susan Norman (Saffire Press, 1997)

* *The Learning Adventure* by Eva Hoffman and Zdzistaw Bartkowicz (Learn to Learn, 1999)

be that they have the ability to make their mates laugh. In my experience, it is not uncommon for teenage girls to value the fact that they are attractive and have no problems getting boyfriends!

Laura and Charlotte began to think about the thing they were most proud of. As they were thinking, I asked them questions and made comments designed to intensify the feeling. I asked them to focus very carefully upon what they saw when they were doing this activity, what they heard and, *precisely*, how they felt. The more I said, '*I bet that makes you feel absolutely terrific.*' and, '*That must make you feel really good – I bet none of your friends could do that.*' – the more their body language and facial expressions changed, confirming just how confident and good about themselves they were feeling.

As they were experiencing such powerful positive emotions, I had music playing in the background. (It was actually Mozart's *Eine Kleine Nachtmusik*.) This music captured their positive mood and would trigger the same emotions whenever they heard it again. Needless to say, I played it at the beginning of every revision session and after a few weeks explained to the girls what I was doing. One day, I asked Laura if she wanted me to play the music in the hall as students were settling down at the beginning of the exam to help her feel positive and confident. '*No need*', she replied, '*I hum it to myself as I walk into every lesson just to make myself feel good and I will be doing it before every exam!*'

It is not just music that can trigger a memory, emotion or feeling. Physical sensations can also trigger an emotion. When a physical sensation is consciously linked to a feeling and used for the purpose of triggering that feeling, it becomes an anchor. Visual images or places will also activate a particular 'state'. Have you ever covered a lesson for an absent colleague and found that students that you teach behave completely differently in a different setting?

Anchors can be a very powerful way of influencing the state of our students. Not only can we trigger feelings of confidence and an '*I can do this*' attitude, we can also use anchors to help students relax and/or feel safe and secure. Imagine how useful it would be if, just as you were about to leave your comfort zone – for an interview or a major presentation, for example – you could recreate the feelings of safety and contentment that you felt when you were snuggling up to your favourite Grandad as he sat with his arm around you on the sofa. Well you can! All you need to do is to find something that will trigger the emotion and consciously use it when you need to relax.

Find out what they are good at

One day I heard the sound of fantastic drumming coming from one of the music practice rooms. I investigated and was amazed to find that the drummer was none other than Steph (see page 63).

Here was the girl who thought she couldn't learn, co-ordinating hand, eye and foot to make the most incredible sound. I made a point of listening to Stephanie whenever she practised and made sure that all staff were aware of her remarkable talent. Gradually, and significantly, our discussions changed from '*I can't do*' conversations, to '*I can do*' celebrations.

Our first priority, particularly with students who fear failure and perceive themselves as failures, is to give them a taste of success.

Interestingly, when we first talked about her ability in maths, before the drumming discovery, Stephanie had rated her ability to learn in the subject as one out of ten. A year after the drumming incident, her personal rating had risen to seven.

- Find out what they're good at (sometimes we have to tell them, because, sadly, they don't know).
- Let every teacher know.
- Let the students know that we know.

Take an interest in their achievements outside your classroom

Acknowledge that students have a life outside your classroom. Asking them how the netball team got on, praising their performance in the school play or congratulating them on raising money for charity gives powerful, *'I care about you as a person'* messages. This is a particularly important strategy for keeping the self-esteem of students who find your particular subject difficult intact.

Bulletin board/self-esteem wall

In order for David's English teacher (page 35) to have a positive impact upon his mood by choosing to enquire about his motorbike at the start of a lesson, she first had to know that David's passion was motorbikes. The problem for many teachers, especially in large schools, is to keep track of what is going on. If you don't know that Stephanie is a great drummer or that James has just been selected to represent the county, you cannot use this information to your advantage.

Create a bulletin board or a self-esteem wall in the staffroom so that tutors and teachers can keep the entire staff updated. Any snippet of information that teachers can use to have a positive impact upon the mood of a student and to let them know that they are valued as a person, irrespective of their ability in a particular subject, is valuable.

Imagine that you are finding a student surly and unco-operative and that you are searching for a way of improving the situation. You glance at the self-esteem wall for any information that might help. Imagine the positive impact on a student, if you greeted them at the beginning of the next lesson with, *'Congratulations on your hat-trick last night Joe!'* or *'How are your guitar lessons going Alison?'*

Success

Success breeds success. When people do well, they are encouraged, often praised, and go on to try that much harder on the next occasion. This increased effort enhances the prospect of further success and an upward spiral of achievement is set in motion.

Conversely, failure, or perceived failure, is dispiriting and can often persuade the learner – even at a subconscious level – not to bother. After all, if we don't try something, we can't fail. A lack of effort the next time around will almost certainly doom the learner to further failure; possibly accompanied by criticism and even punishment. It is a depressing downward spiral that is hard to break.

It means that our first priority, particularly with students who fear failure and perceive themselves as failures, is to *give them a taste of success*. No matter how we contrive it,

Progress wheel: the French flag

I know that . . .

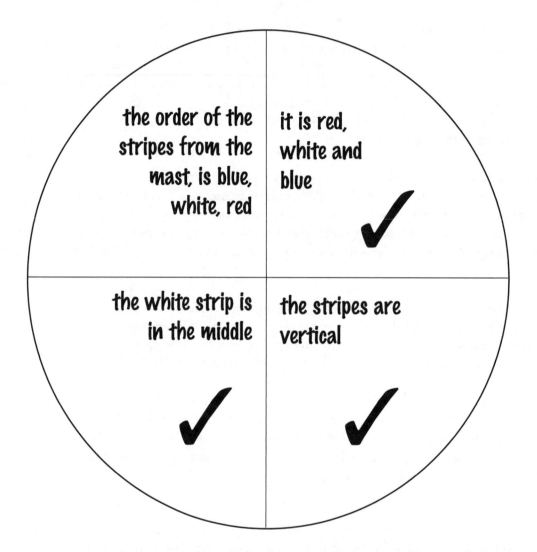

Any task or unit of work can be broken down and represented in the form of a progress line or wheel. It is a simple idea designed to give students a sense of progress and help them focus upon what they know. It can be a useful tool for moving them out of an 'I can't do this' or 'I don't know this' state.

early success has to be our conscious goal, even if it means taking a few steps sideways or even backwards, and laying aside the scheme of work for a while. Setting a piece of work that you know an individual will do well, or publicly asking them a question that you have previously checked in private they can answer, is a strategy designed to motivate and build self-esteem. It will be well worth it in the long run.

The key is that students feel successful. What messages and clues do we give our students through our choice of language, non-verbal communication and written feedback about their relative success or otherwise? Remember: if they perceive themselves as failures, all is lost.

Success book

Many children drift through school being successful without even realizing it! Issue all students – or at least students who suffer from poor self-concept – with a small notebook for them to record their successes. Do not confine success to academic progress; we are simply trying to help students realize that they are capable and worthwhile. Students jot down anything they are pleased with – from answering a question in maths to remembering their PE kit. Make sure that tutors and teachers regularly make time to chat through and congratulate the student on their successes.

Progress line/progress wheel

When a student says, *'I can't do this'*, they rarely mean it. In the vast majority of cases, they simply mean that they are struggling with a specific aspect of the work. Sadly, the focus, all too often, is on the bits that cause the trouble.

For example, Rachel (see page 271) told me that she *didn't know what the French flag was* yet she knew that it consisted of three vertical stripes of red, white and blue and that the white strip came in the middle! Not bad for someone who, 'didn't know'! All that she was unsure about was the order; red, white, blue or blue, white, red. She had 90% knowledge, yet chose to focus upon the 10% that she wasn't sure of.

Switch the focus by drawing conscious attention to the parts of the work that the students *can* do, by using a progress line or wheel (a line may appeal to a sequential learner while a wheel may be more appropriate for a random thinker – see page 78). It is a simple idea and can be operated at a variety of scales. Break a topic, lesson or task into a series of small steps or components. Record these in the segments of a wheel or along a line. Students then plot their progress through a unit or a task. Keep drawing attention to the bits that they can do and try to convey a sense of progress and optimism – crucial factors in motivation.

How would you like your success to be recognized?

I have yet to meet anyone who does not want to succeed. I have met many young people who *claim* that they don't want to succeed or who are so scared of failure and looking foolish that they do not even take part. Sadly, I have also met many children, particularly boys, who do not want their successes to be publicly recognized, fearing that they will become the target for peer ridicule. The thought of having to go up to the front during assembly is enough to make the toughest Year 9 boy turn to jelly!

You'll never hit a target you can't see.

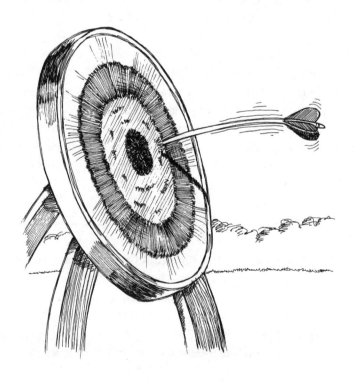

Strategies for Closing the Learning Gap

To combat this, ask children how they would like their successes to be recognized. Some, of course, will relish the formal rewards such as merit slips that culminate in an award being made in assembly. However, many won't. Others opt for their awards to be made privately in the Head's office. (One young boy insisted on bringing the SENCO with him, who dutifully applauded as he received his certificate!) Often, older students tell me that all they want, or need, is for the teacher to acknowledge their achievement unobtrusively. Many tell me that a smile and a 'thumbs up' is sufficient recognition.

One Year 8 girl actually told me that the fact that I had asked her was all the recognition that she needed!

Goal setting

Success is a key to motivation – yet success is relative. Sally's first reaction when she was handed her GCSE results of eleven A*s and one grade B was, *'Oh, I really wanted an A for maths!'* Compare this with Jane, who was crying with relief and delight after securing four grade Cs and five grade Ds. Crucially, Jane had achieved the four C grades that she required to pursue the college course that she had set her heart on, while Sally had failed to achieve the clean sweep of A grades that she had personally targeted.

Success is all about achieving a goal. In this example, Jane did; Sally didn't. Tom just shrugged his shoulders when he was asked if he was pleased with one grade A, four grade Cs and four grade Ds. He didn't know if he'd succeeded because he didn't know what the target was. It means that setting goals – personal goals – plays a central role in being successful. Without them, we have nothing to measure achievement against.

Setting goals and shorter-term targets should be part and parcel of school life. However, target setting in schools is often done badly and, the more that teachers are required to do it, reluctantly. Often, the reason why target setting is all too often ineffective, is that targets are not sufficiently *specific*, nor are they *owned* by the individual. Generally speaking, targets are too general!

Use the following principles as a guide when setting goals and targets with students:

- *Goals are longer-term aspirations* – a grade B at GCSE.
  Targets are shorter-term and more specific – I will achieve at least 7/10 on this exercise.

  Encourage students to set both on a regular basis. Make target setting a feature of every lesson you teach. Use prompts such as, *'By the end of this lesson, I will …'* note the positive statement, *'I will'*. Discourage the use of phrases such as, *'I hope to'* or *'I might'* or *'I'll try'*. *'I'll try'*, gives permission to fail; *'I will'* conveys expectation.

- To have any meaning, goals and targets must be owned by the individual. Make them personal!

  Many people refer to the significance of the WIIFM – 'What's in it for me?' – factor. This means essentially that the individual has to accept the relevance and importance of the goal in order to act upon it.

- For some individuals, it may well be that we have to look beyond school to see how the goal will benefit them. I once spent many hours trying, to no avail, to persuade a particularly demotivated Year 11 student that GCSEs were important. By accident, I discovered that his burning ambition was to join the army. When he

By the end of this lesson I will...

In order to achieve this I must...

discovered that he needed qualifications to be accepted into the army, he had a goal and began to work hard to achieve it. Needless to say, he only started working hard in the subjects that he required and went on to pass them all. The goal was not the GCSEs; the goal was the army. GCSEs were just a step to get there.

● Make them specific. *'I will improve'* or *'I will do better than last time'* are meaningless targets and will have little or no impact upon achievement. Targets do not have to be grand, large-scale affairs. There is nothing wrong with small but precise targets such as, *'I will answer three questions today'* or *'I will check the spelling of any word I'm uncertain of on the word wall'*.

● Encourage students to visualize success. Sportsmen and women do it as a matter of course. Encourage students to picture themselves achieving their goals. Use prompts: *'How do you know that you've been successful?' 'What do you see?' 'What do you hear?' 'How do you feel?'*

● Follow up targets by encouraging students to consider what they need to do in order to achieve them. What will they need to do differently in order to achieve a target for the first time. Use prompts: *'By the end of this lesson, I will...' 'In order to achieve this, I must...'*

● Initially, students will need considerable help and guidance when setting personal targets for a lesson. It is an investment well worth making, for targets that are relevant and personal provide a focus and can lead to enhanced motivation and effort. When they are reached, the student has succeeded – and nothing motivates quite like success.

Feedback

Students need to know when they have been successful and this involves providing feedback. The brain thrives on feedback. For optimum learning, feedback must be immediate, frequent and positive. However, given the constraints of the classroom, feedback is rarely as immediate or as frequent as the student or teacher would like. Reducing class sizes or restructuring the curriculum is not within our control, so we focus upon what is possible under our current working conditions.

Feedback is not the same as marking

Do not underestimate the impact of a smile or the 'thumbs up' sign to reassure a student that they are on the right lines and making progress. Think of how many ways in which you could provide feedback without actually marking an individual's book.

Use the 100 per cent rule
Do not be distracted by other students – *'Excuse me Miss where are the scissors?'* – when you are giving feedback. Giving 100 per cent of your attention for a few seconds is worth more to the student than a few minutes of your attention when you are constantly being distracted by others.

Use other students to provide feedback
'OK folks, stop what you are doing. Show your work so far to the person sitting next to you. Explain what you are doing and why. Ask them what they think. Then swap roles'.

Success credit for your use of ICT

In this essay, I will explain why so many people died in the Kobe earthquake.

The Kobe earthquake took place in Japan. Japan is a rich country and one of the most technically advanced in the world; it has a population of 124 million people and a density of 310 per square kilometre. During the earthquake, the port of Kobe was destroyed. The Japanese government were shocked by the earthquake. Kobe has a new and an old town the new town is much more technically advanced and prepared for earthquakes. The old town however is much more vulnerable in earthquakes and not well prepared at all.

Success Promising introduction

Tip Include a map

Tip Begin a new paragraph a short way in ⟶

Kobe has a major port, ship building and rubber productions are also an important part of the city. Many other things are produced in Kobe e.g electrical equipment, railway cars textile and sugar being a few.

Think Would it be better to give the date and time in the introduction?

Kobe hadn't had a major earthquake since 1956 which meant that many people were not expecting another one so Kobe grew larger and more populated. At 5:40 am on January 17th the earthquake struck. When the ground shook, some buildings collapsed but some just swayed. All of Kobe was blacked out. Over 5000 people died and 35000 were made homeless.

Target for higher levels, explain your statements. Use "because phrases" to explain <u>why</u> things happened.

Thanks to Mike Davis of Casterton Community College, Stanford for both the strategy and the example.

Address the whole class

'If you are left with seven or more cards after the second activity, then you are very much on the right lines.' Body language will tell you which students aren't!

Make praise and feedback specific

Praise is very important (see 'Catch them being good', page 101) and should not be used in a mean-spirited way. Provided that it is genuine and sincere and says, at an emotional level, *'my teacher cared about me today'*, you can't overdo it. When was the last time you felt too good?

However, praise has only limited value without a frame of reference. Supposing, in response to a student hitting a tennis shot just out of court, the teacher says, *'Great effort. Keep trying'*. While this may help them feel a little better, it doesn't contain any useful information about how to improve.

On the other hand, if the teacher says, *'Great effort. Take the ball a little earlier and keep the racket head moving through the shot'*, a frame of reference for the next effort has been provided that will help improve performance and help the student feel optimistic. Encouragement therefore, is a way of giving objective, non-judgmental feedback that connects the student to the future possibility of success.

Marking

How would you feel if you had spent hours slaving over a piece of work, only for it to be returned covered in red ink? Brilliant – if the red ink indicated the things that had been done correctly! I first came across this approach in *NLP for Lazy Learning* by Diana Beaver and immediately tried it in the classroom. The effects were stunning! Students who thought they 'couldn't do geography', and frequently had their mistakes pointed out to them, were suddenly getting a very different message and a massive boost to their self-belief. It is a very different way of looking at the whole issue of marking and, even if you can only manage it once a year, can have a powerful impact upon individual students.

An alternative, is to label the comments 'tip', 'target', 'success' and 'think' in the margin. It is a highly effective way of providing feedback and direction to the student, without giving a negative, 'you can't do this' message.

Provide choice

If the feeling of not being in control (see page 59) is a major source of stress, the provision of choice can be a great motivator. When people believe that they have made a positive choice, motivation is likely to rise. Provide as much choice – or perceived choice – as you can in your lessons. Use the phrase, *'your choice'*, or *'you decide'*, at every opportunity:

- *Do you want to convert that into a diagram, cartoon strip or flow diagram? – You decide.*

- *How would you like to demonstrate that? – Your choice.*

- *You can either work on your own or discuss it first with the person sitting next to you. It's up to you.*

The Average Child

I don't cause teachers trouble
My grades have been OK
I listen in my classes
And I'm in school every day
My parents think I'm average
My teachers think so too
I wish I didn't know that
Cause there's lots I'd like to do.
I'd like to build a rocket
I've a book that shows you how
Or start a stamp collection
Well no use trying now
Cause since I found I'm average
I'm just smart enough you see
To know there's nothing special
That I should expect of me
I'm part of that majority
That hump part of the bell
Who spends his life unnoticed
In an average kind of hell.

First presented at the 1979 National PTA Convention by Michael Bucemi, Quest International
published in *The Learning Game*, by Michael Barber (Orion, 1997)

Their response will start, *'I want to…'*, which is a powerful motivator!

Engineer a 'thank you'

Select a student who lacks confidence and suffers from a poor self-image. Ask them to pop next door and fetch a pile of books – even if you do not need the books. You have consciously created an opportunity for eye contact, a smile, recognition and a 'thumbs up'. I know – it's 'a drop in the ocean'!

Appropriate challenge

When the task is too easy, students are bored. When the task is too hard (or they perceive it to be) – students are demotivated.

When the task is challenging and on the edge of the 'comfort zone' but, crucially, the student believes it to be within their grasp, they are motivated.

Students, and indeed adults, rise to a challenge. Use the phrase, *'I bet you can't'* and the natural human instinct, is to respond with, *'Just watch me'*. Challenges can be particularly effective when set at the beginning of the lesson – see page 191.

Opportunities to work in their preferred style

Everyone has a preferred learning style (see Section Three). Some people prefer to see information (visual learners), some prefer to hear information (auditory learners), while other people prefer to learn by doing (kinesthetic learners).

While most students are sufficiently multisensory to learn even when working outside of their preferred style, the question remains, do they really want to? All teachers know by the response that they get, whether a task motivates a student. Different types of task will motivate different types of learner, which means that teachers must ensure that they are providing variety and choice in the way in which they are asking students to learn.

Use first names

For children to feel good about themselves they have to feel that they are being valued and recognized by their teachers. Schools are big places and it is very easy for individual children – and it is children who we teach – to become 'lost'. A genuine smile and warm welcome can do much to positively influence students of any age. Using their first names – at the beginning of the sentence – conveys an important message that, even among a large school population, *they* are important.

Reflect for a moment upon the children who are frequently addressed by their first name:

- *Jonathon! Jonathon will you sit down. Jonathon, how many times do I have to tell you? JONATHON!*

- *Jonathon, that was another excellent piece of homework.'* (warm smile and other 'I like teaching you' messages) *'I am absolutely delighted with your progress. Well done Jonathon!*

When they walk into my room, they'll walk into France. They'll see, hear, smell and 'feel' France. They'll speak French, they'll feel French – they'll almost be French.

Modern languages teacher

Strategies for Closing the Learning Gap

The 'Jonathons' of this world are certainly recognized – for all sorts of reasons – but what of the children who cause you no trouble, never seek attention, work quietly and unobtrusively and produce steady rather than spectacular work? These are the 'average children' described in the poem on page 86. How many times during the day are they addressed by their first name? If you kept a tally chart for a few weeks, recording how many times you used the first name of every student you teach, what would it look like? Would there be some children who have been addressed by their name infrequently, or even not at all? What effect do you think it would have on their learning if you made a conscious effort to use their names more often?

How would an expert do it?

This is a simple strategy, but a very effective one. Students take on the role of an expert and approach an activity or task in that guise. It is an approach that Win Wenger refers to as 'borrow a genius' or 'put on the head of a genius'.

For example, imagine you are:

● Monet – how would he paint it?

● Venus Williams – how would she play a top-spin backhand?

● William Shakespeare – how would he write the poem?

● Albert Einstein – how would he approach the problem?

When students 'borrow a genius', they are encouraged to think, act and feel as the expert would. Tasks are often viewed in a different light and negative beliefs of 'I can't do' are by-passed as the expert, rather than the student, engages in the activity.

For more information see:

● *The Einstein Factor* by Win Wenger (Prima Publishing, 1994)

● *Beyond Teaching and Learning* by Win Wenger (Project Renaissance, 1992)

● *The Inner Game of Tennis* by W. Timothy Gallwey (Pan, 1986)

The significance of the environment

> *When they walk into my room, they'll walk into France. They'll see, hear, smell and 'feel' France. They'll speak French, they'll feel French – they'll almost be French.*

Modern languages teacher

A young modern languages teacher, seeking her first job, spoke these words at interview. She was true to her words. Within days of arriving at the school, her classroom – now with a red, white and blue wall – had been transformed into a French oasis in an English school. No one – student or teacher – could fail to notice both the transformation and the message of optimism and enthusiasm that the room conveyed. It was not long before the other language teachers asked for their rooms to be decorated in a similar fashion.

Step one

Create an environment that is physically comfortable – this will enable students to learn.

Step two

Create an environment that is stimulating, reassuring, interesting and informative – this will enhance learning.

Most teachers do not have time to reflect regularly upon, never mind change, the appearance of their classroom. Teachers quickly become accustomed to their teaching room – a room where they spend anything up to six hours of every working day – and can easily become almost oblivious to the impact that the environment has upon students. Yet the classroom sends out subtle messages that influence the state of every student each time they walk through the door. It is an opportunity to positively influence the students' mood, which we would do well to exploit.

Classrooms are more than the rooms where we teach; they are the environments in which young people learn. At their best, they can inform and inspire; stimulate and reassure. At their worst, they can actually prevent learning from taking place.

All classrooms will have an impact, intentionally or otherwise, on:

- the physical state of students
- the emotional state of students.

Our first challenge is to create an environment that is *physically comfortable* and does not distract students from their work. This is a prerequisite for effective learning, for when students are thinking about how cold or hot they are, they cannot be thinking about the task in hand and they will not learn.

Getting the physical environment right *enables* the students to learn. Once basic comfort has been established however, we have an opportunity to operate at a completely different level and to use the environment to positively influence the emotional state of the students. We have all been in ordinary, adequate classrooms, in which learning is possible. Less frequently we have been privileged to enter an environment that is, in classroom terms, a different world. In these classrooms, learning, while not quite being inevitable, is significantly *enhanced*.

Stage one – creating an environment that enables learning

Many things – some outside our direct control – limit, or even prevent, learning. These have to be addressed before students can settle to their work. In particular, students will not learn effectively if they are:

- too hot or too cold (If you teach in the same classroom all day, you will become accustomed to the temperature – how does it feel to students walking into your room for the first time?);
- blinded by sunlight;
- uncomfortable (You may not have control over the furniture, but you can choose to allow or require students to stand up and stretch at regular intervals.);
- inaccessible or unable to move (Teachers need to be able to reach the desk of every student with ease if they are to provide them with the individual help and attention that all students require. Students need to be able to move around, to collect resources, to break state, to work collaboratively and so on.).

Classrooms should be...

- physically comfortable
- welcoming – is there a welcome sign on the door?
- relaxing – do you play music as students arrive for a lesson?
- attractive and cheerful – plants and flowers make a difference
- reassuring and emotionally safe – use affirmations, put a question box by the door so that students can ask questions without embarrassment
- stimulating and motivating – include motivational posters
- informative – display keywords and key information around the room – some experts believe that 99 per cent of learning is subconscious
- interactive – use wall displays to ask questions and stimulate thought
- novel – change your displays and your room layout at regular intervals
- neat and tidy – what messages are given off by the state of your desk/room?

Strategies for Closing the Learning Gap

Stage two – creating environments that enhance learning

- **Display key information around the room**

  Many experts believe that a significant amount of learning is done subconsciously. When key information is displayed around the room, the brain will absorb it without the student even realizing. Display, just above eye level, keywords, facts, formulae, maps and diagrams that are relevant to the topic being studied. (The eyes look up when the brain is in visual mode – see page 124.)

  You will often see a student in an examination or just working independently, pause and glance upwards. They are quite literally looking for the answer, their eyes instinctively going to the place where they could see the relevant information from their seat in the classroom.

- **Display keywords**

  What are the keywords of your subject? Display them prominently and refer to them regularly. Use big, bold, colourful letters. In modern language classrooms, reinforce basic vocabulary by labelling the features of the room appropriately – window, door, table and so on.

- **Use giant learning maps**

  Students need to put the lesson in context. A learning map of a course or unit of work allows all students to chart their progress and to see how a particular lesson fits into the scheme of work (see pages 211 and 267).

- **Reinforce good habits**

  Display key questions:

  What? When? Why? How? Who? Where?

  Refer to them constantly and encourage students to ask them independently (see page 55).

- **Stimulate curiosity**

  A poster, new information, a question or a challenge on a classroom wall can stimulate curiosity. Leave some gaps in the information provided to jolt the brain into action. When faced with part information or something that doesn't quite make sense, the brain will naturally seek an answer or solution. When students are curious, their attention levels will increase significantly as they seek to make sense of something that is puzzling them (see page 189).

- **Use affirmations**

  Affirmations can inspire and reassure (see page 73). Displaying quotes and phrases such as the examples on page 72 does much to positively influence the attitude and mood of students.

- **Change your classroom regularly**

  The human brain is stimulated by novelty. When students walk into a classroom in June and find it exactly the same as they did the previous September, do not be surprised if they seem to lack a little sparkle. Any change in the classroom – the layout, the orientation, the wall displays – will be stimulating and bring about a positive reaction in students.

Summary – State

People will learn best when they are in an appropriate state to learn.

People need to be in an appropriate physical and emotional state to learn.

Self-esteem and motivation play a key role in learning.

We do not have control over a student's self-esteem and motivation, but we do have an influence.

Everything we do and say has an influence over our students.

We must make sure that we are exploiting every opportunity to exert a positive influence over students.

We are seeking to 'put enough drops in the right ocean' – we are more likely to do so when we act consciously, consistently and congruently.

Self-esteem and motivation are whole-school issues that demand a whole-school response.

Does your school have a Head of Self-esteem or a Head of Motivation, or both?

If the answer is no, what made you decide not to appoint one?

Aim to change your classroom in a significant way at least once every half-term. There is no doubt that this is a demanding aspiration. Equally, there is no doubt that regular change will have a positive impact on the quality of learning.

The role of the headteacher

We often hear that the headteacher is, or should be, the lead learner in an institution. Similarly, it could be said that the headteacher should be the lead 'praiser'. When a teacher recognizes a student and praises their work, the student receives a boost. When a headteacher recognizes and spends some time with an individual, the boost can be considerable. Make it part of your motivation policy to send students to see the head when they have produced good work. Good work is relative and the efforts of modest academic attainers should be recognized every bit as much as the high fliers. Whatever the head is doing, even if they are meeting with the Chair of Governors (particularly when they are meeting with the Chair of Governors!), interrupt them with a steady stream of students to be praised.

Do not worry that you are distracting them from more important matters, for there is nothing as important as the self-esteem of young people. Headteachers will be delighted to put down the budget or the initiative of the moment to remind themselves why they entered the profession in the first place. They will be imagining the look on the youngster's face as they get home and tell their mum that they were sent to the head with 'good work'. They will know that they have made the child feel special – and they are.

Whole-school approach

Although we do not control a student's self-esteem and levels of motivation, the fact that we have an influence places the onus upon schools and teachers to ensure that the influence that they exert is a positive one. It is an individual and collective responsibility that demands an individual and collective response.

Positively influencing self-esteem and levels of motivation involves putting enough drops in the right ocean to begin to make a difference. We are more likely to be successful if we set about this task:

- consciously
- congruently
- consistently.

At an institution level it means that all teachers are consciously adopting the kind of strategies outlined in this section. Anyone who has ever worked with a young person with damaged self-esteem will confirm that just one critical look or negative comment – however inadvertent – by a solitary teacher on a Thursday afternoon, can destroy the good work of the ten teachers who been consciously and painstakingly exerting a positive influence all week.

We cannot, of course, guarantee that all teachers will be boosting self-esteem and motivation – even when they are trying to. However, by adopting a whole-school approach, co-ordinated by a Head of Motivation, we make it more likely.

'Until these kids behave properly, we can't do anything interesting.'

'Until these kids do anything interesting, it is unlikely that they will behave properly.'

Which is more likely:

● that students will arrive at your next lesson with a totally different attitude?

● that you will decide to use a different strategy in the classroom?

Focused

> *I've come to the frightening conclusion that I am the decisive element in the classroom.*
>
> Haim Ginott

All teachers are concerned with classroom management. They are right to be – few students will learn effectively in a noisy classroom with the teacher spending the majority of the lesson struggling for quiet. It may seem like stating the obvious but a well-managed classroom which is structured, orderly and empowering is crucial if we are to engage students in the learning process as effectively as possible.

Consequently, the ability to manage children is greatly valued among the teaching profession. We have all been mortified when a senior colleague has walked into our noisy classroom – the fact that the students have been on task and the noise generated by animated group discussion is scant consolation. Similarly, we all hold opinions about our colleagues. It says much that our respect is often gained, not by colleagues' ability to help children learn (in many cases we haven't even seen them teach!), but because *they stand no messing*.

However, two things are worth remembering.

- Managing children is not our ultimate goal, but helping them learn is. Establishing a controlled and orderly classroom environment is not an end in itself; it is simply a necessary platform for helping children learn and make progress.

- Behaviour is significantly improved when students feel good about themselves, are fully engaged in their learning and are experiencing regular success.

Establishing and maintaining a disciplined working environment is a central issue for schools. Indeed, concerns about poor behaviour and the fear of losing control can often be strong enough to prevent teachers from trying many of the strategies outlined in this book.

This section has been written to address these concerns. While many will argue that behaviour will be significantly enhanced when students feel valued and successful both as learners and as people, we can also considerably increase the likelihood of establishing an atmosphere conducive to learning by adopting a range of techniques and strategies designed to provide positive discipline without confrontation.

It is not intended to provide comprehensive coverage of positive behaviour management issues – that is beyond the scope of this particular book – but is simply a collection of practical approaches and techniques that seek to maintain the focus on learning. These are strategies that are essentially designed to prevent poor behaviour rather than deal with it.

For a comprehensive collection of practical behaviour management strategies see:

- *Confident Classroom Leadership* by Peter Hook and Andy Vass (David Fulton, 2000)

Good teachers manage the behaviour of most of the children most of the time.

The belief that, *'good teachers control the behaviour of all the children all the time'*, is highly damaging and yet extraordinarily common among teachers. *It is also completely false!*

The only thing that we can actually work to be in control of in a classroom is ourselves. The reality of teaching is that, *'good teachers **manage** the behaviour of **most** of the children **most** of the time'*.

In setting a powerful and supportive agenda, the belief that the only thing we can control in the classroom is ourselves is both realistic and empowering. However, given the naturally stressful nature of the job it is easier said than done!

All teachers will be familiar with the physiological changes that occur when a student acts outside the appropriate agenda – a tightening of the stomach, an increase in breathing rate, a dryness in the throat and so on. These physiological changes occur through stress and the belief that the agenda has moved away from us and towards the student.

What do we do? We interact verbally with the student – we say something designed to reclaim the agenda and reduce our stress. In other words we go straight from the physical feeling to the verbal exchange. Bill Rogers, a specialist in behaviour management, refers to this as the 'guts to gob' style of behaviour management. There are three key things about the 'guts to gob' approach.

1 It is reactive rather than proactive.
2 It almost always makes things worse.
3 It doesn't work!

Parents and teachers alike can empathize totally with this experience. However it begs the question, *'how do you avoid being drawn into this reaction?'*

What has proved most consistently successful in avoiding this reaction is having something else to say or do instead. In other words, a collection of strategies to support the crucial belief that because you can't make students do something you have to act in a way that makes it more likely that they will. We do this on our good days by modelling, guiding, encouraging, persuading and using strategies that reflect our intent to protect mutual rights *and* individual self-esteem and dignity.

All of the above form part of our *plan* for good behaviour. Good behaviour does not happen accidentally and is too important to the learning process to be left to chance. In constructing your plan you will recognize that students calling out, being off task, not having equipment, being rude to you and each other are all daily experiences in class. It therefore self-evident that being *consciously* aware of a wide range of strategies that you can call on to hold on to your self-control is a powerful and effective way of leading and influencing students with integrity at the same time as maintaining the learning climate. The more options and flexibility you have, the more likely you are to retain control over a situation.

It is all too easy, however, for even the most effective strategies to get lost or sidelined in the fast pace and natural stress of today's classrooms. Having a framework within which these strategies can be utilized increases the likelihood that a teacher will choose to employ them in times of stress.

Nine core principles for effective behaviour management

1 Plan for good behaviour.

2 Actively teach rights, responsibilities, rules and routines.

3 Separate the (inappropriate) behaviour from the child.

4 Use the language of choice.

5 Keep the focus on the behaviour of concern rather than personal argument.

6 Actively build trust and rapport.

7 Model the behaviour you wish to see.

8 Always follow up on issues that count.

9 Be proactive in repairing and restoring relationships.

Such a framework must reflect the beliefs and values that guide our choice of response. For example, if we believe strongly that dignity and respect are fundamental then sarcasm, verbal threats and 'in your face' shouting are totally incompatible strategies. This is called *congruence*.

Essentially, congruence is about the ways in which we present ourselves to others. When we are congruent it means that both our words and our non-verbal behaviours are conveying the same message. The impact and effectiveness of the message depends on this. Just how easy is it to notice when someone claims to be pleased to see you but actually isn't? How many times have you given praise to a student just for the sake of 'jollying them along' and it hasn't worked?

Congruence is heavily dependent on the beliefs and values that drive what we do and what we say. It is about total sincerity.

The nine principles for effective behaviour management described opposite – originally developed by Peter Hook and Andy Vass for the DfEE National Training Programme (DfEE, 2000) – provide a framework within which effective strategies for classroom management can be employed. This framework emphasizes:

- a clear and fair agenda within which we *all* operate

- a rationale for our management of the classroom climate

- principles which underpin our actions

- a structure that helps maintain a positive focus.

The strategies in the following section carry no guarantees, but they do make it more likely that students will behave appropriately in the classroom. In using these strategies we ask ourselves a key question: *'What is it we are consciously aware of doing that contributes to students **wanting** to come back to our classrooms?'*

Proactively build rapport

You cannot influence or lead anyone from a distance. Make an effort to smile. Get to know about your students and their likes and dislikes and show a personal interest in them. Acknowledge them and chat to them outside class. A brief *'How's it going?'* in the lunch queue goes a long way.

Keep unspoken but explicit promises to treat them fairly, to give them supportive feedback and to keep them safe from embarrassment, shame or humiliation.

Demonstrate in all you do, that despite the mistakes and poor choices that students make, you hold an unconditional belief they can be winners.

Catch them being good

Notice and acknowledge what they do well far more than you notice what they don't do. *It is important to do this for things that we may **expect** students to do just as much as when they put in the extra effort.* Turning up in uniform, having the right equipment, following

What do you see?

●

Most people will notice the dot and ignore the blank space.

The same can often be true in the classroom. Our attention is easily drawn to the things that are going wrong and incidents of inappropriate behaviour, rather than to the things that students are doing well.

instruction and completing work set are all expected of students. However, showing appreciation of these things does no harm and recognizes that our lives are made easier when they happen.

At first, saying things like *'Good to see you ready'* and *'Thanks for settling down now'* may seem unnatural. It's only by making a conscious effort to do this that it becomes a positive habit. However, unless you really believe that this is worth doing then it will inevitably sound forced and insincere.

Place posters or affirmations on the classroom wall so that they become your trigger to comment positively. Again this can take many forms:

- smiles, nods, thumbs up and so on
- verbal comments and feedback
- stars and smiley face stamps
- written comments on work.

Never underestimate the power of these to provide a positive boost to motivation. As long as they convey the message that *'my teacher cared about me today,'* they will work. Remember that when you look beyond the designer clothes and attitudes you will find children, and children like to be noticed whatever their age. Year 12 students have been known to argue over whether their work was worth a penguin or an elephant stamp!

Of course, sensitivity and understanding the context play a part. Saying out loud to a Year 10 class, *'I wish everyone could work as well as Duncan'*, will not endear Duncan to them!

Give them a way back

Getting it wrong and making poor choices or mistakes is an essential part of learning. It is and always has been the role of children (especially adolescents) to test and challenge boundaries. Part of our role as teachers is to accept this as a normal phenomenon and to work to get children to make better choices through, among other strategies, modelling.

Modelling conflict resolution means that *we* act to repair any potential damage to the relationship. Although it is not possible to disguise feelings of frustration, hurt or annoyance, we must recognize that such displays have the potential to cloud subsequent interactions with the student. It can be difficult, but our objective must be to start with a clean sheet each time. Talking to the student after class about their behaviour can finish with an optimistic, *'Next lesson I'd like you to choose to use a polite tone of voice when you speak to me. I'm sure we can sort this out together.'*

In class, after we have corrected a student, simply coming back to them in a minute or two and asking, *'How's it going? Do you need a hand?'*, lets them know that whereas you don't accept the behaviour, as a person they are OK.

Because teachers can't make students do things, their responsibility is to:

- influence
- guide
- encourage
- persuade
- negotiate
- model
- cajole
- manage
- assert
- build trust and rapport
- 'catch them being good'
- direct
- hold high expectations
- convey confidence and belief
- enhance self-esteem.

Increase non-verbal directions

Non-verbal directions can be powerful for a number of reasons.

- There tends to be less ambiguity about them as most gestures are universally understood. Putting an open hand up towards someone will convey the message 'stop' to most people.

- Because they are visual, the brain processes them much faster. No thought needs to be given to tones or inflection as it does with spoken language.

- Where appropriate they can be used less intrusively than spoken instructions. Catching a student's eye across the room or even calling their name in a conversational tone can be followed with a finger to the lips for 'quiet' or miming writing to get back on task. Either causes minimal intrusion on the rest of the class.

- When used correctly, non-verbal directions tend to be slow movements and support calmer interactions.

Use positive directions

As far as possible, describe what you want someone to do rather than what you want them to stop. Reframing language from 'don't' to 'do' is a very powerful way of communicating.

- *'Don't run'* becomes *'Walking please'*.
- *'Stop calling out'* becomes *'Hands up'* or *'One at a time'*.

This works at two levels. It actually describes a positive, *alternative* way of behaving which increases the choices available to the student and redirects them back to being successful without confronting or criticizing.

Now, don't think of something blue!

What happened? In order not to think of something blue you first had to consider blue. The reason for this is that the word *'don't'* only exists in language. It has no sensory experience. Can you hear, see, smell or touch a *'don't'*?

Imagine what thoughts and experiences your students have when you say:

- *'Don't forget your homework'* or *'Don't speak to me rudely!'*

Use take-up time

This is a skill that avoids what Jacob Kounin refers to as 'overdwelling'. Give your instructions briefly and positively in an assertive tone whilst making eye contact with the student(s), then *immediately* turn away and carry on with the lesson. If you are 'up front', then look at the far side of the class and scan slowly back to the centre at the same time as continuing your information giving. If you are walking round the room, walk away and go to talk to a student who is *working well*.

With 'heavy' instructions, give the directions then go and find someone to help, *whether or not they want it!* This gives both the teacher and the student time to catch their breath and think of what would be a good choice next.

Have you ever been driving home after a heated exchange and, as you replayed the situation in your mind, identified exactly what you wished you had said at the time?

It is all too easy to be wise after the event when we are in a calm and rational state. However, when we find ourselves in an emotional and challenging situation, rational thinking goes out of the window as instinct and emotion take over.

It is therefore helpful if there are phrases and language patterns such as maybe... and... (page 111) that we have consciously decided to use in certain situations before they arise.

They offer no guarantees, but do make it more likely that our words and actions will defuse situations and help students make good choices.

Maintaining eye contact or staring the pupil out just adds heat to the transaction and in some situations students will read into this a power challenge that is effectively saying, *'Come on then if you think you're hard enough!'* In a public setting, especially in front of peers, they are in a 'no win' scenario.

Turning away and reclaiming the lesson indicates that you are confident they will comply, it's not worth pursuing and you are actively protecting their dignity by using the least intrusive approach.

Thanks

Adding *'thanks'* or *'thank you'* rather than *'please'* to the end of a direction implies confidence that your instructions will be followed. In business, letters often end by thanking people in advance for their co-operation. This is simply the verbal equivalent. When combined with take-up time it is a very powerful and successful strategy.

Planned ignoring

We all know that ignoring some instances of poor behaviour can be a useful strategy. The emphasis, however, is on the word 'planned'. This is not the same as pretending it's not happening or *hoping* it'll go away. As part of a range of strategies, it is worth deciding:

- what kinds of things you can ignore (never ignore racist, sexist or dangerous behaviour)
- how long you can ignore them for
- what are your options when ignoring it doesn't work.

It's also important to ignore *at the same time* as praising appropriate, on-task behaviour from others nearby.

If your planned ignoring doesn't have the effect you want, then the following two strategies offer a 'plan B'.

Proximity

Moving alongside a student in class and standing so you are *just* in their peripheral vision can be effective in stopping unwanted behaviour. As you do this, keep your instructions to the rest of the class going so that the movement appears natural rather than targeted towards the particular student.

Be aware that staying there for too long or standing too close can make someone uncomfortable.

Casual questions

Refocusing attention through the use of casual questions is a non-intrusive way to retain control of the agenda and to redirect student behaviour. Simple questions for the 'up-front' phase be:

The teacher notices that Mark is looking idly out of the window and wishes to redirect him back to his work.

A comment such as:
'OK! So what's the answer to number 6 Mark?'
or
'What did I just say Mark?'
will result either in Mark giving the correct answer (which is highly irritating!) or, more likely, a defensive or even a flippant response. There is a risk that a confrontation may develop and the agenda will be diverted away from learning.

A better alternative would be:
'That's right isn't it Mark?'
Mark's attention is restored without diverting attention away from learning.

- *How many ideas can you add, Karen?*

- *Does everybody know what to do here? Erin – OK?*

- *I'm not sure how well I explained that. Does that make sense Damien?*

In using a casual question to refocus a student, always look for opportunities to preserve dignity. Putting students on the spot by suddenly asking, *'What did I just say Terry?'* will gain his attention but also contribute to his embarrassment. This sometimes manifests itself in a surly, *'I dunno!'*

It also adds to our sense of irritation when students are able to recall exactly what we did say!

It is possible to use casual questions as a way of refocusing or redirecting students and still keep dignity and self-respect intact, as illustrated opposite.

Or, in moving to a desk you can ask:

- *Everybody on target?*

- *How's it going? Do you need a hand?*

- *Can I see your work please, Jack?*

When... then

'When... then' is more positive and empowering than *'no you can't until'*. It can be used in many situations where you wish to retain control of the situation by deferring your decision.

- *When you're in your seat with your hand up, then I'll check your work.*

- *When you've finished this paragraph, then you can go out to break.*

- *When I've finished helping Andy, then I'll be over.*

- *When I've settled people to work, then you can have your say.*

'Double what' questions

Questions that ask a student why they did something are not helpful within the context of a fast moving and multi-dimensional classroom. Very rarely do they actually know anyway!

'Double what' questions are designed to give responsibility to the student for their behaviour and to refocus or redirect without attacking the behaviour. The two questions are: *'What are you doing?'* followed by *'What should you be doing?'*

Agreement frames

Student:	I've finished the graph Miss. Is this OK?	
Teacher:	Well Steph, let's see. You've got a title, labelled the axes and plotted the points correctly. You understand graphs don't you?	As the teacher points out what the student can see it is very likely they will begin nodding, internally or externally. It is merely a suggestion, but having begun nodding because she can see the title and so on, it is likely she will continue to agree. This will confirm or enhance her belief about her capability with graphs.
	I imagine you're pleased with this.	Again, keeping the agreement going but this is different to 'I'm pleased with you.' It generates internal or intrinsic motivation.
	Crack on with the next bit. Yeah?	I wonder just what emotional state she will be in, what beliefs will be in place and what level of motivation present as she moves on to the next part of the task?

This strategy is equally effective when the work is not complete:

Student:	Is this OK?	
Teacher:	Well Steph, let's see. You've got a title and most of the points are plotted correctly. What do you need to remember here?	'What do you need to remember?', pointing at the unlabelled axes, is more empowering than, 'What have you forgotten?' If she can say what's missing then it's further evidence of her ability. If she can't, the teacher can say, 'Axes always need a label. I probably didn't make that clear enough.' In other words, the teacher can take the blame so that Steph can keep 'shuffling'.

T: *I notice you're out of your seat Jake. What are you doing?*
S: *Just getting a pencil!*
T: *What should you be doing now?*
S: *These boring questions.*
T: *OK back to work. I'll be over to see how it's going in a minute or two.*

At this point it is not sensible to pick up on the 'boring' challenge but to use take-up time.

Use agreement frames

Agreement frames are a method of quickly establishing rapport – and therefore influence – with someone. Simply, they are a way of constructing the language you use so that people feel able or comfortable to begin to agree with you. An agreement frame occurs when someone says:

- what you can see to be true
- what you know to be true
- what you believe is true
- what is compatible with how you are feeling.

When one or more of these things occur, we tend to signify our agreement by nodding, either internally or externally.

- *'Teachers deserve better pay and conditions.'*
- *'Teaching is an increasingly stressful profession.'*
- *'We have less and less choice over what we do.'*
- *'Raising the morale of teachers is about demonstrating trust in our professionalism.'*

Once this is established, it is possible (with honesty and integrity) to add bits that you would like people to agree to.

'Thanks for staying behind.' (acknowledgement of his co-operation) *'I imagine you're a bit annoyed at having to miss part of break, Jack ...'* (Too right I am!) *'... and it's important this work is finished.'*

Because the first parts are within Jack's experience, it is possible that the next part will be more acceptable.

Agreement frames also offer powerful ways of giving encouraging feedback to students (see opposite).

Maybe... and

Have you ever told a child that you didn't care? It is easily done and is often the instinctive response when students go for the 'last word syndrome' or moan about what they are being asked to do.

For example, when a student is asked to face the front and listen, to stop talking or put their chewing gum in the bin, they will often seek the last word with a reply along the following lines:

Influencing - state

- What strategies do you use to get and keep students in an appropriate physical state to learn?
- Do you give students an opportunity to stand up and move around during a lesson?
- How do you get students into a state of relaxed alertness at the start of your lesson?
- Do you welcome and smile at students as they enter your classroom?
- Do you address all students by their first name?
- How much choice do you provide for your students?
- Do you use positive, stress-free language?
- Do you say 'test' or 'quiz'?
- How do you consciously convey the message to students that you believe they can succeed?
- Do you say 'when' or 'if'?
- Do you encourage students to set personal targets?
- Do you emphasize success and ensure that students know when they have achieved?
- Which bits do you emphasize – the things that students do well, or the things that they do badly?
- How do you let students know – without saying a word – that you care about them?
- Would all of your students say that you cared about them and believed in them?
- What do you consciously do today that makes students want to come back tomorrow?

- Award yourself a mark out of ten (ten being the highest) for the way in which you influence the state of your students.
- Identify one thing that you could do differently that would enable you to increase this score by one mark.

- *'They were talking too.'*
- *'I was only talking about the work.'*
- *'Other teachers let us.'*
- *'This is boring.'*

To avoid responding with the damaging and potentially confrontational phrase, *'I don't care'*, we need a better alternative. *Maybe… and…* is a powerful agreement frame and can be used to defuse these frustrating situations and ensure that the focus of the lesson remains on learning:

- *They were talking too.*
 Maybe *they were* **and** *I need everyone facing the front and listening now. Thanks.* (followed by take-up time)

- *I was only talking about the work.*
 Maybe *you were* **and** *I'd like you to face this way and listen now. Thanks.*

- *Other teachers let us.*
 Maybe *they do* **and** *in this class it's gum in the bin. Thanks.*

- *This is boring.*
 Maybe *it is* **and** *it's what we're doing today. Can I help?*

Most people are not in the habit of using agreement frames and language patterns such as *maybe… and…*. They can, however, be learned. Try and build one of the phrases suggested in this section into your behaviour management repertoire and practise using it for a couple of weeks. When you begin to hear yourself using it quite subconsciously, simply add another phrase.

However powerful and effective these language patterns are, they do not guarantee that students will behave appropriately in your lessons. They do however make it *more likely* that confrontation will be avoided and that students will choose to behave in a manner conducive to learning.

For a detailed explanation of *why* this is so effective, see:

- *Confident Classroom Leadership* by Peter Hook and Andy Vass (David Fulton, 2000)

REPORT A   Wouldn't it have been nice...

Mike is gestalt brain dominant and will only readily absorb the details of a piece of work after he has a firm overview of the topic. He is a random thinker and often suggests alternative ways of looking at an issue. Not surprisingly, he relishes and excels in situations that allow him to exploit his exceptional creative talent. He has a thirst for knowledge and constantly asks questions that frequently extend beyond the confines of the curriculum. Mike thinks deeply about the work that we are doing and often goes 'in to himself' in order to consider and make sense of the material.

As a kinesthetic learner, Mike learns best by doing, responding particularly well to 'hands on' activities and any work involving movement. He works in intensive spurts, punctuated by bouts of relaxation and internal reflection. He is very conscious of the world around him and is quick to pick up events and conversations that are taking place in the classroom. His written work reflects the speed and the random nature of his thinking. He has a lively mind and quickly sees the connection with a piece of work and a new area for investigation.

He is an interesting boy with an unusual learning style. I hope that I am doing enough to help him fulfil his enormous potential.

REPORT B   How it was written

Michael finds it hard to follow simple instructions and pays insufficient attention to the details of his work. He occasionally has some interesting ideas, but sadly these bear very little resemblance to the work that we are doing.

He finds it hard to sit and listen and constantly interrupts during oral work. Michael is a daydreamer and spends too much time looking out of the window. I constantly have to remind him to get on with his work. Michael fidgets too much, distracting himself and others - he really must learn to sit still and improve his concentration. Too much of the lesson is wasted with Michael being more interested in what other people are doing than in his own work.

Michael's written work is untidy, rushed and riddled with errors. He must learn the value of checking his work for mistakes before dashing off to the next piece of work. He has been in detention four times this term for fidgeting – but still he hasn't learned to sit still. He is wasting his ability.

Section Three: Style

"*There is nothing so unfair than the equal treatment of unequal children.*"

Thomas Jefferson

It simply isn't fair! How can it be? We are all very different, yet each one of us is treated in exactly the same way. If the way in which you are taught, happens to coincide with the way in which you learn, congratulations! You will learn and make progress. If you are talented in the areas emphasized and measured by schools, congratulations! You will be considered a success.

If, however, the way in which you learn is incompatible with the methods being used to 'teach' you, and your talents lie outside the narrow academic confines of the formal education system, then you will have to wait until you leave school to be successful. Sadly, many people can't wait that long and will have long since been consigned – by society and themselves – to the education scrap heap.

Michael (see opposite) is one such student. His preferred style of learning and the way in which he thinks and processes information are at odds with the way in which the teacher works and the orderly, structured environment of the classroom. Children like Michael are the 'fidgeters' and can be frustrating to teach. Often they are labelled as naughty and inattentive. Not surprisingly, many become bored and demotivated and make relatively little progress.

People learn best in different ways. Each one of us has a preference for the way in which we receive information and the way in which we processes it. In a nutshell, *we all have different preferred learning and thinking styles*. When we are given frequent opportunities to work in this way, *learning will be optimized*. A conscious attempt to allow individuals to work in the style that best suits them must lie at the heart of any attempt to improve and accelerate learning.

Although, in recent years, increased attention has been given to the fact that there are visual learners, auditory learners and kinesthetic learners, this is not the only way in which thinking and learning styles can be classified. Indeed, Gordon Dryden and Jeannette Vos in *The Learning Revolution* claim that there are around 20 different methods of identifying learning styles.

> **In this section we will look at three of the most frequently used classifications of learning style. Of all the different approaches, these are arguably the most useful, certainly for the classroom teacher.**
>
> ➡ *visual, auditory and kinesthetic learners*
> ➡ *right/left hemisphere dominance*
> ➡ *multiple intelligences*

The classification of learners into visual, auditory and kinesthetic, focuses upon the way in which people prefer to *receive information* and, as such, is a particularly helpful distinction for teachers who have a significant amount of influence over the way in which they transmit information in their lessons.

Think of ten students you teach who irritate you and/or are underachieving.

Underachievement can be identified systematically, for example using a scattergraph as on page 120 or through a 'gut feeling'. Most teachers will have little difficulty identifying the students who irritate them!

This exercise can be done by the whole staff by increasing the number of students to 20. (At this scale, it is highly likely that the same ten names will appear on everyone's list.)

Two things will be apparent:

● The students who irritate you will probably be underperforming.

● The students who irritate you and are underachieving will probably be kinesthetic learners.

Hemispheric dominance is essentially about the way in which people prefer to *process information* and to think. Arguably, it is more difficult for teachers to have influence in this area. It is, however, essential that all teachers are aware that students in their class are all processing information in a variety of ways.

Multiple intelligences is concerned not with how people prefer to receive and process information, but with the ways in which they are intelligent. By recognizing and capitalizing upon individual strengths, learning can be maximized.

Further information regarding thinking and learning styles can be found in:

- *The Learning Revolution* by Gordon Dryden and Jeanette Vos (Accelerated Learning, 1994)
- *Superteaching* by Eric Jensen (Turning Point, 1994)
- *Righting the Education Conveyor Belt* by Michael Grinder (Metamorphous Press, 1991)
- *In Your Hands. NLP in ELT* by Jane Revell and Susan Norman (Saffire Press, 1997)
- *An Introduction to NLP* by Joseph O'Connor and John Seymour (Mandala, 1990)

Visual, auditory and kinesthetic learners

Some people prefer to see information – these are *visual* learners. Some prefer to hear information – these are *auditory* learners. Others prefer to be physically involved (touching, doing, feeling) with their learning – these are *kinesthetic* learners. As a rough guide, approximately one-third of students in your class will be visual learners, one-third auditory and one-third kinesthetic.

We can further subdivide; some visual learners will prefer to see text, while others will respond better to diagrams and visual images. Kinesthetic learners also come in two categories; kinesthetic tactile or *haptic* learners, who need to touch and feel during learning and kinesthetic internal learners being the people who learn best when their feelings and emotions are activated through stories and metaphor.

This VAK classification is the result of the work done by Richard Bandler and John Grinder, the co-founders of the discipline known as Neuro-Linguistic Programming (NLP), and is particularly useful for teachers as it focuses on the way in which information is *received* by the learner. This, of course, is a direct result of the way in which the teacher *chooses* to transmit information and therefore we have considerable influence in this area.

Translators

It is important to remember that we are talking about learning *preferences*, with most students being multisensory enough to learn outside of their preferred style. However, there are two important considerations:

1   A kinesthetic learner, for example, may be able to learn from a visual or auditory stimulus, but do they want to? When students are required to work outside of their preferred style for long periods, there is a real danger that they will become bored and demotivated.

2   Although most people can learn outside of their preferred style, there are a handful of students who will only be able to do any meaningful learning when working in their favoured mode.

A teacher once commented that virtually all the children in her bottom set appeared to be kinesthetic learners. Almost immediately, she posed the question – was this a coincidence, or had they found their way into a bottom set because they had made little progress working consistently outside of their preferred learning style?

Interesting, don't you think?

Strategies for Closing the Learning Gap

Michael Grinder highlights the significance of the *only* students; that is, those who will only learn effectively in their preferred style. He talks about the 'visual only', the 'auditory only' and the 'kinesthetic only'. children. When an 'only' – someone with a very strong preference for receiving information in a particular way – receives information via a different sense, they will internally translate the material into their preferred mode. For example when a 'visual only' hears a piece of information, they will create a visual image in their brain. These students, he refers to as 'translators'.

Translators are faced with a major problem in the classroom because while they are translating information they will miss the next thing that is being said and end up with significant gaps in their knowledge. Michael Grinder suggests that over 65% of 're-teaching' time (this is different from time spent reinforcing or reviewing) is spent with translators.

For further information try:
- *Righting the Education Conveyor Belt* by Michael Grinder (Metamorphous Press, 1991)

Mismatch between learning styles and teaching approaches

All teachers have a preferred teaching style which will often correlate strongly with their own preferred learning style. It is an approach to teaching that they will instinctively revert to in times of pressure. When there is a mismatch between the preferred learning style of the student and the preferred teaching style of the teacher, there is every likelihood of underachievement, boredom and even misbehaviour.

In general terms, schools cater better for visual and auditory learners, for students who are left-hemisphere dominant and for those people who naturally prefer to work in linear, sequential manner. Many of the experiences and the majority of lessons are organized along these lines.

Kinesthetic learners, right-hemisphere dominant students and random thinkers, however, have significantly fewer opportunities to work in their preferred style. For many of these people learning is 'messy' and unstructured; yet the majority of teachers seek to keep lessons neat and tidy. '*You **all** have 15 minutes to **write** your answer to question 7*', might make perfect sense for an organized lesson plan, but makes no sense whatsoever from a learning perspective that takes into account a wide variety of learning preferences.

Kinaesthetic learners are disadvantaged

Michael Grinder makes the point that the initials 'KO', for 'kinesthetic only', are particularly appropriate as it is those children with heavily kinesthetic preference that are likely to be 'knocked out' of the education system, disadvantaged by the relatively few opportunities to work in their preferred style. It may be a generalization, and there will clearly be exceptions (PE, art, technology) but it is an area worth exploring in some detail.

Place a piece of paper on your desk, labelled:

V

A

K

Graph showing predicted GSCE grades against CAT scores

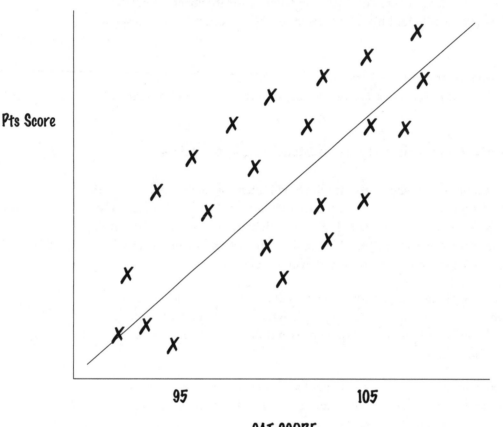

Pts Score

95   105

CAT SCORE
(Cognitive Ability Test)
Graph showing predicted GCSE Grades against CAT Scores.

The predicted grades were based upon all available evidence at the end of Year 9 (SATs, CAT scores, URQ scores and so on). Not surprisingly, students with a higher CAT score were predicted to achieve a high points score at GCSE and vice versa.

22 students were identified in the CAT range 95–105 below the line of best fit. These students were forecast to achieve D grades and/or 4 grade Cs.

Close analysis revealed that 20 of the 22 had strong kinesthetic learning preferences. It is interesting to speculate that if these students had more opportunities to work in their preferred style, they would go on to achieve C and B grades. If so, an increase in the school's 5 A–C figure of 13 per cent would be possible.

Every time you hear yourself say, *'What I want you to do now, is...'* or, *'The next task is to...'*, make a note – is it an opportunity for a visual, auditory or kinesthetic learner? Keep a record for a couple of weeks to gauge the relative opportunities for different types of children. In the secondary classroom – with the exceptions of the subjects mentioned on page 119 – the ratio could well be something like:

V   卌 III

A   卌 II

K   III

Primary classrooms are often very different and offer significantly more opportunities for kinesthetic learners – this is one of the reasons why some children who have been successful during the primary years begin to 'go off the rails' at secondary school. Some primary colleagues suggest that the number of opportunities for kinesthetic learners at primary school, while still greater than at secondary school, has declined in recent years with the introduction of the Literacy and Numeracy Strategies. Food for thought.

Review schemes of work

An alternative way of gauging the relative opportunities for different types of learner is to sit down and analyse your schemes of work. Use highlighter pens in three different colours to identify any opportunities for visual, auditory and kinesthetic learners.

- What pattern emerges?
- Is there a difference between subjects?
- Is there a difference between teaching sets?
- Is there a difference between Key Stages?

The students that make the difference

The scattergraph opposite (which is an actual example compiled in a comprehensive school in 2000) shows the predicted achievement of students at GCSE, based upon their results in Key Stage 3 SATs, Cognitive Ability Tests (CATs) and the students, performance in the classroom. It shows quite clearly that students of similar ability (based upon their performance in CATs) are likely to go on to achieve significantly different results at GCSE.

Scattergraphs constructed after GCSE exams showing CAT scores and actual performance at GCSE will reveal a similar pattern. The value of working with predicted results, is that it is not too late to do something about them!

In crude terms, it can be said that the x below the line points represent students who are underachieving in relation to their potential. Students to the extreme right of the graph are probably achieving A and B grades when students with similar CAT scores are achieving A*s. Children towards the left of the graph are gaining F and G grades, compared to the D and E grades achieved by students in the same ability range. But it is the students in the middle of the graph who are of particular interest in school improvement terms. All children are important; however, we have to start somewhere and students in the CAT range of 95–105 are the children achieving D grades but could, and arguably should, be achieving at grade C and above. It would appear sensible to focus upon this group, at least initially.

The key for teachers and schools is to:

- be aware of different learning styles and the impact that a mismatch between learning style and teaching approach can have upon behaviour, motivation and learning

- make lessons multisensory

- offer variety and choice in learning activities.

'What, read that? No chance guv – I'm an auditory!'

Out of a cohort of 160 students, 22 fall within the CAT range 95–105 and are achieving below their anticipated level (below the line). There are, of course, many possible reasons for this apparent underachievement. However, I would suggest that it is significant that, upon close examination, no less than 20 of these students, revealed strong kinesthetic preference.

Dryden and Vos in *The Learning Revolution* suggest that the mismatch between preferred learning style and teaching approach is '*possibly the biggest single cause of school failure*'. It would certainly appear that they have a case and that the correlation between relative achievement and learning style is significant. It is interesting to speculate that had these 22 students been given more opportunities to work in their preferred learning style, they may well have achieved C or even B grades rather than a string of D grades, making an *overall impact on the school's 5 A–C per cent of around 13 per cent!*

Whatever drives you – the quest for school improvement and progress up the league tables or the fact that individuals matter and that currently many children leave school having achieved only a tiny fraction of their potential (their only crime being the way in which they learned best was at odds with the practices and procedures in the majority of classrooms) – this is an area that cannot be ignored. Interest and research into the impact of learning style on achievement has, surely, only just begun.

Keep it in perspective!

Although there is an understandable temptation to group students by learning preference and teach them accordingly, I believe this is an overreaction to the situation, unnecessary and even unhelpful. We are talking about preferences – most students being multisensory enough to survive and flourish in a typical classroom environment, even when required to work outside of their mode.

We are also in the business of preparing young people for life and survival in a multisensory world. The last thing that young people need is another label and to be pigeon-holed in a particular category. I also have an image in my mind of a Year 10 student replying to a teacher's request to read page 16 with the reply:

'*What, read that? No chance guv – I'm an auditory!*'

The key for teachers and schools is to:

- be aware of different learning styles and the impact that a mismatch between learning style and teaching approach can have upon behaviour, motivation and learning
- make lessons multisensory
- offer variety and choice in learning activities.

How to determine learning styles

There are a number of ways to determine an individual's preferred learning style. It is advisable to use a number of approaches simultaneously. In particular, do not rely solely on the results of a learning style questionnaire – some people do not learn particularly well from a visual prompt and here we are providing a visual stimulus to determine their preferred learning style! Questionnaires have their place; but be wary.

Determining learning styles

There are a number of ways of determining an individual's preferred learning style. It is advisable to use a number of approaches simultaneously. All will give you clues rather than a definitive answer.

1 Ask them
If you had to spell a word that you were unsure of, would you:

a   scribble it down or picture it, to see if it looked right?

b   say it quickly to yourself, to see if it sounded right?

c   trace it in the air, to see if it felt right?

2 Observe them
How do they respond when given a particular task? With enthusiasm, or with a sigh? These are big indicators. Close observation of body language will reveal other, more subtle clues. In general:

● visual learners follow you with their eyes, talk quickly and have relatively shallow breathing

● auditory learners often tilt their head to the side and repeat what you have just said under their breath

● kinesthetic learners speak slowly, breath deeply and fidget.

3 Watch their eyes
● Visual learners will tend to look up.

● Auditory learners tend to have level eye movement.

● Kinesthetic learners tend to look down.

4 Learning style questionnaires
These are quick and simple to use. Treat them with caution, however – remember that some people do not respond well to a visual stimulus!

An easy-to-use questionnaire can be found on pages 126 and 128.

For more information about body language and 'eye accessing clues', try:
● *Introducing NLP* by Joseph O'Connor and John Seymour (Mandala, 1990)
● *In your hands – NLP in ELT* by Jane Revell and Susan Norman (Saffire Press, 1997)

For general information about learning styles, try:
● *Righting the Education Conveyor Belt* by Michael Grinder (Metamorphous Press, 1991)

Nor should we label a student on the basis of observing their eyes move or hearing them make a comment such as, *'That rings a bell'*. Use a combination of the techniques opposite to ascertain someone's preferred way of learning. All of them will give you clues rather than a definitive answer.

Piecing together all of the clues for every student that you teach is a daunting prospect. Start by focusing upon the students who are causing you particular concern – they will probably be students who are displaying clear signs of a strong learning preference. As you become more proficient at reading the telltale signs of different thinking and learning styles, extend your observations to a wider range of students.

It is highly likely that students will display the characteristics of all three thinking modes as they weave in and out of the various styles. We are looking for the students who consistently favour a specific mode and who show a particularly strong preference for a *particular* way of thinking and learning.

Ask them

Ask the student how they would spell a word they were unsure of:

'Imagine that you have to spell the word Antarctica *– what would you do?'* (Use different words for various age groups.)

'Would you picture the word or scribble it down, to see if it 'looked right'? Would you say the word slowly, either out loud or in your head, to see if it 'sounded right'? Or would you write it out in the air, to see if it 'felt right'?'

The way in which an individual answers that question gives you a big clue as to their preferred way of working.

Observe them

When are they really engaged and working well? How do they respond when set a particular task?

When a student responds to the instruction to read page 17 with a sigh and a look on his or her face that says, *'Oh not again – I hate reading!'*, they are giving you a message. When the same student reacts enthusiastically when asked to work with three other students and turn a paragraph about exfoliation into a short mime, you get a pretty big clue about their learning preference!

Close observation of body language and behaviour will reveal other, more subtle clues. They represent the way in which a person is thinking (in visual, auditory or kinesthetic terms) at any particular moment. When a student frequently displays these characteristics, they are giving the teacher a big clue as to their preferred way of thinking and learning. In general terms:

- *Visual learners will often follow you with their eyes* as you move around the room. They tend to talk quickly (to keep up with the visual images in their brain) and often have relatively shallow breathing.
- *Auditory learners will often tilt their head* slightly to one side – sometimes they will rest their head on their hand. Sometimes you will notice their lips moving as they repeat what they have just heard under their breath.
- *Kinesthetic learners will often speak slowly* and you may notice them breathing deeply. They will often fidget – teachers can usually spot this!

Questionnaire – How do you learn best?

We all learn in many different ways – we see things, we hear things and we do things. However, most people have a preference – sometimes a very strong preference - for a particular way of learning.

People who prefer to see information are often referred to as *visual learners*, people who would rather hear information are known as *auditory learners* and people who prefer to learn by doing are called *kinesthetic learners*.

It helps to know what kind of learner you are, as people will generally learn best when they work in their preferred learning style. This questionnaire will give you a clue as to your learning preference. Remember, it is only a preference; we all learn in many different ways.

Answer each question as honestly as you can. Award a mark between 3 and 0 for each statement.

3 – That's definitely me! Absolutely agree. All the time.
2 – That describes me quite well. Largely agree. Some of the time.
1 – That doesn't really describe me. Generally disagree. Very rarely.
0 – That's not me. Totally disagree. Never.

Visual

If I have to spell a tricky word, I write it out to see if it looks right.   _____
I remember things best when I write them down.   _____
I take a lot of notes of what I read/hear.   _____
I always look at the teacher when they are talking – it helps me concentrate.   _____
I find it easy to understand maps, graphs and diagrams.   _____
When I am doing a test I can often picture my notes or the textbook.   _____
I am able to visualize pictures in my mind.   _____
I talk quickly – I tend to talk more than I listen.   _____
I prefer to see a map than be given spoken directions.   _____
I say things like, 'I see what you mean' or 'I get the picture'.   _____

TOTAL   _____ /30

(continued on page 128)

Listen to their language

The words that students use are another clue as to the way in which they prefer to take in information. They are simply talking in the way in which they are thinking.

When in visual mode, people often use phrases like, *'I see'*, or *'that looks good to me'*, *'it appears to me'*.

In auditory mode people might say, *'I hear what you say'*, or, *'that rings a bell'*, or, *'in a manner of speaking'*.

Phrases such as, *'that touched a nerve'*, *'I've got a handle on this'*, *'I can't get a grip of this'*, or *'I'm not with you'*, often indicate someone is in kinesthetic mode.

Watch their eyes

'Eye accessing clues' have their origin in Neuro-Linguistic Programming (NLP). People move their eyes in systematic directions depending on how they are thinking. Experts believe that the reason for this is that people are accessing different parts of the brain when in different thinking modes. These movements happen quickly and can be very subtle, but by observing someone's eyes very closely, we get important clues as to how they are thinking.

Note that some people do not fit the generalizations below – for example people who are left-handed. However, all people will consistently 'look' to the same place when they are in a particular thinking mode. For example, the majority of the population will look upwards and to the right when they are asked the colour of their bedroom wall when they were a child. This is because they are remembering a visual image. The small minority of people who look in a different direction will always look to that place when remembering a visual image.

For the majority of the population, however, the following model holds true.

- Visual learners tend to look up.
- Auditory learners tend to have level eye movement.
- Kinesthetic learners tend to look down.

We can be even more specific than this: when someone looks to the right (as you look at them) they are remembering and when they look to the left, they are constructing. So, for example, when someone looks up and to the right, they are recalling a visual image; when they look up and to the left, they are constructing a visual image.

Try practising by asking a partner some questions and watching where their eyes go to search for the information. For example:

- What did your bedroom look like when you were a child?
- What does the back wall of your classroom look like?
- Imagine what a bright orange triangle inside a pink circle looks like.
- Sing 'Happy Birthday' to yourself.
- What does your favourite piece of music sound like?
- Imagine what the Queen would sound like if she had a very high squeaky voice.
- What does wire wool feel like?
- How does it feel when you dive into an ice-cold swimming pool?
- How would it feel if rain was really heavy?

Auditory

I prefer to listen to the teacher explaining than read about it in a book.   _____

When I'm doing a test, I can often hear the teacher saying something.   _____

When spelling a tricky word, I say it over and over again, to see if it sounds right.   _____

I say things like, 'I hear what you say' or 'that rings a bell'.   _____

I often tilt my head to the side and/or rest my head in my hand during lessons.   _____

I often talk to myself – say things aloud – when working.   _____

I often repeat instructions to myself under my breath.   _____

I find/would find it helpful to speak my notes on to audio cassette and play them back.   _____

I would prefer people to tell me directions rather than show me a map.   _____

I find it easy to follow a speaker even when I'm not looking at them .   _____

TOTAL   _____ /30

Kinesthetic

I don't like reading or listening to instructions – I just prefer to get on with it.   _____

I need to take regular breaks when I'm working.   _____

If I have to spell a tricky word, I write it in the air to see if it feels right.   _____

I wave my hands around a lot when I'm explaining something.   _____

I say things like, 'that feels right to me' or 'I've got the hang of it'.   _____

I like to learn in real life situations.   _____

I find it hard to sit still – I'm a fidgeter.   _____

I like to explore things – taking them apart and tinkering with them.   _____

I like to walk around when I am reading/talking.   _____

If I had to assemble a piece of furniture, I would just work it out by
trial and error, rather than follow the instructions   _____

TOTAL   _____ /30

Now complete the graph below – what clues does it give you about the way that *you* learn best?

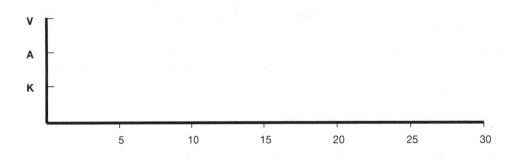

Learning style questionnaires

These are a useful tool and can give an instant indication of a person's preferred learning style. Treat them with caution however; they are simply another indicator and should not be considered as the definitive answer.

A comprehensive, easy-to-use questionnaire can be found opposite.

A hierarchy of response to individual learning styles

The diagram on page 130, loosely based on Maslow's hierarchy of human need, illustrates a staged response to the issue of learning styles. Where do you currently stand – as a school? As an individual?

Level 1 – no planned response

At level 1, teachers may or may not be aware that their students have individual learning preferences. In general terms, even the teachers who are aware of this vital issue, do little or nothing about it. By that, I mean that there is no systematic, consistent response. Opportunities for kinesthetic learners are *random* and *ad hoc* and *largely dependent upon chance.*

If a kinesthetic learner happens to have a teacher who provides frequent opportunities to learn in their preferred style, they will probably do well. If they happen to have a teacher who doesn't provide these opportunities, they will probably struggle. It's as simple as that. It is clearly, however, much too important an issue to be left to chance and the whim of individual teachers.

The first challenge is to ensure that *all* teachers are *aware* that different students will learn best in different ways, each one having a preferred learning and thinking style. Teachers should also be aware of their own favoured approach to teaching. Beware – what you think you do in the classroom and what you actually do, are often totally different. You need an objective reflection – better still detached observation – to establish the strategies that you employ on a regular basis.

Remember, it is safe to assume that whatever activity is going on, up to two-thirds of the class could be working outside their preferred style! If you employ a narrow range of teaching strategies and favour a particular approach, it will be the same two-thirds every lesson!

Knowing that there will almost certainly be a mismatch between the way in which you are teaching and the way in which some of your students learn, helps. It may well explain a lot! However, it is only the start; having made teachers aware, we must do something about it!

Level 2 – focus on students causing concern

At level 2, teachers and schools focus their attention on students who are causing concern. The two chief causes of concern are *relative underachievement* and *behaviour problems*. Consideration is given to the extent to which the problem of underachievement and/or poor behaviour stem from a mismatch between preferred learning style and the way in which the student is being taught.

There are a number of ways of doing this exercise – see page 116.

Response to the issue of learning styles

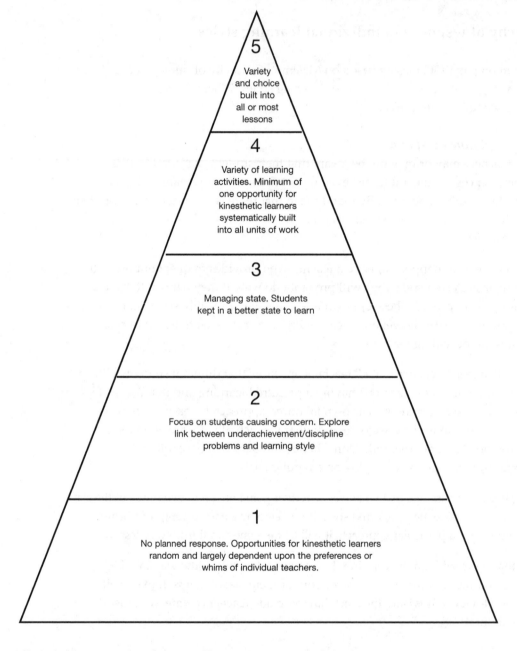

5
Variety and choice built into all or most lessons

4
Variety of learning activities. Minimum of one opportunity for kinesthetic learners systematically built into all units of work

3
Managing state. Students kept in a better state to learn

2
Focus on students causing concern. Explore link between underachievement/discipline problems and learning style

1
No planned response. Opportunities for kinesthetic learners random and largely dependent upon the preferences or whims of individual teachers.

Where are you at – as an individual and as a school?

What do you need to do to reach the next level?

What will you do immediately? (The first step is the hardest but the most significant.)

What do you need to do during the next academic year?

At an individual level, teachers can pick out two or three children in each class that they are concerned about. Alternatively, the analysis could be extended to consider the entire school population or to focus upon students in a specified year group. Teachers of course have a 'gut feeling' for underperformance; however, a more objective analysis based on the scattergraph on page 120 may prove to be beneficial.

Many of these students identified will inevitably have a very strong kinesthetic preference – the students who Michael Grinder describes as 'kinesthetic only'. What kind of diet do they get in your classroom(s)? To what extent does their heavily kinesthetic learning preference contribute to, or even cause, their current difficulties?

It is interesting to discover whether the problems exist across the curriculum. I once had an interesting conversation with an English teacher who had just completed a cover lesson in technology and had been amazed to find that a Year 10 boy, with whom she frequently had problems in English, had behaved perfectly well in the workshop. '*He was a different boy*', she said over and over again, adding, '*He's a little so-and-so for me – he can never sit still*'.

If we identify that a student causing concern is a kinesthetic learner, floundering like a fish out of water in a predominantly visual and auditory environment, we can begin to address the issue. Many teachers are understandably wary of the classroom management issues of catering for kinesthetic learners; the prospect of 30 students wandering around as they read is enough to give any teacher nightmares. By targeting students in this way, we are limiting the classroom management issues; asking one student who would particularly benefit from walking down the corridor while they read a passage from a book, is a significantly different proposition from having 30 people wandering around the classroom!

Having established a link between students causing concern and their preferred learning style, we are seeking to do two things:

- manage the 'state' of kinesthetic learners (level 3)
- provide regular opportunities for kinesthetic learners to work in their preferred style (level 4).

Level 3 – managing state
If we give students frequent opportunities to move around in a controlled, managed way, we can significantly increase the likelihood that they remain in an appropriate state for learning (see Section Two).

All students benefit from regular 'state breaks' and frequent opportunities to move around and increase the flow of oxygen to the brain. However, it is the kinesthetic learners who will particularly benefit. If we accept the fact that these children need to move around and fidget and we plan for this, we can both ensure that they remain focused and on task for longer periods and significantly reduce the disruption that they cause to those around them.

For example: Adam is a kinesthetic learner. Not surprisingly, he is a great 'fidgeter' who finds it hard to sit still for any length of time. When he fidgets he distracts students sitting near him. By asking him to move – to pop next door and collect a pile of books (even when they are not needed) or to bring his work out to the front – the teacher is consciously managing his state to reduce his unplanned fidgeting and to optimize his learning and that of others.

Summary scheme of work

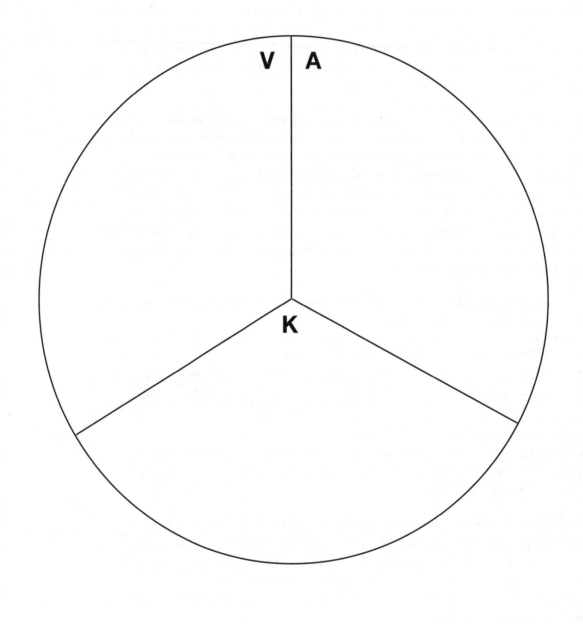

Strategies for Closing the Learning Gap

These strategies (see page 139) are designed to manage and have a positive influence upon the *state* of kinesthetic learners. They help to reduce boredom and the chances of misbehaviour and increase the likelihood that the students will learn and make progress, even when asked to work outside of their preferred style. Although these strategies are not giving kinesthetic learners opportunities to learn in their preferred style, it is a start!

Level 4 – provide a variety of learning activities

Providing a variety of learning activities is the key for ensuring that all types of learner have extensive opportunities to learn in their preferred style. Quite simply, the more variety that we can build into our lessons, the better. Our ultimate goal must be a variety and choice of approaches *within each* and *every lesson*. However, as a minimum provision, ensure that opportunities for different types of learners exist within each unit of work.

Consider these four strategies:

- Write schemes of work in three different colours to represent VAK opportunities.
- Produce a summary of each scheme of work.
- Increase the number of collaborative planning opportunities.
- Rotate teachers.

Schemes of work

Write schemes of work in three different colours to represent learning activities that suit visual, auditory and kinesthetic learners. You can now tell at a glance if any group is disadvantaged.

This technique works best when schemes of work are written by a group of three teachers. Remember, teachers have a preferred teaching style; most will naturally provide more opportunities for one of the three kinds of learner. The ideal situation is, of course, for a teacher who is highly visual in their approach to teaching to plan schemes of work with a teacher who is predominantly auditory and another who provides frequent opportunities for kinesthetic learners. Even if you do not find yourself in this ideal situation, it is still helpful to plan work in groups of three; each teacher taking responsibility for ensuring that there are frequent opportunities for the learning group that they represent.

Summary schemes of work

For each scheme of work, include a summary that focuses upon learning activities rather than content. You could use a proforma such as the one on page 132. It is simple to use, quick to complete and very versatile. It can be used as a planning tool, a checklist or a monitoring device. In whatever guise it is employed, it will force teachers to consider the range of learning opportunities that are being provided during any unit of work.

Increase the opportunities for collaborative planning opportunities

I have worked with many teachers who are sympathetic and willing to introduce more opportunities for kinesthetic learners into their lessons. However, they lack the practical, subject-specific strategies to do so. Often, the irony is that a colleague just down the corridor is already successfully employing these techniques!

The key to meeting the needs of the many different types of learner is variety. But variety does not happen by chance – it has to be planned for.

It can be very difficult for teachers to create learning activities in a style that is completely alien to their natural way of working and so it is *crucial* that teachers are given regular opportunities to plan collaboratively and swap strategies. For example, we need meetings like this:

> *'We are just about to start a six-week unit on the Romans. I know I'm a 'highly visual' teacher and struggle to provide opportunities for kinesthetic learners. Can you give me some advice about the kinds of activities that I might use?'*

As I write, I can almost hear teachers exclaiming that they do not have the time for such luxuries. Maybe teachers don't currently have the time to plan work in groups. However, as you reflect on the scattergraph on page 120 and consider that in this real example an improvement of around 13% would have been the result of ensuring that kinesthetic learners had more opportunities to work in their preferred style, you may just conclude that making some time available for group planning and swapping strategies should be a school improvement priority.

In *Closing the Learning Gap*, a number of strategies are suggested for creating time to focus upon improving the quality of learning. Two of the most effective are:

- **Ban meetings.** Replace them with planning and developmental sessions. What would be the impact if teachers didn't attend meetings for a whole year? Would the quality of learning deteriorate? I suspect not. What would be the impact of spending regular slots swapping teaching strategies and planning work in groups so that all types of learner are given equal opportunities? Would the quality of learning improve? I suspect it would – particularly for the kinesthetic learners.

- **Take INSET days in pairs.** There is nothing more frustrating than an interesting and inspiring training day that has no impact upon the classroom because teachers do not have the time to prepare resources. Imagine the impact if you took an INSET day to consider the effect of individual learning preferences upon progress and achievement in your school, immediately followed the next day with time to swap strategies and to plan units of work collectively.

Rotate teachers

Why not? I have heard it said that a major reason for a teacher teaching a group for a year is to allow them to get to know each student well. Why then is there a mismatch (in many schools) between learning styles and teaching approach? Is it that we get to know them really well – that is, we are aware who irritates us and who is underperforming – but do nothing about it?

Maybe I am being cynical; maybe I exaggerate the point. Maybe. If I am, kinesthetic learners must be getting the same amount of opportunities to work in their preferred style as visual and auditory learners. Is this the case in your classroom? Is this the case in your school?

If a school or department is aware that a particular teacher is highly visual or particularly skilled at providing for kinesthetic learners, is not rotating teachers an option worth considering? I do not advocate that teachers switch groups on a weekly basis. The aim is to provide a *minimum of one opportunity, per unit of work, for each student to learn in their preferred style*. This can either be achieved by equipping all teachers with a range of strategies or by occasionally switching teachers. It is certainly an option worth considering as part of a conscious strategy to cater for individual learning styles.

Keep it in perspective!

All learners learn best through multisensory experiences.

If you were teaching a group of students automotive engineering, would you:

A) put the visual learners in a room and show them a diagram of an engine, put the auditory learners in a room and tell them how an engine works, and put the kinesthetic learners in a room and allow them to work on an engine, taking it apart and putting it back together?

OR

B) allow all students to *see* the engine, *hear* the explanation and *explore* the engine, taking it apart and putting it back together?

We must guard against an over-the-top reaction to the issue of learning styles. While we must acknowledge differences in style and preference and make allowances for individuality, we must also recognize that *all* learners benefit from multisensory learning experiences.

Level 5 – provide a variety of learning activities in every lesson

This must be our ultimate aim. Not only does it mean all students have an equal opportunity to learn in their preferred style, but such learning will be multisensory and will so activate the multiple memory systems described on page 249. By aiming high, we will almost certainly significantly increase the range of activities that we use in our teaching, even if we fall a little short of our ultimate goal.

The key to achieving this situation is to equip all teachers with a range of learning activities that extend beyond their preferred and natural approach to teaching. There is an implication here for:

- professional development
- collaborative planning
- sharing good ideas
- team teaching and peer observation opportunities.

Consider how useful it would be to establish a *bank of learning activities* and publish them in your departmental and/or school handbook. Much of the expertise will already exist in-house. This can be supplemented by external advisors, colleagues from other schools and the range of strategies suggested on pages 139–153.

Not only do teachers need a range of strategies at their disposal, they also need to develop confidence and expertise in utilizing them. It is very helpful for teachers to see a strategy in action, prior to trying for themselves. For example, observing a teacher managing a class who are converting a paragraph of text into a play is very different from reading about it. For many teachers, the reassurance of having the support of an extra adult in the classroom when trying a new strategy for the first time, can be hugely beneficial and can sometimes be the difference between a teacher trying something new and fighting shy of making a change.

Level 5 will take time to reach. Teachers who have been teaching in a particular style for a number of years will not feel comfortable using very different teaching strategies in the classroom overnight. We must build gradually until providing multisensory learning experiences in every lesson becomes second nature. For the vast majority of schools, level 4 represents a significant improvement on the current situation – level 5 is the icing on the cake.

In many respects, the key to progress through the five levels is *strategies*. We can raise awareness and consciously plan for individual learning styles, but unless teachers have a range of practical, easy-to-implement strategies at their disposal, little will change. Visual and auditory learners tend to get a good deal in schools, the majority of teaching approaches traditionally used in the classroom being compatible with these learning styles. There are a number of possible reasons for this: firstly, teachers often teach in a similar style to the way in which they were taught. Secondly, teachers have been successful in the visual and auditory world of secondary and higher education in order to become teachers, and their teaching style is simply an extension of their preferred learning style.

Strategies for kinesthetic learners

By their very nature, some subjects (PE, technology) and some activities (working on an engine in automotive engineering, handling a fossil in geology) lend themselves to a kinesthetic approach.

Other strategies that may appeal to kinesthetic learners can be grouped into four main categories. The challenge is to adapt them to suit your particular subject and identify opportunities to use them in the classroom.

Paper based
- Write notes/key words on post-its, post cards or scrap paper then use to arrange, organize, plan, sequence, classify and prioritize.
- Use post-its and cut-out words to create maps, diagrams and learning maps.
- Sequence an event, process equation or poem.
- Turn any diagram into a jigsaw.
- Classify 'cause and effect' statements.

Role play
- Create mimes, friezes, and short plays.
- Re-enact an event. Act an equation, mime a subduction zone or role play molecular movement in solids, liquids and gases.
- Recreate the trial of Charles I, enact the death of Romeo etc.

Models
- Use classroom objects – homework diaries, pens, pencils, ties, shoelaces – to create models, 3D plans etc.
- Make a waterfall, plan a battle, create a diagram of the human heart.

Movement
- Move to different areas of the room for different skills – listening, speaking, writing, etc. – or to research a different aspect of the subject – different stages of the nitrogen cycle, different acts or characters in a play, advantages/disadvantages, roving reporter.
- Create timelines, historical events, stages of a process or fiction.
- Respond to a statement – strongly agree on the right side of the room.
- Punctuate a sentence.
- Dance the world map.
- Snowballing and 3/4/5.

A further contributory factor is the undoubted and understandable concern that providing opportunities for kinesthetic learners will increase the likelihood of discipline problems. This is the result of a tendency to equate kinesthetic learning with leaping around the classroom. This, however, is a misconception. *Strategies that would appeal to kinesthetic learners do not necessarily involve large-scale movements.*

Nevertheless, it is right to acknowledge that there is a greater classroom management challenge involved in setting up active learning opportunities than there would be if we asked students to read and write in silence. It is also right to point out that the alternative is to demand that kinesthetic learners sit and read and write – and then to get frustrated when they fidget! After a while these students will become bored and demotivated, with many of them going on to become significant discipline problems. On top of that, they will not be learning much! Managing activities for kinesthetic learners may require a higher level of classroom management skills but, by engaging and motivating the student, they can actually make life easier in the long run.

The key is to find suitable strategies that can that both appeal to the learner and be manageable within the constraints of the classroom. The following are such strategies. The list is not by any means exhaustive; they are simply strategies that have proved successful and effective in the classroom. They are flexible and can be adapted to suit the age and ability of the student and the subject that is being taught. They are more than strategies that appeal to kinesthetic learners; they are effective learning activities in their own right and are designed to challenge students to think and so develop understanding.

Many are combinations of strategies – for example by reducing *Romeo and Juliet* to five key events and depicting each one in a frieze, we combine the thinking strategy of reduction (see page 199) with a technique for engaging kinesthetic learners. When we ask to students to explain out loud which event from the play they are illustrating and why they think it is important, we further develop understanding and create a memorable multisensory learning experience.

Strategies for kinesthetic learners

Manage state

Use the strategies such as time-outs described in Section Two for managing the state of your students. Pay particular attention to the students who you have identified as having a strong preference for kinesthetic learning. Give these students regular reasons to move. For example:

- fetch a pile of books from next door
- give out resources
- collect work in
- bring their work to the teacher's desk.

Resist the understandable temptation to respond to a kinesthetic learner who is being particularly fidgety by demanding that they sit still and in silence. Instead find a reason – any reason – for them to move... *on your terms!*

Case study

As part of an Action Research project, Clayton Hughes, a modern languages teacher at Denbigh School in Milton Keynes, sought to enhance student motivation and ultimately attainment, by enabling students to take more ownership of their learning.

One of the lessons in the project involved *the students deciding how they were going to learn* present tense verbs in preparation for a test. The students brainstormed possible approaches for different types of learner. Their ideas are presented below.

Visual	Learning maps; posters; post-it notes; made-up games; look-cover-write-check
Auditory	Record verbs on to a tape and listen to them before going to sleep; practise with partners; make up a song; shout them out; repeat verbs to a partner
Kinaesthetic	Clap as you say each one; use dice (choose one of the verbs to practise, number each part of the verb, then as you roll the dice, say the part of the verb corresponding to the number thrown)

At the end of the lesson...

Teacher: This has been one of the best lessons I've ever had with this class.

Student: I enjoyed this lesson because we did a lot of useful things that will help me in revision.

Student: This has possibly been the most useful and interesting lesson we've had in a long time.

At the end of the project. . .

Grade	Predicted	Actual
A*	0	5
A	8	11
B	12	4
C	7	7

Results first published in *Topic*, Autumn 2000

Drum roll

Announce a key point in the lesson with a roll on the drums. Students simply perform the drum roll by banging their knees. All students benefit when key points are highlighted in this way – kinesthetic learners benefit additionally from the physical activity. Needless to say, it is a strategy that has an age limit!

Provide choice

Providing regular opportunities for students to choose how to attempt a task, significantly increases the chances of students working in their preferred style. Choice is also a key to relieving stress and motivating students (see page 85).

Whenever possible, allow the students to select how they want to go about a piece of work... for example:

- *You can do this on your own or work together in pairs – your choice.*
- *Would you like to draw this or use the resources on the back table to construct a simple model – you decide.*
- *You can present your findings as a written newspaper report or perform it as a TV news report or record it as a radio news report. It's up to you.*
- *You can write about this, draw a labelled diagram or draw a 'learning map'. If you wish, you can 'make' a learning map (see page 267). Your decision.*

Make learning multisensory

Not only does multisensory learning ensure that all students – visual, auditory and kinesthetic – have an opportunity to take in information through their preferred sense, it also increases the chance of something being remembered (see page 249). Different sensory memories are stored in different places in the brain and by receiving information in a variety of ways, we ensure that it is stored in a number of different places.

Quite simply, the more ways in which we receive information, the greater the likelihood that it will be recalled. Whenever possible, ask students to verbalize what they can see or what they are doing. Ask students to visualize what you are describing. Ask students to read out loud as they are walking. The more senses that we can engage simultaneously, the better.

On page 125, I posed the question: how would you spell a word that caused you difficulty. Here is the multisensory learning strategy, using the example *Antarctica*.

1   Identify the part of the word or the single letter that you confuse. (Often it is the first c.)

2   'Write' the word in the air with your finger. When you get to the letter c, use your whole arm and make an exaggerated movement. Do this three or four times.

3   As you are 'writing' the word, say the letters out loud. When you get to the letter c, emphasize the letter in some way. For example you could say it using a high or low voice or in a different accent or as if you were freezing cold.

4   As you 'write' the word, picture it. Picture it above your head. Imagine the large letter c is written in your favourite colour. Imagine the rest of the word in a different colour. As a finishing touch, imagine that the letter c is flashing on and off.

You have now seen, heard and felt the word. It will have taken less than two minutes.

Multisensory learning

All types of learner benefit from multisensory learning experiences.

Providing multisensory learning experiences need not be as difficult as it might sound. Here are two simple strategies.

1. Simply invite students to describe aloud what they are *doing* and you have engaged a number of senses (describing something aloud as you do it is a powerful strategy for developing understanding – see page 197).

2. Use learning maps. Encourage students to 'walk' their fingers along the branches of their map, describing it aloud as they go. They see the map, hear the description and feel the movement, in a powerful multisensory experience.

(This strategy is described in more detail in chapter 6 of *Mapwise* by Oliver Caviglioli and Ian Harris.)

Many of the strategies that follow can, and should, be made into multisensory learning experiences. Simply by asking students to describe and explain out loud what they are doing as they do it, will significantly develop understanding and improve memory (see page 197).

Use post-its!

Any activity that involves moving notes around – sorting/sequencing/rank order/arranging – will appeal to kinesthetic learners. Use post-its, index cards, or cut-up pieces of scrap paper to write key words, facts or ideas. Then use the notes to classify, sequence, rank order and so on. Use this technique when planning any piece of work – from writing a poem to a major piece of coursework – so that you can constantly rearrange and alter your plan.

This is a particularly useful and versatile strategy. Use it to sequence historical events, the steps of a mathematical function or the lines of a poem. Alternatively, use it to arrange and construct a diagram by writing or drawing the key components of the diagram on post-its and then physically constructing it. Maps can be constructed in a similar way, by writing the name of a place with a suitable symbol on a post-it. Simply arrange them to create a map. (Kinesthetic learners will often use the post-its to 'make' the feature – don't be surprised if you get three-dimensional maps!)

Roving reporter

Your challenge is to present a 30-second news report for a radio station. You can spend the lesson moving around the room to collect the information that you will require for your report. Summarizing material in a 30-second report is a valuable learning experience as it requires students to prioritize and summarize information. It is a strategy that could be used to report on:

- a natural disaster such as an earthquake
- an event from history
- the birth of Christ
- a scientific or medical breakthrough
- the death of Romeo.

Group mime/play/frieze

Converting an event into a short play or mime should not be restricted to the nativity. Traditionally, certain subjects – for example English and history – have appeared to be suitable for this approach. What about maths? Why not? There are literally hundreds of opportunities to use this strategy or a variation of it. For example:

- *English*. Reduce *Romeo and Juliet* to five key events. Represent each one with a frieze. Explain out loud the scene that you are depicting, and why you thought it was important.

- *Maths*. Act out a quadratic equation, providing a commentary. The key aim here is to require students to think carefully about what they are doing and the sequence of operations. It is the process rather than the performance that is of particular value.

- *Science*. Turn a diagram of tectonic plates colliding into a 'mime'. As you perform the 'mime', another member of the group provides a commentary. (Auditory learners often volunteer for this role.)

Use ordinary classroom objects - homework diary, pencil case, ties, to transform a diagram of the Battle of Marston Moor into a 'model' (see Transformation on page 201).

Rupert's cavalry

Royalist cavalry

Royalist infantry

Royalist cavalry

Ditch with Rupert's musketeers

Cromwell's cavalry

Parliamentary infantry

Parliamentary cavalry

- Transform a diagram into a model using ordinary classroom objects - label with post-its.
- Use text and historical source to 'enact' the battle, showing relative positions halfway through and at the end of the conflict.

Learn to spell using a rhythm

Click alternate fingers or swing your arms from side to side as you chant the letters of the word. For example, spell 'Mediterranean' by chanting M... E... D... , accompanying each letter with a click. Double click for double R.

Spelling cards

This is simply a version of Scrabble and can be played in any language. Write letters on individual cards and get students to rearrange them to create words and practise spelling. This can be an effective technique with young students and/or students with spelling difficulties.

Ties

Ask students to take off their ties and use them to create a shape. For example, use a tie(s) to create the shape of a country or continent. When students work in groups they will also be forced to discuss the challenge; they will have talked about the shape, they will have seen it and they will have 'made' it. A multisensory learning experience that takes about three minutes and requires no preparation!

Graphs

Ties can also be used to 'make' a line graph. Alternatively, ask students to 'walk' the graph. These exercises can be made multisensory by asking students to describe the shape of the line and the trend of the graph out loud as they are walking 'along the line' or laying out their ties.

Make a diagram

Extend the 'ties' and 'graph' exercises by including other classroom objects – pen, shoe, watch, homework diary and so on – to create a diagram. For example, create a diagram to show:

- the structure of the human heart
- a plan of the Battle of Marston Moor
- an electrical circuit.

Make a model

This is a further extension of 'make a diagram'. We are not looking for an elaborate model – it is the process of creating a model in collaboration with other students that develops understanding and particularly appeals to kinesthetic learners. You do not require a vast array of resources; just add some card, coloured paper, glue and so on to the everyday items found in the classroom. For example:

- Give students a diagram illustrating how waterfalls are formed. (visual)
- Provide a brief explanation of the diagram. (auditory)
- Students make a model of the diagram. (kinesthetic) The process of creating the model and discussing the challenge in small groups, develops understanding.
- Students demonstrate their model and explain how waterfalls are created to a visitor (member of the support team, a Governor, another teacher). (visual, auditory and kinesthetic)
- Explaining out loud is a very effective technique for developing understanding.
- The quality of the model (the thinking behind it rather than the quality of the construction) and the explanation gives the teacher a wonderful opportunity to assess the depth of understanding.

A kinesthetic learning strategy for maths

$$3 (x + 5) = 39$$

$$3x + 15 = 39$$

$$3x = 39 - 15$$

$$3x = 24$$

$$x = \frac{24}{3}$$

$$x = 8$$

1 Cut out each line of the equation.

2 Students have to sequence them correctly.

3 When done in pairs, there is the added advantage of students articulating their thinking.

Progression

1. Cut the lines again.

2. Colour-code the cards to help students arrange them, e.g. the sections of line 2 are all in orange, line 3 is in green etc.

3. Progress to having all cards in white.

4. Next, include some blank cards for students to complete.

5. Finally, students 'make their own equations'.

$$3 \ (x + 5) \ = \ 39$$

$$\boxed{3x} \ \boxed{+ 15} \ = \ \boxed{39}$$

$$\boxed{3x} \ = \ \boxed{39} \ \boxed{- 15}$$

$$\boxed{3x} \ = \ \boxed{24}$$

$$\boxed{x} \ = \ \boxed{\frac{24}{3}}$$

$$\boxed{x} \ = \ \boxed{8}$$

Role play

An old favourite in modern languages classrooms. Is there anyone who hasn't ordered a drink from a 'French café'? This is a strategy that can also be applied in other curriculum areas. For example:

- re-enact the trial of Charles I
- act a scene from *Macbeth*
- role-play the molecular movement as a solid turns into a liquid and then into a gas

Sequencing

Cut a piece of text into a series of sentences or phrases (approximately 12 statements). Mix up the sentences. Have 12 students sit at the front. (Ensure that you select the kinesthetic learners for this task.) Give each a statement. Students stand and read their statement. As the statements are out of order, the text will make little or no sense. The rest of the class have to rearrange the students so that the text makes sense. (For example, Alison needs to sit near the end. Jonathon needs to sit by Stephen, and so on.) Allow the class to make three adjustments and then have students stand and read the statements again. Repeat the exercise until the text makes sense.

Underline or highlight keywords

The simple act of putting down a pen and picking up a highlighter helps a kinesthetic learner. The student's choice of keywords also gives the teacher valuable information regarding the level of understanding.

Walk while you read

It doesn't have to be the whole class, just the one or two heavily kinesthetic learners who would particularly benefit. *'Adam, walk down to the corridor to the double doors and back. While you are walking, read page 16 and come back and tell me which you think the most important sentence is.'*

Reading is not an activity confined to classrooms; make sure that students who are kinesthetic learners are aware of the benefits of walking while they read as they are revising for exams/learning at home, and so on.

Dance

An interesting extension of turning information into a play. Create a 'dance' to illustrate a diagram or sequence of events. For example, illustrate the movement of water in the hydrological cycle in the form of a dance (music is optional). Or compose and perform a dance to illustrate Napoleon's retreat from Moscow (music compulsory!).

Why not? Because students who normally find history boring would enjoy it?

Another possibility is to dance the world map:

'Stand up. When I say North America, point upwards and to the left. When I say, Australia, point downwards and to the right. Build up a rhythm – turn it into a dance!'

As a kinesthetic learning strategy in GCSE PE, combine a sequencing activity with transforming a diagram into a model.

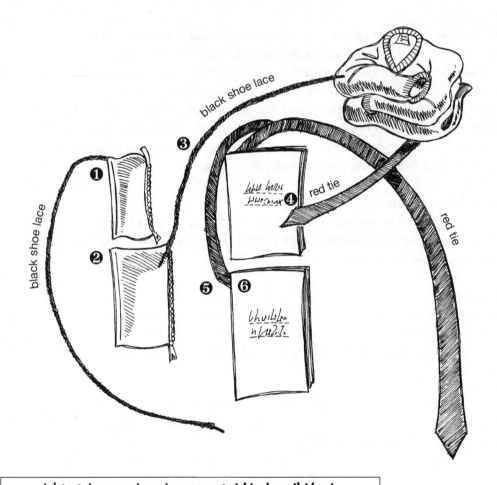

right atrium receives deoxygenated (dark red) blood

right atrium pumps blood into right ventricle

blood pumped into lungs to regain oxygen

freshly onygenated blood flows into left atrium

left atrium pumps blood into left ventricle

left ventricle pumps oxygenated blood around body

By asking students to describe the 'model' and the process aloud we can create a multisensory learning experience.

Blindfold box

Place artefacts in a box, so that students can feel an object without looking at it. Ask them to describe what they feel. The rest of their group has to identify the object from the description. This could be done with, for example, religious artefacts or mechanisms in technology or science. We intensify a sense by isolating it, and by asking students to describe what they feel, we are encouraging them to pay a great deal of attention to detail.

Demonstrate to a deaf person

This is a variation of 'describe to a blind person'. In this exercise, students are not allowed to use words or diagrams. Students have to think deeply (developing understanding) about what it is they are trying to convey before they even start.

Charades

An extension of this strategy is to play charades using key words and phrases. This can be an effective review activity at the end of a unit of work.

Take something apart

The best way to understand anything is to take it apart! A useful strategy in science and technology.

Put an action to a keyword or phrase

For example the phrase 'plunge pool' is accompanied with a bend of the knees and a movement of the arms, in a shape that resembles a plunge pool! Jolly Phonics – a teaching method in which actions are ascribed to particular letter sounds – is such a strategy and is being increasingly used with young learners.

Ben's stepping stones

A good technique with younger children. Create stepping stones to help students across the room (or shark-infested sea) by writing numbers on pieces of card and spreading them around the floor. Children use the stepping stones to cross the ocean, *but only if they can correctly identify the number on the card*. This can be developed into an addition/ subtraction exercise as they progress.

For older students, position questions across the room. Progress across the room is dependent upon correctly answering the questions (not unlike *Blockbusters*).

Three-four-five

Students identify what they consider to be the *three* most important points of the lesson. They then have *four* minutes to move around the class and tell *five* different people their key points. This is an excellent review strategy.

A variation is to ask students to identify three things they wish to find out about the topic that they are about to study. (Or the world's leading expert on volcanoes is visiting the class next lesson. Think of three questions that you would like to ask them.) Students then have four minutes to move around and tell five people the information that they would like to discover. This is an excellent strategy for the start of a lesson or unit of work (see page 189).

Snowball effect

'Think of three reasons for... / examples of... Now swap your ideas with the person sitting next to you. Aim to get four ideas between you. Now move to the desk next to you and put all of your ideas together. See if you can get six ideas.'

Accommodate different learning styles through cross-curricular co-operation

Inevitably, it will be easier to appeal to a particular type of learner in some subject areas in others.

Consider the distinctive contribution that subjects such as art, music, drama and English could make to a science-led piece of work on the planets.

Cross-curricular liaison will not meet all of the challenges posed by different learning preferences, but it can make a contribution.

Thanks to David Grikis of The Deeping School for this suggestion

You can continue increasing the size of the groups in order to increase the number of ideas that are generated. This strategy can also be reversed.

'Think of a reason/example/solution... Now tell your partner your idea. Let them tell you theirs. Decide between you which idea is the best.'

Pairs then join together, swap ideas and again decide which is best. You will be left with two ideas that the whole class must consider, before deciding upon the best idea.

Move around the room to work stations

Languages classrooms can be arranged around the four skills: reading, writing, listening and speaking, with students physically moving to a discrete area of the classroom when working on a particular skill. Sometimes, the content of the lesson lends itself to this approach and this arrangement can be replicated in other curriculum areas. For example, students move around the room to:

- discover what happens at various stages of the carbon cycle
- research background information about different characters in a play
- consider an issue from a particular viewpoint.

Move to the correct position

- Students, each holding a word, stand in line to make a sentence. *'Jason, you are a comma. Alison and Ian, you are speech marks. Now go and stand in the correct places please. Sally, you are an apostrophe, please go and stand in the correct place.'* (A variation is to give children the individual letters that make up a word.)

- *'Imagine the classroom is a grid square.'* (Label the corners appropriately.) *'I am going to give you a card showing a six-figure grid reference. When I say, "go", go and stand in the correct position.'*

- *'Imagine the classroom is Australia. You all represent the entire population of the country. Please distribute yourself appropriately.'*

Timeline

Any lesson involving a sequence of events can be physically constructed. A timeline, for example, can be represented by a long piece of paper, or rope, or simply by the space between two classroom walls, with students physically moving to positions to indicate the timing of events. There are obvious possibilities for using this strategy in history and RE lessons but it can also be used, when studying the events of a play, story or poem or when studying the component parts of a physical process or reaction. A variation is to consider a statement, such as, *'parliament was right to execute Charles I'*. Students move to the side of the room (right-hand side = strongly agree, left-hand side = strongly disagree) according to their views. As their views change during the debate, they adjust their position accordingly (an effective strategy in PSHE).

Jigsaws and board games

Any form of diagram can be made into a jigsaw. Kinesthetic learners will benefit from both creating and doing a jigsaw. Board games are also useful for engaging kinesthetic learners. Creating and constructing a board game based on a particular theme for younger children, demands that students think deeply about the topic as well as the board game. As such, it is an excellent strategy for both developing and assessing understanding.

Two hemispheres of the neo-cortex – a summary

Logic hemisphere (usually the left):	Gestalt hemisphere (usually the right):
processes from parts to whole	processes from whole to parts
logical	intuitive
linear	random
sequential	spontaneous
symbols	colour
lyrics of songs	tunes of songs
number	rhythm
	images

For a more detailed analysis, see *The Dominance Factor* by Carla Hannaford (Great Ocean, 1997)

Strategies for Closing the Learning Gap

Catch the bean bag

When a student catches the bean bag, they have to answer a question. This is a strategy often used in language lessons and is a particularly useful warm-up or 'state break' activity.

Cut out key words

Rather than making notes by writing down key words, give students a photocopy of a page from a textbook and ask them to identify the keywords and cut them out. Then they can physically arrange the keywords and use them to make notes. Although this may be considered an expensive technique and too time-consuming for every lesson, it is an activity that will appeal considerably to kinesthetic learners and is well worth including once in every unit of work.

Physically make a learning map

Learning maps are increasingly being used in the classroom (see page 211). Extend the strategy above and use the cut-out key words to build a learning map. Kinesthetic learners will relish the opportunity and will be constructing three-dimensional learning maps in no time at all. Although this is a strategy that can be used at any time, it may be particularly beneficial to use this technique at the end of a unit of work.

Hemispheric dominance

The neo-cortex is divided into two hemispheres; the right hemisphere controlling motor movement in the left-hand side of the body, with the left hemisphere being responsible for motor movement down the right-hand side.

While it is important not to oversimplify and exaggerate the role of the respective hemispheres – the brain operates holistically with both hemispheres involved, to a greater or lesser degree, in virtually all forms of thinking and human activity – it is important to recognize that the *two hemispheres operate and process information in very different ways*. The 'gestalt hemisphere' (in the vast majority of people this is the right hemisphere) likes to deal with the overview or big picture and works randomly and intuitively. It operates from 'whole to parts'. Carla Hannaford in *The Dominance Factor* talks about the *'spontaneous, curious nature of the right brain'*, adding that it processes through image, rhythm and movement.

The 'logic hemisphere' (usually the left side of the brain) processes information in pieces and is more concerned with the detail than the overview. It is sequential and works in a linear, logical manner and works from 'parts to whole'. It is responsible for dealing with the pieces and symbols of language and maths.

We each have a dominant hemisphere, which influences the way in which we think and this dominance becomes particularly noticeable in times of stress. Quite simply, some people prefer to see an overview of the situation and naturally work in an intuitive, random way, while others prefer to focus upon the details and are comfortable working in a logical and sequential manner. For convenience in this book, the 'logic' hemisphere is referred to as the 'left' hemisphere and the 'gestalt' as the 'right' hemisphere – simply because this is situation in the majority of the population.

Do you recognize yourself?

If you are *gestalt hemisphere dominant*, you will probably answer 'yes' to most of these questions:

Do you:

- get irritated and frustrated when trainers cover up an OHT during INSET and reveal the slide incrementally?

- when faced with assembling a piece of furniture or programming a new video, follow an intuitive, trial and error approach?

- prefer someone to draw you a map when giving you directions?

- get bored following step-by-step instructions?

- follow your hunches, responding to situations intuitively and adopting the course of action you instinctively feel is right?

- get satisfaction from having a good idea or conceiving a master plan but get frustrated by implementing the detail and finishing a project?

If you are *logic hemisphere dominant*, you will probably answer 'yes' to most of these questions:

Do you:

- not mind, or even prefer, trainers to cover up an OHT during inset and reveal the slide incrementally?

- when faced with assembling a piece of furniture or programming a new video, religiously follow the step-by step instructions?

- prefer someone to give you step-by-step instructions when giving you directions?

- get 'lost' when ideas and plans are holistic and too vague and are happier following detailed, step-by-step instructions?

- think through your response to a particular situation and follow a logical course of action?

- enjoy implementing the details of a plan and ensure that projects are finished properly?

Strategies for Closing the Learning Gap

Determining hemispheric dominance

You do not need a theory to tell you that some people are methodical and pay great attention to detail, while others are much more random and 'scatterbrain'. All teachers will almost certainly recognize students in their class who are gestalt hemisphere dominant and those who have a dominant logical hemisphere. As a rule of thumb, a person who is gestalt hemisphere dominant, when confronted with the task of assembling a piece of furniture, will simply begin the task following their instinct. People who have a dominant logic hemisphere however will methodically follow the instructions, working step-by-step. Naturally, both will have a piece left over when they finish!

There are two, more formal, objective measures of hemispheric dominance.

- *Questionnaire*. A simple hemisphere dominance indicator can be found opposite.
- *Muscle-testing*. This is a simple technique used in educational kinesiology or Brain Gym® and when used by an experienced practitioner can illicit a response to a question from the body itself. Briefly, a question is asked – in this case regarding the dominant hemisphere – and then gentle pressure is applied to a muscle (usually the deltoid muscle). The way in which the muscle resists and responds to the pressure indicates the body's subconscious response to the question. We are dealing directly with what Carla Hannaford calls the 'truth detector'.

For further information, including instructions how to determine hemisphere dominance, try:
- *The Dominance Factor* by Carla Hannaford (Great Ocean, 1997)

Brain dominance profiles

In addition to a dominant hemisphere, we also have a dominant eye, ear, hand and foot. This 'lateral dominance' or preference for one side of the body over the other, is, according to Carla Hannaford, 'basically innate' and can be easily established by muscle testing. The various combinations (there are 32) of dominant hemisphere, eye, ear, hand and foot, make up your *dominance profile* and influence the way in which you think, behave and learn. For example, people with a dominant eye opposite their dominant hemisphere will often have a preference for taking in information and learning visually.

Teaching students with different brain dominance profiles

A student who has a dominant logic hemisphere and a dominant right eye, right ear, right hand and right foot, will prefer a structured learning experience and an orderly, sequential presentation of information. They will appreciate details and have little difficulty following step-by-step instructions. They will, however, be less comfortable with an overview and will often have difficulty grasping how details fit into the Big Picture.

However, students who have a dominant gestalt hemisphere, with a dominant left eye, left ear, left hand and left foot, will learn in a very different way. These students will quickly see the Big Picture and absorb the main idea but will often have difficulty following a sequential approach or step-by-step instructions. Although they may have a comprehensive understanding of a subject, they may have difficulty communicating their understanding in a linear, logical way. These learning characteristics are particularly acute during times of stress – a major disadvantage during examinations!

It is important for teachers to be aware of their own dominant hemisphere and preferred teaching style.

Which students tend to do well in your classroom?

To what extent is this the result of the way in which they are being asked to learn?

Strategies for Closing the Learning Gap

You will have both of these students – and others with different Brain Dominance profiles – in your class!

For more information regarding Brain Dominance Profiles, try:
● *The Dominance Factor* by Carla Hannaford (Great Ocean, 1997).

Mismatch between teacher and student hemispheric dominance

Seventy-five per cent of teachers are sequential, analytic presenters… And 70 per cent of all their students do not learn that way.

Eric Jensen

Teachers too have a dominant hemisphere and a preferred way of thinking and learning. Often this is reflected in the way in which they prefer to teach. All teachers have a preferred teaching style, which will become particularly noticeable in times of stress. When there is a mismatch between the teaching style and the hemispheric dominance of the student, learning will inevitably be impaired.

In general terms, students who have a dominant right hemisphere and are random, intuitive and divergent thinkers are disadvantaged when lessons are arranged in a logical, sequential manner, emphasising detail at the expense of the Big Picture. This approach is quite simply incompatible with the way in which they think and learn. For them, learning is 'messy' and unstructured, yet many lessons are precisely the opposite. Think of a bright student who complains of being bored and is underachieving in your class; there is every chance that they are right hemisphere dominant.

There are many teachers who are left hemisphere dominant – not surprisingly as they have succeeded in the world of formal education and linear, sequential learning. There are also many classrooms in which reading, writing and listening – primarily, although not exclusively, left brain activities – are the staple learning tasks. Students with a dominant left hemisphere, who prefer to process information sequentially, have a considerable advantage when working in these conditions.

It is therefore important for teachers to be aware of their own dominant hemisphere and preferred teaching style. Which students tend to do well in your classroom? To what extent is this the result of the way in which they are being asked to learn?

Be aware – without labelling

Teachers need to be aware that students will quite naturally think and learn in different ways. It is a factor that will often explain behaviour and apparent learning difficulties. However, we must be careful not to label students and be aware that this is not an issue about which style is better, it is simply about differences.

RELAX!

The importance of being relaxed when learning is well established. Students, however, have to face many stressful situations during their school life, not least examinations. There are many techniques that people can use to help them calm down a little and put them in a better state for learning – unfortunately, techniques that involve lying on a blanket and listening to gentle music are inappropriate for the examination hall!

This technique is suitable for the most formal of situations – even students who would never admit to doing something as 'uncool' as using relaxation techniques can do it and no one will know!

Sit straight in your chair and place your feet firmly on the floor. Now push your toes into the floor, as if you were making a hole on the beach. Do this to the count of five and then slowly let go. Next, push your heels into the floor as hard as you can and count to five. As you slowly let go, notice how relaxed your feet have become.

Now, imagine that you are holding a rubber ball in both hands. Squeeze both hands as tightly as you can while counting slowly to five. As you slowly release the pressure, notice how relaxed your hands are and how much slower your breathing has become.

Push your back against the chair, concentrating upon keeping your back straight. Hold this position as you count to five. Slowly let go.

You will notice how much more relaxed your body has become and much calmer your breathing is.

Try it, the next time you are stressed!

Strategies for Closing the Learning Gap

Keep it in perspective!

All types of learner, irrespective of hemispheric dominance, will be required to grasp both an overview and the detail of a topic. The issue here is about the various ways that individuals will arrive, and will want to arrive, at this endpoint. Teachers need a range of strategies at their disposal in order to cater for different learning preferences among their students. By consciously providing *variety* and *choice* in the learning activities that we employ in the classroom, we significantly increase the chances of ensuring that all students have regular opportunities to work in their preferred learning style.

Strategies for whole-brain learning

The strategies that we can adopt in the classroom address four broad issues:

1   People learn best when the two hemispheres of the neo-cortex communicate with each other.
2   All learners need both an overview and the detail.
3   Learning is enhanced when both sides of the brain are engaged.
4   Students will approach certain situations in different ways.

Encouraging hemispheric communication
Relax

The two hemispheres of the neo-cortex do not work in isolation. They are linked together by the corpus callosum, a bundle of nerve fibres that allow the two sides of the brain to communicate with each other. This allows the brain to work and think holistically; both hemispheres simultaneously engaged, yet processing the information in a very different way.

When you are relaxed, communication along the corpus callosum allows the whole brain to be involved in the learning process, in effect, simultaneously digesting the detail and the overview.

During times of stress, however, communication is impaired and the dominant hemisphere takes centre stage. This is sometimes referred to as *unilateral state* and essentially limits the learner to their preferred hemisphere. For example, people with a dominant right hemisphere will struggle to see detail, particularly in times of stress.

This makes consciously relaxing students a key strategy in 'whole-brain learning'. (See Section Two for a range of techniques designed to induce the optimum learning state of 'relaxed–alert'.)

Cross crawling

This activity, used in Brain Gym®, is designed to stimulate communication between the hemispheres of the neo-cortex by marching on the spot and placing the wrist on the opposite knee as it is raised (see page 44).

By simultaneously activating the right and left hemisphere in order to control motor movement in the opposite side of the body, communication between the hemispheres is encouraged. In simple terms, this acts as a kick start to the non-dominant hemisphere to begin processing in conjunction with its dominant partner. When both hemispheres are processing in tandem the brain is said to be in a *bilateral* state and learning will be optimized.

Strategies for whole-brain learning

Encouraging hemispheric communication:
- relax
- cross crawling.

Providing an overview and the detail:
- Big Picture first
- learning maps
- summarize
- give reasons
- use templates.

Engage both sides of the brain:
- transforming (see page 201)
- keywords in different colours
- put it to music.

Allow students to approach learning activities in different ways:
- problem solving
- seek alternatives
- be creative.

Providing an overview and the detail
Give the big picture first
All students will benefit from this strategy, particularly those with a dominant gestalt hemisphere.

Begin lessons by providing an overview of what is to come (see page 185). When right hemisphere learners have a clear grasp of the Big Picture, they will find it significantly easier to grasp and digest the details that will follow. (This is often likened to the need to see the picture on the front of the jigsaw box before the individual pieces make any sense.)

Extend this strategy and provide students with an overview of each unit of work or two-year exam course before they embark on it. Students will find work easier to grasp if they can see how it fits into an overall scheme. Use a learning map to give students a clear picture of the structure and content of a course and use it to indicate progress through the work. Learning maps are being increasingly used with students – and don't forget, teachers can use them too.

Learning maps
One of the great benefits of using learning maps is that they allow us to simultaneously absorb the Big Picture and the details of any particular topic. It is precisely because of this that they are of enormous benefit to all types of learner. Learning maps also utilize colour and visual images, thus engaging the whole brain in a way that traditional linear notes do not. Learning maps can be used:

- *by students,* to record and summarize key information as an alternative to taking notes. Teach students how to construct learning maps and encourage them to use them whenever appropriate. They allow gestalt-hemisphere dominant students to fit the detail that they sometimes struggle with into the Big Picture. They also allow the logic hemisphere learners to see beyond the detail and grasp the overview.

- *by teachers,* to provide an introduction to a course or unit of work. Construct a giant learning map on the classroom wall. In a sense, it is a giant course plan or advanced organizer. Students will benefit from knowing the material that is to come before they encounter it (see page 187). Refer to it at regular intervals so that students can track their progress through the course. By doing this students will find it easier to see how each particular lesson and/or piece of work fits into the overall scheme.

- *as a summary, or revision aid.* Reviewing material and selecting the key points is a useful learning exercise in its own right. Summarizing these points in the form of a learning map is both an effective revision activity and revision tool.

See page 267 for further information on learning maps.

Summarize
Asking students to summarize their learning at the end of a lesson or unit of work, is helpful to all types of learner. Gestalt-dominant learners will find summarizing is part of their natural approach to learning while the exercise will help logic-hemisphere dominant students place the detail with which they are comfortable into a wider context.

Detail – Summary template

Use at the end of each unit of work

Summarize this unit in 30 words

List the five key points from this unit

1

2

3

4

5

Strategies for Closing the Learning Gap

Give reasons

Ask students to give reasons (specify a number – this will depend upon the precise nature of the work) for their answer. Logical, linear learners should have no problem with this activity, while intuitive, random learners will be forced to consider the detail behind their instinctive answer.

Use templates

Use templates, such as the one opposite, to get students into the habit of seeing both the big picture and the detail. Substitute *lesson* for *unit* as appropriate. Some students will find it easier to provide the summary while others will be more comfortable giving reasons, details and examples. Offer two versions of the template: one like the example opposite with the summary at the top of the page, and another with the space for the details above the summary. Providing students with a choice will illicit an 'I want to' response and is part of a wider motivation strategy described in Section Two.

Engage both sides of the brain

Activities that connect the hemispheres

Both hemispheres are likely to be engaged in cognitive activity whenever students are required to change the information that they encounter in some way. These transformation strategies are described in more detail on pages 201–203.

We are attempting to exploit the interconnectivity of the brain by consciously providing learning experiences that will simultaneously engage both hemispheres of the cortex. This is not as difficult as it sounds: some activities that do this are described on page 164.

Key words in different colours

Students write key words in different colours. When they read back through their notes, the left hemisphere will decode the symbols of the words, while the right hemisphere will process the pattern of the different colours; the hemispheres are connected and learning is enhanced.

The benefits of this strategy go beyond linking the hemispheres. The words selected by students as 'keywords' give the teacher an instant indication of the extent to which the student has understood a piece of work. By forcing the student to use a different colour for these words they dwell on the key points for a crucial split second longer – increasing the chances that it will be remembered.

Put it to music

We are all able to remember vast amounts of information in the form of songs, rhymes and jingles. Even songs that we have not sung since our childhood can be easily recalled whenever we hear the tune, simply because songs and rhymes simultaneously engage both hemispheres of the neo-cortex in an excellent example of 'whole-brain learning'. For while the logic hemisphere is engaged with the lyrics of the song, the gestalt hemisphere focuses upon the tune.

Activities that connect the hemispheres

- Describe out loud (left) a picture or diagram (right).

- Describe out loud (left) a learning map (right). (A particularly effective strategy to cement memory is to get students to describe their learning map to a partner.)

- Visualize (right) a written description (left).

- Describe (left) your visualization (right).

- Convert text (left) into a picture (right). (Converting material is an effective technique for developing and assessing understanding – see page 203.)

- Turn key words (left) into a song or a poem (right).

(NB. Left and right refer to the gestalt (right) and logic (left) hemisphere – which is the situation in the majority of people.)

Putting keywords to music or creating simple raps and jingles of key information is therefore a very powerful way of helping students remember material. Anything can be put to music or given a rhythm – use simple, well-known tunes such as 'Happy Birthday', 'One man went to mow' or 'London's Burning'.

Allow students to approach learning in different ways
Problem solving

Open-ended, problem solving activities can appeal to different types of learner, simply because there are a variety of ways to solve a problem. Problems can be solved intuitively or logically, allowing all students to work in their preferred style.

Seek alternatives

Gestalt-hemisphere dominant students will relish opportunities to seek alternatives as it appeals to their tendency to think divergently. Ask students to come up with an alternative answer/approach/classification and so on. Challenge them to think of three different ways.

Be creative

A variation to seeking alternatives is to ask students to be creative and invent something a response, a way of working and so on. Although it would seem that this activity would favour gestalt-brain thinkers – for many years, the gestalt hemisphere was considered the creative side of the brain – it is also possible to adopt a logical, step-by-step approach to creativity.

Story of Ernie the elephant

Once upon a time, in a jungle far away, four friends; Martha monkey, Charlie cheetah, Kevin the kangaroo and Ernie the elephant were playing. After a little while, Martha had an idea; 'I know', she said, 'let's hold the animal Olympics'. 'Great idea', said Kevin. 'I love sports', added Charlie. And so it was agreed, and the Olympics began.

The first event was running. Martha and Kevin were fast, but Charlie ran like the wind and won easily. A long time after everyone had finished, Ernie lumbered in last. 'I'm the fastest of all the animals', exclaimed Charlie proudly as the others clapped.

The next event was jumping. Charlie was quite good at jumping as well and leapt high into the sky. Martha bounced up and down enthusiastically but Kevin, shouting with glee, jumped higher then everyone. Poor Ernie was so heavy that he couldn't get off the ground. Everyone applauded Kevin as Ernie sighed – he had been last in both events.

After a brief rest, the friends moved on to tree climbing. Kevin, buoyed by his success in the jumping, quickly bounded on to the first branch but found that he could go no further. Charlie leapt effortlessly to join Kevin on the first branch and proceeded gracefully from branch to branch until he was halfway up the tree. At that point, the branches became too thin to support his weight and he was forced to stop. Martha had no such problem and within seconds had scampered her way to the top of the tree where she looked down on all of her friends.

Ernie began to cry. He couldn't even climb to the first branch and was firmly rooted to the floor. 'I'm useless', he sobbed, 'I'm no good at anything'.

Before anyone could answer, they were enveloped in a cloud of thick black smoke that left them coughing and spluttering. 'It's a fire!' yelled Martha from her vantage point, high in the tree, 'and it's coming this way!' She was right. The smoke got thicker and flames danced all around them as the heat became unbearable. They tried to escape but in every direction they were beaten back by a wall of flames. 'It's no use', wailed Charlie, 'we're surrounded'.

Kevin, Charlie and Martha sat down and began to cry. They could see no way out of their dilemma. Ernie meanwhile looked around and, as he spotted a small lake in the distance, he had an idea. Slowly, he trundled towards the lake and was soon lost from sight, obscured by the thickening smoke. When he returned a short while later, his trunk bulged with water which he squirted with all his might on to the fire.

Many times he made the trip, using his trunk to collect water that he would use to fight the fire. It was hard work, but gradually the flames began to subside. Hours later, the job done and the fire extinguished, Ernie, exhausted, sat down, by his friends.

'Thank you Ernie', said Kevin, 'you saved our lives'. 'Well done', said Martha, patting Eric on the back, 'none of us could have done that'. 'You're the best', added Charlie softly.

Everyone clapped and cheered. Ernie smiled.

Multiple intelligences

> *It's now time for educators and parents to quit asking the old question, 'How smart are you?' … the new question is, 'How are you smart?'*

Eric Jensen

David didn't enjoy school. He considered himself 'thick', struggled with basic literacy skills, rarely received any feedback from teachers other than criticism and stumbled from one incident of misbehaviour to the next. The education system regularly confirmed and reinforced David's low opinion of himself as a learner. Every time he sat an examination or test and in the majority of lessons, the message was unequivocal: *'You're a failure'.*

Yet David is a gifted mechanic and has been from a very young age. Even when he was 11, he could take an engine apart and put it back together with a skill and dexterity that few adults could match. He once told me that I had a problem with my car and correctly diagnosed the fault simply because he had heard the engine as I drove into school. His talent, skill and knowledge were all the more remarkable because David – the boy who was useless at learning – had taught himself.

Stephanie – see page 63 – had a similar experience at school. She would be the first to tell you that she was *'useless'*, *'no good at maths'* and *'in the dummy groups for everything'*. It is no great surprise that she has reached this conclusion; not a school day goes by without her being reminded that she finds reading and writing difficult. No teacher has, to my knowledge, ever told her she was 'thick'. They don't have to; she is provided with all the clues she needs.

Interestingly, no teacher, to my knowledge, has ever told her that she is special. Yet Stephanie is talented, even gifted, and has an incredible ability to learn. But Stephanie's particular talent does not count for much in our education system. She is a drummer. It is a lousy system that leaves someone with such exceptional hand, eye and foot co-ordination and sense of rhythm, feeling that they are 'useless'.

For David, Stephanie and countless others like them possess talents outside the narrow confines of intelligence as defined by our education system. They will have to wait until they leave school before they find success. That is, if they can wait. For many succumb long before they leave school, the constant negative feedback and perceived failures eroding their self-esteem to the point that they are devoid of ambition, motivation and feelings of worth.

Success at school is heavily – some would argue totally – dependent upon being literate and numerate. This is not to say that literacy and numeracy skills are not important, simply that there are other skills, talents and attributes that are also of value. This is the heart of the theory commonly referred to as 'multiple intelligences'.

First postulated by Dr Howard Gardner, multiple intelligence theory has been around since the early 1980s. It offers hope to the Davids and Stephanies of this world and offers an alternative perspective on the notion of intelligence.

Schools expect students to learn in a certain way, and student who do not fit this type are often viewed as inferior instead of merely different.

Carla Hannaford

The theory has are two key elements:

- Intelligence is not fixed. It can and does change throughout an individuals lifetime. A single IQ measurement is therefore meaningless.
- There are different types of intelligences. We all possess each type to various degrees in, what amounts to, our personal intelligence profile.

Gardner initially identified seven main categories of human intelligence: verbal–linguistic, logical–mathematical, visual–spatial, bodily–kinesthetic, musical, intrapersonal and interpersonal. He subsequently added an eighth – naturalist. He argued that every individual possesses all of these 'intelligences' in varying amounts. Some people excel in one of these areas at the expense of the others, while others have a more balanced profile.

1   *Linguistic.* People with a well-developed linguistic intelligence are good with words. They learn best through listening, writing, reading and discussion. They are usually good listeners and effective communicators both orally and in writing. Not surprisingly, they tend to flourish in the majority of classrooms.

2   *Logical–mathematical.* This form of intelligence centres on reasoning and the ability to see patterns and relationships. As the name suggests, people who are strong in this area are good at maths. They are also logical and are capable of working sequentially. They often enjoy and excel at problem-solving activities.

3   *Visual–spatial.* People who are strong in this area can visualize easily. They have the ability to imagine and to create and recreate scenes and images in their mind. They will be comfortable with graphs, maps and other forms of visual representation. People with a well-developed visual intelligence will learn effectively through observation.

4   *Musical.* Musical intelligence involves the ability to discern patterns in sounds and pick out individual instruments in a piece of music. It is associated with a well-developed sense of rhythm. These people are extremely sensitive to music and will often experience strong emotions when listening to music.

5   *Bodily–kinesthetic.* This intelligence involves the skilful use of the body. People who are strong in this area include sportsmen and women, dancers, builders, surgeons and others who are 'good with their hands'. These people have excellent co-ordination, balance and dexterity.

6   *Intrapersonal.* This intelligence refers to the ability to know oneself. People who are strong in this area are very aware of their beliefs, emotions and feelings. These people are often highly self-motivated.

7   *Interpersonal.* This intelligence refers to the ability to get on well with other people. People who are strong in this intelligence work well in teams, are generally good listeners and can build and maintain relationships.

Learning maths through musical intelligence

An Area Rap

Area of a square, times the length by itself
The side of a die on the shelf

Rectangle is a shape that's hard to rhyme
Multiply length by the width this time

Area of a triangle, base times height
Halve it, to get it right

The circle is radius squared times pi
Remember that and your marks will be high

A parallelogram is height times base
Learn it or I'll smash your face!

Multiple intelligence theory offers schools a great opportunity to redefine intelligence and success and to smash through the straitjacket of the reading, writing, reasoning education system. All students have a right to:

- learn *about* multiple intelligences
- learn *through* multiple intelligences.

Learning about multiple intelligences

Making students aware that there are different forms of intelligences can have a powerful effect on their self-esteem and attitude towards learning. Essentially, we are helping students to recognize and value their particular strengths and talents.

In *'multiple intelligent schools'* all students are smart, just in different ways. In schools where students are taught about multiple intelligences, you will frequently hear them refer to the ways in which they are intelligent. *'I'm music smart'*, is a very different way of saying, *'I'm useless at maths'*.

Multiple intelligence theory recognizes that all students are intelligent. Don't you think they should know that?

Learning through multiple intelligences

Multiple intelligence theory does not stop at pointing out that individuals have different strengths. Its potential extends far beyond the obvious – someone with a well-developed musical intelligence will be good at music while someone strong in the logical–mathematical area will be good at maths.

Rather, we can draw upon our knowledge of individual strengths to teach *through* multiple intelligences. For example, by using music and musically orientated strategies in a maths classroom, we can help students who are strong in musical intelligence but relatively weak in the logical–mathematical area to learn maths!

All students are strong in particular intelligences. When they learn through these they will learn more effectively, their self-esteem will be enhanced and their motivation will increase. It is a wonderful opportunity, but one that can only be fully exploited by:

- *strategies* – teachers need to identify the strategies that they can use in the classroom that take account of a range of intelligences
- *planning* – multiple intelligences have to be built into schemes of work.

Strategies for learning through multiple intelligences

The following strategies are effective learning activities in their own right. They are classified under the various intelligences simply because they will particularly appeal to people who are strong in that area.

Linguistic

- Any activities involving reading, writing or speaking
- Writing reports and summarizing
- Class or group discussion
- Class debate

We have long recognized the need to differentiate between levels of ability.

Why has it taken us so long to differentiate between types of ability and learning style?

- Describe out loud what you are doing as you do it. Explain what you are doing and why (see page 197).
- Describe something, either in writing or orally, in your own words.
- Make up rhymes, jingles and so on.
- Use mnemonics – see Section Five.
- Make audio tapes of key points and summaries of each unit of work.

Logical–mathematical

- Predict – what will happen next/what will happen if…
- Sequencing activities and timelines.
- Use statistics to find a pattern/reach a conclusion.
- Use flow charts.
- Classify information.
- Use diagrams and lists.
- Use learning maps.
- Set problem-solving challenges.

Visual–spatial

- Visualize outcomes (see page 187).
- Visualize information (see page 261).
- Use peripherals – display key words and key information around the room just above eye level.
- Use learning maps.
- Attach pictures or images to keywords/information to improve memory.
- Convert text/key information into a picture or a diagram.
- Drawing and using graphs.

Musical

- Use music at the beginning of the lesson to influence state.
- Use music to set the lesson in context, for example African music in a geography lesson on Africa, historical pieces in history and/or English lessons.
- Students make up songs, raps, rhymes.
- Using rhythm to learn key information – see the spelling strategy on page 145.
- Put key words to a familiar tune, for example 'Happy Birthday'.
- Acknowledge and praise performances and success in extra-curricular music activities.

Bodily–kinesthetic

- See pages 139 to 153 for kinesthetic learning strategies.
- Acknowledge and praise success in extra-curricular sporting activities.
- Use 'state break' activities (see Section Two) to keep students in an appropriate learning state.

Intrapersonal

- Individual work.
- Silent work.
- Personal target setting.
- Keep a learning diary or learning log. Focus not just on what has been learned, but also *how* it was learned.
- Reflect on work. Prompt students to consider why they attempted it in a particular way, to what extent was it successful and so on.
- Reading.

An average teacher reaches 60–80 per cent of students.

A great teacher reaches 60–80 per cent of students.

The difference is that average teachers reach the same 60–80 per cent all the time, while great teachers reach a different 60–80 per cent every lesson.

adapted from Eric Jensen

Interpersonal

- Group work.
- Role play.
- Discuss your plans/ideas/answers with a partner.
- Class discussion/debate.
- Peer teaching/helping another student.
- Team challenges/problem solving.
- Reporting back presentations.

Planning

Eric Jensen suggests that average teachers 'connect' with between 60 and 80 per cent of their students every lesson. Given the huge diversity of learning and thinking styles, this figure is remarkably high and not, by itself, a problem. However, the fact that teachers have their own distinctive teaching approach, coupled with the literacy- and numeracy- dominated education system, means that it is the same 60–80 per cent of students that the teacher connects with almost every lesson!

It means that a significant minority, of around 20 per cent of students, rarely or never have opportunities to work in a way that is compatible with their particular blend of intelligences. Students who are strong in the linguistic and logical–mathematical intelligences have plenty of opportunities. They are in the 60–80 per cent. It is those people whose personal profile favours the musical and bodily–kinesthetic intelligences that have so few opportunities – outside of music and PE – to work to their strengths. Little wonder that they become dispirited and underachieve.

The aim must be to provide sufficient variety of learning activities so that students of all intelligences have frequent opportunities to learn – in all subject areas – in a way that appeals to their particular strengths. Students who struggle to learn effectively when asked to work in a particular way may well flourish when given an opportunity to work in a different style. By providing a variety of activities, we effectively give students more than one chance to learn.

No one is suggesting that teachers can accommodate every intelligence in every lesson. A more realistic goal would be to ensure that every 'intelligence' is included in all units of work. This can only be achieved with planning and the sharing of good practice. A simple planning sheet (similar to the one on page 132, but divided into eight sections) can be useful for this purpose. Use it to:

- plan new units of work and ensure that there are learning activities that will appeal to every type of intelligence (see page 176)
- review existing units of work – are there any intelligences not represented?

In reality

The thought of accommodating seven or eight different intelligences is a daunting prospect for even the most effective teachers. It needn't be. For the vast majority of teachers, just teaching normally and balancing individual activities with pair and group work, will ensure that students who are strong in the linguistic, logical–mathematical, interpersonal and intrapersonal intelligences, will have plenty of opportunities to work in their preferred style.

Planning for multiple intelligences

Activity/strategy	Intelligence	Lesson	Scheme of work
Display key words, pictures and diagrams around the room	visual	✓	✓
Display a giant learning map of the entire scheme of work on the classroom wall	visual/ logical–mathematical	✓	✓
Use music to influence state and mood	musical	✓	
Set individual targets	intrapersonal	✓	✓
Visualize outcomes	visual	✓	✓
Set problem-solving challenges (team challenge)	logical–mathematical /interpersonal		✓
Ask students to predict	logical–mathematical		✓
Convert text to diagrams / attach a visual image to keywords	visual		✓
Visualization activities	visual		✓
Classify/sequence information	logical–mathematical		✓
Put key words into familiar tunes	musical		✓
Students make up raps, rhymes or jingles	musical		✓
Keep a learning log	intrapersonal	✓	✓
Construct learning maps	visual/ logical–mathematical	✓	✓

Strategies for Closing the Learning Gap

We must then incorporate a variety of strategies into our teaching to provide opportunities for those students who are strong in the bodily–kinesthetic, visual and musical intelligences. Some of these strategies will be, or at least, *can* be features of *every lesson*, for example:

- the use of music to influence state – musical
- keywords, posters and giant learning maps on the wall – visual
- setting personal targets – intrapersonal
- individual use of learning maps – visual.

Meanwhile we should aim to employ others *at least once during every unit of work*, for example:

- problem-solving activities – logical–mathematical
- prediction – logical–mathematical
- visualizations – visual
- converting text to a picture/diagram – visual
- putting keywords to a familiar tune – musical
- making up raps, rhymes, jingles – musical.

Use the checklist opposite as a starting point for ensuring that all learners have sufficient opportunities to learn in their preferred style. It does not include reference to linguistic learners – these students are already exceptionally well catered for. Nor does it include strategies for kinesthetic learners; a comprehensive range of strategies for them can found on pages 139–153.

Provide choice

It is not necessary for all students to turn keywords into a song during every unit of work. The important thing is that all students have the opportunity to do so. Providing choice is a powerful teaching strategy. Providing choice for students can:

- relieve stress
- boost motivation
- enable all students to learn in their preferred style.

For example, after students have studied a piece of text and identified the keywords, they could then be given the choice of using the keywords to:

- write a 30-word summary – linguistic
- construct a 30-second news report – linguistic
- draw a flow chart to explain what happened – logical–mathematical
- classify the words – logical–mathematical
- convert the text into a diagram – visual
- change the text into a model – bodily–kinesthetic
- draw a learning map – visual/logical–mathematical
- cut out and construct a learning map – bodily–kinesthetic/visual/logical–mathematical
- change the text into a play/mime/frieze – bodily–kinesthetic
- put the keywords to music – musical
- turn the keywords into a poem – musical.

NB. The above strategies are all effective learning activities in their own right. All require the students to think about the text and are based on the strategies on reduction and/or change outlined on pages 199–203.

Summary – style

- People learn in different ways. It is helpful to be aware of the way in which your students prefer to learn – without labelling!

- Learning is enhanced when students can learn in their preferred style.

- There is often a mismatch between the way in which students prefer to learn and the way in which they are taught.

- This mismatch can cause demotivation, misbehaviour and underachievement.

- Keep it in perspective! All learners learn best from multisensory learning experiences.

- If we provide *variety* and *choice* in our lessons and our schemes of work we ensure that all learners will have frequent opportunities to work in their preferred style.

- Variety and choice do not just happen – they have to be planned for.

Award yourself a mark out of ten for the way in which you provide for students with different learning cycles.

Identify one thing that you could do differently which would enable you to raise your score by one mark.

Subject-specific strategies

The very different nature of individual subjects will significantly influence the precise nature of effective learning activities in particular curriculum areas. There is, therefore, a desperate need for us to identify subject-specific strategies that appeal to different types of learner.

Very often, the way in which teachers teach is heavily influenced by the way in which they were taught and the fact that they look at their subject through the eyes of a subject expert.

In order to increase the range of strategies at our disposal, the challenge may well be for us to think laterally and adopt and adapt strategies from other curriculum areas. For example:

- sequencing, a common activity in English, can be used to good effect in maths (see page 146)
- role play is used extensively in French – why can't we role play an equation or molecular activity in solids, liquids and gases? (see page 147)
- *you* might not learn maths by turning everything into a rap, but someone with a very strong musical intelligence might (see page 170).

All teachers welcome good ideas that work in the classroom. They do not necessarily have to be new; simply sharing and adapting techniques and tasks that are already being used is an effective improvement strategy. Schools are increasingly sharing good ideas *within* departments, the next step may well be to share strategies *between* departments.

The four key phases of a lesson are:

Phase one
OVERVIEW

Link the lesson
Provide an overview
Describe the outcomes
Introduce the key learning point
Stimulate curiosity
Set the challenge
Set individual targets.

Phase two
INPUT

Provide new information
Teacher input
Multisensory input – opportunities to
    receive information in preferred style
    – visual, auditory, kinesthetic.

Phase three
PROCESS

Making sense of the information
Activities to develop understanding
Opportunities to process information in
    preferred style – VAK, multiple
    intelligences, hemispheric dominance.

Phase four
REVIEW

Demonstrate understanding
'Know what you know'
Reflect on what and how you have
    learned
Recap and review.

Section Four: Structure

> *No matter how much fun or how stimulating the learning process becomes, it's also vital to work to a cohesive, step-by-step plan.*

Colin Rose

All learners progress through a series of distinct phases or stages while learning. The precise nature of these phases and the specific activities that take place within each one, will inevitable vary with the age and ability of the learner and the focus for the learning, but nevertheless, learning will be firmly based upon progress through these four broad stages.

In this section we will look at each of the four stages:

➡ **gaining an overview of what is to be learned**

➡ **encountering new information**

➡ **making sense of that information**

➡ **reviewing and reinforcing what has been learned.**

When lessons are structured to consciously reflect, and to guide young, immature learners through the natural stages of the learning process, learning is enhanced. The lesson structure shown opposite is based upon these four broad phases. It is a simple template designed to help teachers consciously structure their lessons in a way that reflects how the brain works quite naturally. It is a structure that can form the basis for planning, teaching, monitoring and development.

The structure presupposes that the teacher has used strategies such as smiling and playing suitable music to get the students in an appropriate state to learn before embarking upon phase one. Getting students in the right frame of mind is our first task and the time required for this will inevitably vary with circumstances. When everyone is ready, draw attention to the fact that learning is about to begin: ask a different student each lesson to hang a notice on the door that reads, *'Do not disturb – learning in progress'*. Not only does it remind your students what lessons are all about, it also deters unwanted visitors!

Just as mature learners progress through these stages quite naturally, so too do experienced teachers. There is no suggestion otherwise. We are, however, looking to improve – to tweak – and by consciously addressing something that is instinctive and intuitive, we may find areas for professional development.

There are a number of other principles that must be taken into account when structuring lessons.

1   People remember more from the beginning of a learning experience – when curiosity, anticipation and concentration are greatest – than they do from the middle. This is known as the *primacy effect*. People also remember more from the end of a learning experience than they do from the middle. This is referred to as the *recency effect*.

The BEM principle

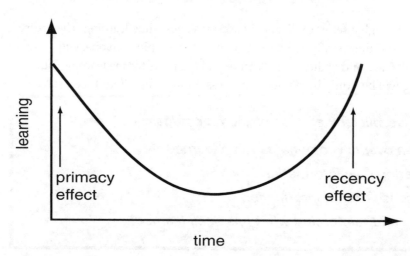

People remember more from the beginning and end of a learning experience than they do from the middle. This is known as the primacy effect and the recency effect.

Exploiting the BEM principle

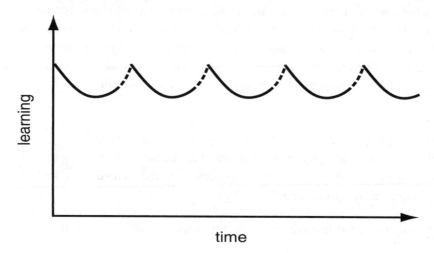

Create lots of 'beginnings' in your lessons to maximize memory and learning.

2   Consequently we should actively seek to create lots of 'beginnings' in our lessons (see diagram opposite).

3   Average concentration span broadly corresponds to chronological age plus one or two minutes. Thus, a typical 12 year old can concentrate for a maximum of around 14 minutes.

4   Learning should therefore be 'chunked' into short bursts of activity, punctuated by 'state break' activities, such as time-outs (see page 43). This approach both creates a number of beginnings in the lesson and is compatible with the brain's natural concentration span.

5   Structuring lessons around a number of different activities provides an opportunity for all students to learn in their preferred style.

6   *It is important that the four-phase lesson structure is not regarded as rigid or restrictive.* Boundaries between the phases will almost certainly be blurred. For example, developing understanding will not be restricted to phase three – helping students to understand material permeates everything that we do – it is simply the part of the lesson when activities to develop understanding become the conscious focus.

7   *Teachers can – indeed should – scroll through the phases more than once during the course of a lesson, particularly in a double period.* For example, an explanation may be given to the students followed by an activity designed to help them make sense of it. There may then be a short time-out or similar 'state break' activity, before the sequence of information and activity is repeated.

Phase one

People remember more from the beginning of a learning experience – the first five minutes of a lesson are therefore crucial as they represent prime learning time. It is during this time that the tone for the entire lesson is set so don't waste it collecting in homework and giving out resources!

Deliver the key learning point

Exploit the primacy effect and *introduce the key learning point right at the beginning of the lesson.* The key learning point is the pivotal point of the lesson – the defining moment. Invariably, it is a piece of crucial information or a key concept that students must grasp in order to progress through the next part of the unit of work. In simple terms, it is the bit that you would do if the lesson only lasted for 60 seconds!

Get into the habit of referring to the key learning point in your introductory remarks.

Link the lesson

New learning is built upon the foundations of existing knowledge and understanding. Before learning can begin therefore, the lesson has to be placed in context. Learners need to know where they have been and where they are going if new information is to make any sense. Linking the learning represents an opportunity to review what has been learned during preceding lessons.

Use a whiteboard

Erect a small whiteboard in each classroom (keep the main board free for teaching and learning) with the permanent prompt:

By the end of today's lesson, you will all...

Begin each lesson by writing the intended learning outcomes. In OFSTED language, it is 'sharing the learning objectives with the students'. In accelerated-learning speak, it is 'giving the Big Picture'. Either way, it helps children learn!

Use phrases such as

'Last lesson we looked at X, next lesson we are going on to look at Y and today's lesson is all about Z'.

Use learning maps

A giant learning map of a unit of work on the wall will help students – and teachers – place the lesson in context. It will also appeal to gestalt- and logic- hemisphere dominant students.

Review previous learning

This can take many forms (see review on page 221). Use a variety of approaches to ensure that the beginnings of your lessons do not become predictable and stale. Possible approaches include:

- *What are the three most important/interesting things that you learned last lesson?*
- *Imagine that your friend missed the last lesson. What three things would he need to know in order to catch up?*
- *What three questions can you answer now that you couldn't answer before last lesson?*
- *Write down one sentence to summarize what you learned last lesson. Include as many key words as you can.*
- *Describe the learning map that you drew last lesson to the person sitting next to you.*
- *You have five minutes to move around the room and tell four different people, three things that you learned last lesson.*
- *Think of three things that you learned last lesson. Swap your ideas with the person sitting next to you. See if you can get four things between you. Turn around and share your ideas with the pair sitting behind you. I bet your group can't think of six different things that we learned.*

Provide an overview

Tell students at the beginning what they are going to learn and how they are going to learn it.

This is sometimes referred to as 'providing the Big Picture' – students will make sense of information far more easily if they can see how it fits into their overall learning. In hemispheric terms, we are accessing the gestalt (global) before the logic (detail) hemisphere. In simpler terms, jigsaw pieces will only make any sense if you have first seen the picture on the front of the box!

Use phrases such as

   'This lesson is all about...'

   'In today's lesson we are going to discover...'

   'The focus of today's lesson is...'

Use learning maps

Learning maps do more than link the lesson, they provide an excellent overview that will particularly appeal to gestalt-hemisphere dominant learners but will be invaluable to all students.

Visualize success

Whatever your goal – completing your coursework, solving a problem, passing your GCSEs – visualize yourself achieving it.

Be as specific as possible. What do you see, what do you hear, what do you feel, at your moment of triumph?

This strategy has such a positive impact because the brain does not know the difference between reality and fiction. When a situation that has previously been visualized is actually encountered, the brain believes that it has already 'been there and done it.'

Visualizations are extensively employed in sport. How many times do you think Steve Redgrave 'won' that gold medal in the build-up to the Olympics? He almost certainly knew exactly what he would be thinking and how he would be feeling before, during and after the race, because he had been over it in his mind so many times. It was an event that was too important to be left to chance.

Visualizations are both reassuring and motivating and can be used to great effect to help students learn and succeed.

Strategies for Closing the Learning Gap

A major source of stress is the feeling of not being in control and not knowing. Telling students how the lesson fits together will help relax them and get them in a receptive state to learn. For example:

'Today's lesson will start with a short video clip that will last for about 10 minutes. Then we are going to do an exercise in pairs that will take about 15 minutes. We'll take our time-out after that and finish off with some individual work. You'll have a choice of doing a written explanation or drawing a labelled diagram.'

Describe the outcomes

This is an extension of providing an overview and makes explicit what each student will achieve by the end of the lesson.

Use phrases such as
'By the end of today's lesson you will all...
... know the difference between...
... understand that...
... be able to explain...
... be able to calculate...
... be able to answer these three questions...
... have completed a diagram to show...'

Use language that conveys expectation of success. Be as specific as possible, so that all students know precisely what is expected of them.

Visualize outcomes

Encourage students to imagine what their completed task will look like. Invite them to speculate how they will feel when they have successfully finished the learning activity. Ask them questions such as:

● *'How will know that you know?*

● *'How will you know that you understand?*

For example, if students are drawing a graph, ask them what a good one looks like. Ask them what a great one – or the 'best graph in the world' – looks like. What is the difference between an excellent graph and an OK graph? What will they need to do in order to produce an equally great graph? How will you know that you've drawn a great graph?

This principle can be extended. Show them a great graph and discuss the reasons why it is so good. There is a saying that goes, 'you will never hit a target that you cannot see'. If we want them to produce excellent work, shouldn't we show them what excellence looks like?

Pre-exposure

Telling students what they are about to learn (sometimes referred to as pre-exposure) does more than relieve stress; it primes the brain to notice important pieces of information. For example, you might begin a lesson by saying, *'Your homework tonight will be to identify three reasons why the treaty failed.'* Students will then be more likely to 'notice' the reasons as they come along during the lesson. If we fail to alert the brain in this way there is a danger that important pieces of information will be missed, simply because the brain does not register them as important.

Getting students to ask the questions

Display
Display the key questions – what, why, how and when - around the room. Make constant reference to them.

Ask them yourself
The teacher sets the tone. It is up to us to model the behaviour we are trying to establish.

Ask the expert!
'Today we have a visit from the world's leading authority on *Macbeth*. Chose three questions that you would like to ask them.' (Questions can be generated in pairs or groups to avoid putting students on the spot. The expert can be a) the teacher b) another teacher who is a specialist c) a visitor.)

Write the test
'Today's lesson is all about... . Next lesson I'm going to test you (give you an opportunity to demonstrate to yourself on how much you've understood). What questions do you think I will ask?'

'Today we are starting a three-week unit of work on earthquakes. Before we start, I would like you think of three questions that will be included in the end-of-unit test. After questions are generated and collated – in pairs, groups or as a class – announce, 'we now have three weeks to find out the answers'.

Knowing the questions in advance provides the student with a focus for their learning. They are far more likely to pay attention and grasp the significance of a piece of information, if they know in advance that it is the answer to a key question.

I would normally ask a question now
Demonstrations and/or explanations are common in the classroom. Often, they are punctuated by the teacher posing a question. Get students in the habit of asking the questions, simply by saying, 'I would normally ask a question now – can anybody think what it might be?' An alternative is to use a bell or buzzer: every time it is rung, students are required to ask a relevant question.

Question box/wall
An easy way to encourage students to ask questions without embarrassment is to provide a question box or wall. Students simply write down questions as they think of them – anonymously if they wish – and drop them in the box. Often these questions provide excellent extension or research work.

Questions that I need to be able to answer
Students work in pairs or small groups to formulate a list of questions that 'I need to be able to answer before I fully understand this topic'.

Further strategies for encouraging students to ask the questions can be found in *Lessons are for Learning* by Mike Hughes, pages 31–40 (Network Educational Press, 1997).

In simple terms, we are setting a piece of fly paper at the start of the lesson and by so doing, increasing the chances that important information will 'stick' – consciously and subconsciously – when it comes along.

Stimulate curiosity

Easier said than done, but if we can stimulate the curiosity of our students at the beginning of the lesson, then motivation, concentration and effort will be significantly enhanced. Certainly it should be a conscious objective.

Stimulating curiosity and capturing the imagination of students – whatever their age – owes much to the personal characteristics and approach of the individual teacher. It is difficult to inspire if you are not inspired. It is impossible to enthuse if you are not enthusiastic. However, the impact of the teacher's mood and approach can be *significantly enhanced* by employing the simple strategy of getting the students to ask the questions.

Asking questions

Supposing no one asked a question. What would the answer be?

Gertrude Stein

Students spend large amounts of time answering questions. Occasionally, these are deep, open-ended questions that challenge thinking and deepen understanding. All too often, however, they are straightforward, closed questions that contribute more to the assessment than to the learning process.

In contrast, asking questions is fundamental to learning. Young children – expert learners – constantly ask questions, to satisfy an instinctive and insatiable desire to learn. Not only are children born with an inner drive to discover, they have an innate understanding that the starting point for all learning is to ask questions. Answers are merely the catalyst for more questions – the more they find out, the more they want to know.

What a tragedy then, that by the time children – unstoppable learning machines in their infancy – reach secondary school, the curiosity has withered and the questions all but disappeared. As much as we are saddened by this metamorphosis, we should not be surprised. As children become older and progress through the formal education system, their learning becomes increasingly content based while, simultaneously, their personal responsibility for learning is eroded. Far from immersing themselves in their learning as they did while exploring the world as young children, they are distanced from the process as teachers provide the answers for them; the only responsibility of the child being to remember them. Most crucially of all perhaps, the learner-generated questions of the infant years are replaced by the questions provided by the teacher.

We are not seeking to halt or reverse the ageing process. There is no claim that teenagers will bring the same innocence and enthusiasm to learning trigonometry that they once displayed when learning to ride their first bicycle. However, learners of any age will inevitably seek the answers to questions that they themselves have generated with a greater determination and enthusiasm than ones which have been presented to them. Rekindling the flame of curiosity and encouraging students to generate the questions that they want to answer is a key strategy in improving motivation and learning.

Phase one

- Does the lesson begin crisply?

- Does the teacher link the learning?

- Are the learning objectives shared with the students?

- Do the students know what they will be doing during the lesson?

- Are students clear about what is expected of them?

- Is there a sense of curiosity, challenge and expectation?

- Are students encouraged to set individual goals? Are they specific?

- How quickly is the key learning point introduced?

- Does the teacher grab the attention of the students right from the start?

Award yourself a mark out of ten (ten being the highest) for phase one of one of your typical lessons.

Identify one thing that you could do differently that would enable you to increase this score by one mark.

Set the challenge

People respond to a challenge. All students will approach activities and learning tasks in a very different manner when they are couched in terms of a challenge. Boys in particular are quick to pick up the gauntlet and endeavour to prove themselves capable: schools and teachers who are grappling with the relative underachievement of boys would do well to examine the ways in which boys are currently challenged in lessons.

The phrase, *'I bet you can't...'* is a challenge no self-respecting, underachieving boy can ignore!

- *I bet you can't finish by 12.30.*
- *I bet you can't ask me a question about this topic at the end of the lesson, that is so hard, I won't be able to answer.*
- *I bet you can't think of three possible reasons.*
- *I bet you can't do this without making a mistake.*
- *I bet you can't get more than you did last time.*

Three things are important to bear in mind when setting a challenge:

1. A challenge is only motivating when the student *believes* that they are capable of succeeding. The fact that the challenge is demanding and requires maximum concentration and effort does not matter – providing that the student believes the task to be within their capability.

2. We must say *'I bet you can't...'* in a way that means, *'I know you can...'* – and, furthermore, *'I want you to...'*. We are seeking to illicit a positive response and kick-start people into action, not demoralize them.

3. Getting the right level of challenge is crucial. When tasks are too easy, students are bored; when they are too difficult, students are demotivated. A task of the appropriate level of difficulty, communicated as a challenge is necessary to maximize interest, motivation and learning.

Set individual targets (see page 81)

Targets are the stepping stones to larger, longer-term goals. When we are seeking to get students in an appropriate state for a lesson in mid-February, a goal of grade B at GCSE that was set the preceding September and will not be realized until the following summer, will have relatively little impact.

We should encourage students to set, lesson-by-lesson, shorter-term targets. For maximum impact, targets should be:

- generated by the student
- specific
- applicable to the lesson – be related to the desired learning outcomes
- written down.

Strategies for Closing the Learning Gap

Phase two

1   How long does phase two last?

2   How does this compare with the average concentration span of the students?

3   How do students receive information?
    ● visual   ● auditory   ● kinesthetic

4   Are opportunities for students with different learning styles systematically built into schemes of work? How is this organized?
    ● visual/auditory/kinesthetic
    ● hemispheric dominance
    ● multiple intelligences
    ● other

5   Is information delivered in easily-digestible chunks?

6   What is the ratio of time students spend receiving information to time spent making sense of it?

7   To what extent are lessons multisensory?

8   What strategies do you regularly employ for kinesthetic learners?

9   Where would you position yourself on the kinesthetic hierarchy on page 130?

Award yourself a mark out of ten (ten being the highest) for phase two of one of your typical lessons.

Identify one thing that you could do differently that would enable you to increase this score by one mark.

Use the following prompts to help students set their own targets:

'By the end of this lesson I will...
In order to achieve this I will need to...'

Phase two

This is the phase in which the student encounters new information and it is characterized by *teacher exposition* and *information transfer*. In simple terms, it is the part of the lesson when the teacher 'teaches'. New material is outlined and explained and detail is provided to supplement and expand upon the broad overview given during the introduction.

In many respects, this section is the bread-and-butter of the teaching profession and is, not surprisingly, done relatively well. Teachers have a range of resources to call upon when explaining new material. Books, photographs, diagrams, worksheets, whiteboard and computer can all be used to good effect.

Two caveats however:

- Information is transmitted predominantly visually and orally during this part of the lesson. As has been suggested, those students who prefer to learn by 'doing' – kinesthetic learners – can be disadvantaged, particularly when their learning preference is a strong one. In order for all students to learn effectively, information must be presented in a variety of ways during phase two (see Section Three).
- Teacher exposition often lasts too long! Teachers, almost by definition, are good at explaining and it is all too easy for lessons to be dominated by the teacher. Exposition should be kept short and sharp and not exceed the natural concentration span of the students.

The relative length of phases two and three offers an indication of the balance between information being transferred and information being understood. Learning is done *by* people, not *to* them, and this should be reflected in the structure of a lesson. When phase two lasts too long, there is insufficient time for students to make sense out of new material.

In simple terms, phase two is all about teaching while phase three (see page 195) is predominantly about learning.

At the risk of oversimplification, learning is enhanced when students spend longer in phase three than they do in phase two. Yet in many lessons, teachers:

- spend longer in phase two than they think they do
- spend longer in phase two than they do in phase three.

Ensuring that a larger proportion of lessons are devoted to students making sense of information (phase three) would go a long way to enhancing the quality of learning taking place in the classroom.

Consider the following exercise.
Read the text and answer the questions below.

The Boogins are indigenous to the European continent, making their swalts among the shrubs and bushes of former river beds. The male is some 3 cm longer than the female and lives, on average, two years longer. Both are dark in appearance with the female having the slightly longer fur.

Boogins are members of the Tracett family and are closely related to Binks. They are hampdavidons, and live almost exclusively on small bugs and insects. Adult males drink prodigous amounts, particularly during the hours of darkness, to prepare themselves for the long daylight hours which they spend foraging for food.

Boogins are unusual in that they breath through a small opening behind their dun. This makes them vunerable to strong northern winds that blow across the plain. A run of bad winters have left the Boogins threatened with extinction.

Questions

1   In which continent do Boogins live?

2   Where do Boogins make their swalts?

3   Which are bigger, males or females?

4   To which family do Boogins belong?

5   What do Boogins eat?

6   How do Boogins breath?

7   Why are Boogins facing extinction?

Answering the questions correctly is a relatively straightforward task. (If you do it neatly, you will probably get a merit!) Yet how many students would have clue what Boogins are? Equally as worrying – how would the teacher know if they had a clue or not?

Strategies for Closing the Learning Gap

Phase three

" *Turning mere facts into personal meaning is the central element in learning.* "

Colin Rose

Phase three is the phase when students are given the opportunity to make personal sense of the material that they have just encountered. It is the time when information is processed and understood. It is the time when *information becomes learning*.

The brain is designed to cycle between acquiring new information and processing it, and this must be reflected in the way in which lessons are organized. Two things are therefore required:

- Learning must be punctuated by *regular breaks* such as time-outs and other 'state break' activities (see page 41). These provide the brain with some down time and a respite from the constant barrage of information. During these breaks, the brain will be internally processing the information that it has just absorbed. It is a necessary subconscious process that mirrors cognitive activity during the hours of sleep.

- Students must be engaged in activities and tasks that require them to grapple with, manipulate and *think about* the information they have been presented with. For understanding cannot be given or passively received in the same way as information. It is an active process – the product of doing rather than receiving. It is also highly personal, and demands concerted cognitive activity on the part of the individual learner.

The temptation to skip phase three in the pursuit of covering a crowded curriculum is understandable. But it is also misguided, for when the activities that will develop understanding and cement learning are neglected, lessons are reduced to little more than transfer of information. Students may cover the curriculum but it is unlikely that they will understand it – and if it hasn't been understood, it hasn't been learned.

For understanding – the *'ah ha! I get it'*, moment when everything finally clicks into place and begins to make sense – is the essence of learning. It makes phases three arguably the *key section* of the lesson.

For many schools, focusing improvement and professional development programmes upon phase three of lessons will yield significant gains in learning and attainment. Reflect for a moment upon the ratio of time spent in phase two (teacher input) and phase three (student understanding). In many cases, the teacher dominates the majority of the lesson. Yet, in order for students to fully understand material, the majority of the lesson needs to be spent on activities and tasks that enable the learners to manipulate and interrogate information in order to make sense of it.

Assessing understanding

As teachers, we have a responsibility not only to develop understanding, but also to assess it. This can prove difficult, if not impossible, if the nature of the tasks that we set does not allow students to demonstrate how much they have understood.

This is often the case when the task is primarily a note-taking activity or low-level comprehension exercise that involves little more than searching the text for the clues. Sadly, these activities are all too common in schools.

It is no more possible for a teacher to make me understand than for a teacher to digest food for me.

Carol Ann Tomlinson
M. Layne Kalbfleisch

There are no magic wands, no guarantees, we are simply looking for strategies that make it more likely that students will think about and make sense of the material that they have encountered.

Strategies to develop understanding

Understanding is not an inevitable by-product of lessons. Indeed, unless it is consciously planned for, it is unlikely that students will fully digest the information that they encounter. The following strategies are designed to help students make sense of and understand material. The list is not exhaustive; they are simply a range of learning activities that have consistently proved to be both effective and manageable in the classroom. They all have a number of things in common. They are:

- *Generic.* They can be applied, with the minimum of modification, to a wide range of curriculum areas.

- *Based upon what we know about effective learning.* For example, when students are required to change the form of information (see page 201) they will be drawing upon both hemispheres of the neo-cortex (see page 153).

- *Inextricably linked with other learning styles and strategies.* For example, when students are required to reduce information to key words required (see page 199) they might then put them to music, which would appeal to students with a well-developed musical intelligence (see page 169). Alternatively, they may portray them in the form of a mime or frieze, which would be of particular benefit to kinesthetic learners (see Section Three).

- *Designed to simultaneously help the student make sense of material and give the teacher an opportunity to assess the extent of understanding.*

- *Suitable for small groups or individual students.* Working in pairs or small groups can often have the advantage as the process of discussing and debating can help challenge, shape and extend understanding.

- *Manageable.* They work with 9B on a wet Friday afternoon!

Verbalize

> *You don't know what you know until you say it.*
>
> 9 year old (quoted in Robert Fisher, *Teaching Children to Learn*, 1995)

This is arguably the most effective strategy there is to develop understanding and one of the easiest to implement. Simply encourage students to explain aloud, in their own words, what they are doing and why, while they do it. In order to verbalize in this way, the student is forced to process information internally, thus deepening and cementing understanding. To a certain extent, intuition becomes conscious action.

Even the students who are adept at solving quadratic equations or who instinctively punctuate a piece of prose, will benefit from explaining it as they do it. It is an effective strategy whatever the activity – from sawing a piece of wood to understanding Shakespeare!

It is also something that many people do quite naturally. Observe people who stop and ask a stranger for directions. Invariably they will repeat them back! This is a natural action, designed to ensure that they have understood correctly, deepen understanding and, by paying conscious attention, help cement the information in the memory. Something similar happens when teachers participate in ICT INSET.

'What you express is 10 to 100 times more productive of your learning than what is expressed to you!'

Win Wenger, Director, Project Renaissance

Wenger originated the concept of 'pole-bridging', which seeks to simultaneously engage and connect many different sites or 'poles' in the brain. One of the easiest ways to do this is to encourage students to describe aloud what they are doing, while they are doing it. Talking through your thinking in this way helps to develop and deepen understanding and can lead to significant gains in learning.

For more detailed information, see:

● *Beyond Teaching and Learning* by Win Wenger (Project Renaissance, 1992)
● *The Einstein Factor* by Win Wenger and Richard Poe (Prima Publishing, 1994)

The student does not even need to talk to someone else; they can simply talk quietly to themselves as they undertake a task. By listening to what they are saying, however, the teacher can make an instant, informal assessment as to their level of understanding.

There are a number of variations on this theme. Students can explain what they are doing to:

- themselves
- a partner
- the teacher
- a relative or friend – write to all parents and encourage them to listen to their son/daughter explain what they have been doing in school. Outline to them why it is so important.
- a pet, cuddly toy or poster of their sporting favourite – the person does not have to be real: it is the process of verbalizing their thoughts that is powerful; the audience is incidental.

Reduction

This strategy is so effective because it so closely resembles the learning process. Learning is all about cutting through information to identify the core idea or key concept – if you like, 'hitting the nail on the head'.

Strategies that ask students to reduce, require them to *think* carefully about the material and *prioritize* information. The key is to present them with a dilemma which requires them to make a conscious decision. Students will be reassured that there is often no one correct answer, while their response will provide teachers with a clear indication about the extent to which they have grasped a piece of information. For example:

Reduce text	*What is the most important/significant chapter in the book'? What is the most important sentence on the page? What is the most significant/important/interesting line in the poem? What are the six most important words in the paragraph?*
Reduce a diagram	*What is the most important section of this diagram? What is the key word in this diagram?*
Reduce a story or a play	*What is the most significant scene in the play? Who is the key character in* Romeo and Juliet? *You have been asked to cut a whole scene from* Macbeth *so that it can be reduced by three minutes for television purposes. Which scene will you cut so that the meaning of the play is not lost?*

Having prioritized and reduced the information, a number of options are now available. Activities that force the students to change the key words into a different form are particularly valuable as they will require the students to think even more deeply about the information and so further develop understanding. A range of suggestions are given on page 203.

Transforming key words into a poem

Jimmy The Raindrop

Jimmy the raindrop broke into a smile
When he landed in the mountains at the source of the Nile
He's by no means alone, so much rain he might drown
As the raindrops together begin to roll down
A trickle, a stream and into a river
Poor little Jimmy is all of a dither

The river is big now, it's the Nile and it's blue
But hey, what is this, not one Nile but two
A confluence at Khartoum, the blue meets the white
And all of a sudden the Nile takes a right

Into Lake Nasser and onto Aswan
No chance of a flood as Jimmy goes through the dam
Onwards and upwards, how dry is the land
A cactus, a palm tree and buckets full of sand

Tumbling along all helter and skelter
Out of the desert and into a delta
The sand turns to mud as far as you can see
No longer a river, a distributary

It's been a long journey, the longest there is
And poor little Jimmy is all of a tis
He's tired and he's dirty and ready for bed
But the end is in sight, here comes the Med

Rameez, Year 7 student

Impose a limit

- *'Prepare and deliver a 40-second report. Then reduce the time allowed to 30 seconds.'*
- *'Summarize this material in 150 words. Then reduce the words again, this time to 100.'*

Summarizing in this way is an excellent strategy for developing understanding. Every time we reduce the time or words allowed, we force students to prioritize in order to identify the bits they are going to leave out. Depending upon the nature of the material, it may be appropriate to reduce a 100-word summary to just ten words or even one key word. There is no right answer, we are simply trying to get students thinking!

A4 limit

Ask students to summarize a unit of work on just one side of paper. Guide them by asking, if they were allowed to take the paper into an exam, what would they write? Allow students to write in prose or key words and/or to summarize the material in diagrams or pictures in they wish.

Remove a word

Reduce a piece of text, a word at a time, without altering the meaning. This activity works best in groups of three. Two students take alternate turns at removing a word; the third judges whether the removal of the word changes or, more accurately, loses the meaning of the text.

Reduce a unit of work to five key points

Ask each student to identify five key points from a unit of work and write them down on a postcard or strip of paper. The first student places their cards across the front desk. Students then, in turn, consider the five cards. If any of their points match with the information on the card, they simply lay their card on the original.

Not only is it an excellent revision strategy, ideal for the end of a module, the teacher is provided with useful feedback about the way in which the cards are distributed. Three or four substantial piles of cards – providing the information on them is appropriate – will indicate general agreement among the class, indicating that the majority of students have grasped the key points of the unit. Little agreement among the students may mean that understanding has been patchy.

Transformation

> *The very process of transforming requires the brain to process information actively, which in itself provides challenge to the learner.*

David Leat, *Thinking Through Geography*

All too often, students are asked to reproduce information in exactly the same form as they received it. For example, students are asked to write about a piece of text or draw a graph. Not only does this represent very little in the way of intellectual challenge, it is extremely difficult to assess the extent to which material has been grasped.

Retention rates

Lecture – 5%

Reading – 10%

Audio-visual – 20%

Demonstration – 30%

Discussion – 50%

Practice by doing – 75%

Teaching others – 90%

Source: National Training Laboratories, Bethel, Maine

Strategies for Closing the Learning Gap

Forcing students to change information into a different format has a number of benefits:

- Students are forced to think about the material – they have to do something with it.
- The teacher can gauge the extent to which information has been understood.
- There is a every likelihood that both hemispheres of the neo-cortex will be engaged in the process of changing the format of the information.

This is a strategy that can be used in isolation or combined with the strategy of reduction. For example, reduce a piece of text to six key words, then use those key words to compose a song or poem. It is also apparent that these strategies will appeal to different types of learner and various multiple intelligence profiles (see page 169).

Examples of this strategy
(The dominant hemisphere for each activity is given in brackets. G = gestalt hemisphere – for most people the right side. L = logic hemisphere – usually the left. See page 153. The dominant intelligence is suggested in italics.)

- describe (L) a graph, diagram, photograph or model (G) – *linguistic*
- visualize (G) a piece of text or written description (L) – *visual*
- describe (L) a visualization (G) – *linguistic*
- convert a piece of text (L) into a diagram or picture (G) – *visual*
- convert a piece of text into a play, mime or frieze – *kinesthetic*
- convert a diagram into a play, mime or frieze – *kinesthetic*
- convert text (L) into a cartoon strip (G) – *visual*
- put key words (L) to music (G) – *musical*
- use key words (L) to write a poem (G) – *linguistic*
- visualize piece of music – *visual/musical*
- convert text or a diagram into a model – *kinesthetic*
- convert text into a flow diagram – *logical–mathematical*
- mime a poem – *kinesthetic*

> *Transfer the information and it will still be information.*
>
> *Transform it and there is every chance that it will become understanding.*

Teach something

In general terms, we remember around 90 per cent of what we teach compared to just *10–20 per cent of what we read or hear.* This should come as no surprise. In order to teach, we have to:

- make sense of material and process it internally before communicating it
- identify the core idea
- simplify it
- explain something in our own words
- summarize information.

In many respects, the act of teaching combines many of the thinking strategies that develop understanding and begs the question, why don't we require our students to do more of the teaching?! When students are involved in teaching or coaching another student, both children benefit. The 'teacher' has to organise their thoughts and make

Invent a ten-year-old brother or sister, who always asks you what you have done in school.

Whatever you say – 'photosynthesis', 'convectional rain' or 'alliteration' – your sibling enquires, 'What's that then?'

How do you reply?
This can be a written or oral activity and can be completed individually or in pairs.

Strategies for Closing the Learning Gap

sense of the material before they can communicate it to their partner, while their 'student' gets to hear an explanation in 'student speak'.

There are a number of ways that we can put students in to the role of teacher:

- Informally for example during time-outs (see page 43).

- At regular points during the lesson. After each 'chunk' of information, help students make sense of it by giving them an opportunity to teach – explain it in their own words to their partner. Partner A, you have two minutes to teach that to partner B. Then reverse roles.

- Giving students an opportunity to explain their work and demonstrate their understanding to someone at the end of the lesson is particularly beneficial as it ensures that material is reviewed after it was originally encountered (see page 221). Allow ten minutes for the students to move around the room and explain something to three different people – kinesthetic learners particularly will benefit.

- Prepare a learning activity for children two years younger. This can be done individually, in pairs or in small groups. The fact that the children are two years younger is significant – it will encourage students to *simplify* the information. A variation is to specify the learning activity. For example, produce a board game based upon this material for students two years younger.

- Pupils do not have to explain things to another pupil. The beneficial impact of teaching is the same if students have explained something to a kitten, puppet or poster. Make sure parents are aware (write to them or hold an awareness evening) of the benefits of explaining something that has just been learned to another person. Encourage parents to ask their children what they learned in school each day. Not only does this help children organize their thoughts, it requires them to review material within 24 hours (see page 221).

- Use students to teach children who have been absent. This can be done as an individual or group activity. Asking a class to recap the work of the previous lesson for an absent student is an effective way of recapping and linking the lesson to previous work.

- Use students who have finished an exercise and have grasped the key idea to coach students who are struggling with the work.

- Explaining something does not have to be done verbally. Students can write to a sick friend or pen pal and explain what they have been learning in science: *'We have just been learning about photosynthesis. This is when…'* Alternatively, write a *'Step-by-step guide'* to solving an equation, testing for starch, baking a pizza, calculating a six-figure grid reference or whatever. This is a useful homework strategy as it enables students to both review material and to consider how they have done something.

1   Identify something that you understand. (It doesn't have to be in your subject area – it could be a hobby or interest outside of school.)

2   Think back to the time when you were developing that understanding. What were you doing?

3   How do you know that you understand it?

Irrespective of what you have identified, it is highly likely that:

- You were *doing* something – practising, attempting, trialling, rehearsing – as you developed your understanding.

- You know that you understand it because you can *demonstrate* your understanding – i.e. you can *do it*. The positive feedback, in whatever form, whenever you demonstrate your understanding, confirms that you have successfully understood.

Understanding is an active process: the product of doing rather than acquisition.

Sequencing

This exercise works equally well with a story, a series of instructions, a poem, the description of a process or a sequence of events.

Take a piece of text and divide it into sections – sentences, phrases or paragraphs, depending upon the nature of the text. The challenge for the student is to correctly sequence the text so that it makes sense. There are many variations on this theme:

- sequence a poem, process, equation or event
- work individually, in groups or as a whole class
- extend into a flow diagram or storyboard activity.

The ability to sequence implies a degree of logic. Although there is not always a single correct solution to sequencing tasks, we are looking for students to be able to explain their reasoning behind their decisions – if you like, the thinking behind their thinking.

It's like...

'It's like...' is a phrase frequently heard in the classroom, as teachers use analogy and example in an attempt to explain and simplify something.

- *'The world is like an orange. As an orange is surrounded by a thin layer of peel, so the Earth is surrounded by a thin layer of crust.'*
- *'Passing the ball with the inside of your foot is like hitting the ball with a hockey stick.'*
- *'Bandwidth is like different types of roads. The greater the bandwidth, the more information it can transmit, just as motorways – which are wider than ordinary roads – can hold more traffic.'*

The use of analogy is effective as it relates new information to existing understanding. However, it is significantly more powerful if the associations are made by the student. For analogies, to a certain extent at least, are personal. When we tell someone that the world is like an orange, we have a clear picture in our mind. However, it would be dangerous to assume that each student will hold the same picture in their own mind.

For example, what picture comes into your mind when you hear the word *chair*? Are you thinking of a particular chair? A chair in your living room or a favourite armchair from your childhood? Are you thinking of the same chair as I am? I am thinking of a famous fence on the Grand National course at Aintree.

An analogy may make perfect sense to us, but it is dangerous to assume that everyone's understanding will be the same. Analogies will only work if both parties have a shared understanding. However, when the student's perception of the object, image or concept is very different from that of the teacher's, the analogy will be distorted. Worse still, when it does not exist in the child's reality, the analogy will not even register.

To develop understanding, encourage students to consider how they would describe something to somebody else. Use the prompt, *'it's like...'* This is a strategy that works equally well with individual students, pairs or small groups. We are developing students' ability, and assessing the extent to which, they can transfer and apply their understanding to another situation.

Phase three – the key phase

If making sense of information is the central element of learning, phase three is arguably the key phase of the entire lesson. It is the time when information is processed and understood. It is the time when information becomes learning.

Sadly, it is the phase that is most often neglected, sacrificed in an understandable, but misplaced, desire to cover the curriculum. If students are not given time to digest and process information, it is unlikely that it will be understood. And if it hasn't been understood, it hasn't been learned.

For many schools, focusing improvement and professional development programmes upon phase three of lessons, would yield significant gains in learning and attainment.

When we tell someone that the world is like an orange, we have no idea of the extent to which they have understood the point. However, when they tell us that humus is a bit like margarine because it binds all the ingredients in the soil together like margarine does in a cake, we are given a clear indication that the student understands what humus is and what it does.

Predicting

Prediction is a higher-order thinking skill that both develops and demonstrates understanding. It requires the ability to see beyond the immediate and obvious and identify the *consequences* of an event or action.

Prediction can be framed in either the past or the future:

*'What **would** have happened if...?'*
Or
*'What **will** happen if....?'*

And in a positive or negative way:

*'What will happen if X **happens**?'*
Or
*'What will happen if X **doesn't happen**?'*

- *What would have happened if Hitler had invaded Britain immediately after Dunkirk?*
- *What would have happened if Tybalt had not killed Mercutio?*
- *What will happen if I replace it with a negative number?*
- *What will happen if I raise my head when kicking the ball?*
- *What will happen if I add iron to copper sulphate solution?*
- *What will be the likely consequences if we fail to reduce carbon dioxide emissions?*

Classifying

The ability to classify information is based upon understanding and the ability to make connections. In many cases, it is the reasoning behind the classification, rather than the final categorization, that is of most interest to the teacher when assessing a student's level of understanding.

Extend students' thinking by asking them to classify information in more than one way and then to select which method they believe to be the most appropriate for the given context.

There are two broad options open to us:

1 provide students with categories and ask them to assign information as appropriate

2 provide students with information and challenge them to determine appropriate categories and then assign the information accordingly

Lynmouth Flood 1952

One of the worst floods of all time destroyed the Devon village of Lynmouth in 1952. Classify these statements under the headings: be prepared to give reasons for your choice.

What happened?

34 people died, 1000 were left homeless.

Loose rock and gigantic boulders were washed downstream.

Why did it happen?

Much of the surrounding area was made of impermeable rock.

It had rained for 12 of the previous 14 days.
In the morining, upright trees, weighed down by mud and boulders clinging to their roots, were seen floating out to sea.
90 houses and hotels were destroyed.
The gradient of the river was very steep.
Rainfall on the day of the flood was one of the three heaviest rainfalls ever recorded in Britain.
130 cars and 19 boats were lost.
The river flowed through a small catchment basin, with narrow, steep-sided valleys.
The flood occurred at night.

Strategies for Closing the Learning Gap

The range of possibilities for a classification exercise extends beyond subject-specific information. Consider the ways in which the following distinctions could be applied in your curriculum area:

- describe/explain
- compare/contrast
- similarities/differences
- cause/effect
- for/against
- positive/negative
- more likely/less likely
- agree/disagree.

Students do not have to use written lists to classify information. Some alternatives are:

- *Post-its* or pieces of scrap paper – kinesthetic learners, visual–spatial learners and logical–mathematical learners will particularly benefit from moving post-its around as their ideas develop.
- *Cut out words/phrases/objects* from a photocopied handout – expensive, but an alternative strategy which will particularly appeal to kinesthetic learners.
- *Highlighter pens* – issue students with a piece of text and two different colour highlighter pens. Study a piece of text and highlight all the sentences that describe what is happening in one colour and all the sentences that explain why/how it is happening in another.

The ability to distinguish between description and explanation is fundamental to the development of understanding, not to mention to examination success. Encourage students to apply the 'because test' when distinguishing between the two.

- Describe – tells us *what* is happening.
- Explain – tells us *why* or *how* it is happening. When we explain something, we invariably use the word *'because'*.

We can often prompt an explanation by asking the question *'Why?'* or *'How?'*. For example:

T: *What is the climate like at the Equator?* (describe)
S: *It is hot at the Equator.*
T: *Why is this?* (explain)
S: *Because the Sun is virtually overhead all year around.*

Create learning maps

(See page 267 for more information about learning maps.)

Making a learning map is a powerful way to develop and demonstrate learning. In particular, two of the key steps in the process of producing a learning map are effective strategies for developing understanding in their own right.

Desert Island Distillation

Your group has been shipwrecked on a desert island in the Pacific Ocean!

The story so far . . .

You have searched the whole Island for fresh water, but unfortunately you have not found a drop. The Sun is shinning brightly from a cloudless sky - it does not look as if it will rain for weeks. There is not even any coconut milk for you to drink or fruit to eat. All you have found is a tree with waxy leaves and a few stones.

You cannot survive without fresh water (the salt that is dissolved in the sea water makes you sick if you drink it). So you must design a way of getting fresh water from sea water.

Luckily, some items from the shop have been washed ashore. These include:

wooden planks	a ship's compass	waterproof sheets
a knife	an axe	a telescope
rope	sails from the ship	metal tubes
an oar	string	pieces of chain
bottles of rum	clothing	broken pieces of glass
wooden barrels	metal bars	portrait of the captain
a candlestick holder	a scrubbing brush	a metal bucket

You can use all the items in your design, or just a few.

What to do:
1   Talk about your design to get fresh water from sea water.
2   Draw a diagram of your design and label it.
3   Write down how your design will work.

Your group must act quickly, or you will die of thirst before you are rescued!

Step one   *Identify all the relevant keywords and phrases.* This is basically a *reduction* strategy.

Step two   *Arrange the keywords in a meaningful pattern.* Essentially, this is a *classification* activity.

Chapter headings

This is an effective technique for helping students group information and identify the headings for the main branches of their learning map. Alternatively, it can be used as a stand-alone classification activity.

Students imagine that they are writing a book on the topic concerned, for example the Second World War. They then decide upon the chapter titles for the book; for example, 'Retreat from Dunkirk', 'The Battle of Britain', 'The War in the Desert', 'D-Day' and so on.

Learning is all about making connections. The fact that it is not always possible for us to 'see' the connections that are taking place in the minds of our students makes it difficult for us as teachers to resolve difficulties and guide students through the learning process. It is difficult to develop understanding if we cannot accurately identify the misunderstanding.

Learning maps are a significant help in this respect as they enable us to see in an instant:

- the student's overview of the issue – their Big Picture
- the student's detailed grasp of the issue (the way in which they have *reduced* the information)
- the connections and associations the student is making (the way in which they have *classified* the information)
- any misconceptions or glaring omissions from their understanding.

Oliver Caviglioli and Ian Harris use the phrase '*visible thinking*' to describe a learning map. Their book, *Mapwise*, is highly recommended (Network Educational Press, 1999). Learning maps are a highly effective learning tool in their own right. They can be made even more effective, however, when students are required to:

- describe their maps aloud
- explain why they have organized their maps in such a way.

Verbalizing in this way will not only further develop the students' understanding and fix the information in their memory, the teacher will illicit further valuable clues as to the way in which they are thinking and the extent of their understanding.

Problem solving/investigation/enquiry

The brain's search for meaning is innate. This means that when faced with a situation that doesn't quite make sense, the brain will quite naturally seek out an order or pattern, at both a conscious and subconscious level. In simple terms, the brain is always seeking an answer.

This means that problem-solving activities, investigations and enquiries – the label may be different in various curriculum areas, but the principle is the same – are compatible

Consider the following statements

The majority of questions asked during lessons are:

- asked by teachers

- answered by teachers

- closed questions

- for review and to assess understanding, rather than to challenge thinking and develop understanding.

What is your immediate response to these statements?

Pay particular attention to the questions that you ask in lessons during the next two weeks. Do this individually or as a department. How has your response to these statements changed?

with the way in which the brain operates. When these activities are presented in the form of a challenge, we have a powerful and motivating learning activity.

Getting the level of challenge right is absolutely crucial. Teaching is all about helping students take the next step so that eventually they will be able to do something on their own. When the problem to be resolved is beyond their capability, even with the assistance of the teacher, students will, not surprisingly, switch off.

Similarly, when the task does not represent a worthwhile challenge, the problem may be solved but no learning will take place because no progress has been made.

The challenge must be set at a level slightly above the current understanding of the students so that, with the guidance of the teacher and the support of their peers, they can successfully complete the challenge and make personal sense out of the situation. This is the principle of cognitive conflict, the foundation of the Cognitive Acceleration through Science Education (CASE) thinking skills programme.

Effective problem-solving exercises take time to plan and prepare. However, the benefits in terms of learning are more than worth the effort. As a general rule of thumb, include one substantial problem-solving activity in each unit of work.

Rank order

Putting a series of variables – be they events, statements, reasons or objects – into a rank order requires the ability to *prioritize*. It means that a rank-order activity is very much related to the strategy of reduction outlined on page 199. It is impossible to do properly without thinking carefully and comparing the relative value of each variable in turn.

In many respects, it is the *process* rather than the *outcome* that is the real value of rank order exercises. The process, particularly when the activity is organized in pairs or groups, helps the learner to organize their thoughts, with contributions from their peers challenging, shaping and influencing their thinking. Listening to these exchanges helps the teacher to understand the way in which the students are thinking and identify any obvious misconceptions or gaps in understanding.

Questions to make students think

Questioning is a staple strategy of the classroom. Done well, it is a powerful technique that can probe, challenge and extend understanding. However, questions such as:

- *'Who killed Mercutio?'*
- *'When was the Treaty of Westphalia?'*
- *'What is the capital of Peru?'*
- *'What is the large bone in the thigh called?'*

make little direct contribution to the learning process. They are often referred to as 'closed questions' and for the student to answer them, they must have known the answer in advance. They do have a place in the classroom, not least:

- for assessing what students know and already understand
- to quickly recap information from last lesson
- as a review strategy

Phase three

- How much of your lesson is spent in phase three?
- What is the ratio of time students spend receiving information to time spent making sense of it?
- What conscious strategies do you employ to help students understand information?
- What strategies do you use to assess how much has been understood?
- Which of the following strategies do you use regularly?

1   verbalizing – explaining aloud
2   reduction
3   transformation
4   teaching something
5   sequencing
6   'It's like...'
7   predicting
8   classifying
9   creating learning maps
10 problem solving/investigations/enquiry
11 rank ordering
12 higher-order questioning
13 thinking about thinking
14 understanding the question
15 students asking questions

Award yourself a mark out of ten (ten being the highest) for phase three of one of your typical lessons.

Identify one thing that you could do differently that would enable you to increase this score by one mark.

- to boost self-esteem (If you are convinced that a student who normally struggles in your lesson and lacks confidence has grasped a particular point, address a relevant question to the class and then deliberately select the student concerned to provide the answer. When they get it right – as you knew they would – it will do much for their self-esteem and standing in the eyes of their peers.)

However, closed questions such as these will do little to challenge the students' thinking and develop their understanding. This will only be achieved when students are challenged by higher-order, open questions that cannot be answered without deep thought.

There is nothing new in this. Teachers are well aware of the difference between open and closed questions and the very different demands that they place upon students. Both types of questioning have their place in the classroom. The problem arises, however, when too many of the questions that are asked lack challenge and higher-order questions are neglected.

Sadly, I have observed many lessons when the ratio of closed to open questions has been as high as 10:1. I have also observed lessons in which no open questions have been asked. However, almost without fail, the teacher concerned believed that the ratio of the two types of questions had been 50:50.

Perception is often different from reality. For teachers searching for ways that would make a difference and improve the learning of their students, reflecting upon the quality of their questioning can be an effective way forward. It is a process that is of even greater value when a detached, objective observer can provide feedback and hard data about the style of questioning that has taken place during a lesson.

The following approaches can prove beneficial.

- Record lessons so that teachers can hear for themselves the questions that they ask.

- Write down the questions asked by the teacher for later reflection.

- Record each question as an 'O' (open question) or 'C' (closed). A pattern of 'C C C C C C C C C O C C C C' gives a powerful message!

- The observer makes an instant judgement about the extent to which each question challenges the students to think and how it contributes to the learning process. Each question is awarded a mark out of 5. (5 = higher-order question that challenges thinking. 0 = closed question that demands little more than basic recall.) Again, a pattern of '1 1 1 2 1 2 1 1 4 1 2 1 2 1' is revealing.

- Consider whether there is a pattern to questioning. Does the lesson begin with a flurry of closed questions? What is the effect on the students? Does the lack of challenge early in the lesson switch them off or does early success motivate them to proceed?

- When does the first open question appear in the lesson? Is it in the first few minutes to set the tone for the lesson and exploit the enhanced curiosity at the beginning of a learning experience (see page 189)? If the first open question is not asked until 20 minutes or so into the lesson (in excess of the concentration span of the students) there is a danger that many students will have already switched off.

Asking questions to develop understanding

Asking questions is a particularly effective way of clarifying and developing understanding. It is also highly personal and dependent on the current level of understanding of the individual. The most effective questions therefore are often those that are generated by the student.

There are no guarantees, but by consciously adopting suitable strategies, we can increase the likelihood that students will ask the questions necessary to take their understanding to the next level. For example:

Asking questions without embarrassment

Informal

- Use time-outs (see page 43). It is more likely that a group of students will say, *'We don't understand this, can you come and help us?'*

- Provide a question box so that students post their questions anonymously.

Formal

- *'Work in pairs or small groups to identify the question that shows that the person who can answer it really understands. You don't need to tell me the answer, just identify the question'.*
  OR
  'Identify one question that someone of your age would need to be able to answer in order to take their understanding up to the next level'.

- Formalize a time-out. Give a group five minutes to identify three questions that they would like to ask at this point. It is far easier to say, *'Our group would like to know'* than, *'I don't know'*.

Encouraging all students to ask a question

- At the end of any input – exposition, video clip, section of a textbook – all students *must* ask a question. They can be generated individually or in groups and written anonymously to avoid embarrassment.

- Introduce a 'question of the week award' for the most interesting question.

- Begin the lesson by saying, *'I bet you can't ask me a question about today's lesson that is so hard, I won't be able to answer it'.*

The content of the questions will, of course, be subject specific. However, the generic principle that understanding is dependent upon a style of questioning that is challenging and thought provoking, holds true, irrespective of specialism.

Thinking about thinking

Use every opportunity to develop understanding a little further by encouraging students to think about their thinking. This need not be as daunting as it seems. Try the following approaches.

- Explain reasons for your decision. Why did you decide to classify the information/rank order in the way that you did? Why did you choose these key words?
- How else could you have done it? Which other words could you have selected?
- Why do you think that your words/categories/rank order is better?
- If you were faced with a similar task again, how would you go about it?
- How would you know that someone has understood this?
- How do you know that you understand this?
- What three questions do you need to be able to answer before you understand this?
- How could this task have been made harder/easier?

Understanding the question

Often, the problem for students in examinations is not understanding the subject, but understanding the question! If it is unfair that we assess students on their literary skills and their ability to comprehend what they are being asked to do, rather than on their grasp of the subject, it is also the reality that we, as teachers, face.

The following are three effective strategies for helping students to understand examination questions.

1. Students, preferably in groups, rewrite GCSE papers so that they would be suitable for Year 7 students. Thus, 'compare and contrast' becomes, 'in what ways are they similar – in what ways are they different?' 'Evaluate' becomes 'What do you think of… ?'

2. Students produce a mark scheme for specimen examination questions. That is, what information would you need to include in order for an answer to be worth a maximum four marks?

3. Use a mark scheme to actually mark specimen answers. When students can identify that one answer is worth three marks but another answer is only worth one, they have gone a long way to understanding what is required of them in examinations.

Asking questions

Adults will invariably ask questions to clarify, extend and cement their understanding. Some students do the same – but, for various reasons, not all. Yet asking questions is one the most efficient and effective ways of developing understanding.

Teachers face two key challenges: those students who are anxious to ask a question to clarify and extend their thinking but are too embarrassed to speak out, and those students who are not particularly bothered whether they understand or not – they are just going through the motions.

Ebbinghaus curve of forgetting

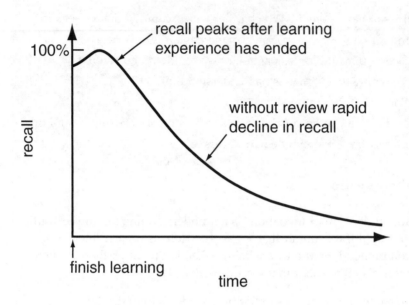

recall peaks after learning experience has ended

without review rapid decline in recall

recall

100%

finish learning

time

Review curve

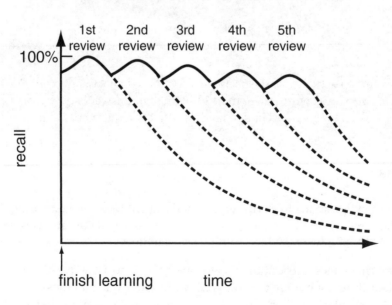

1st review   2nd review   3rd review   4th review   5th review

100%

recall

finish learning   time

We must therefore strive to consciously create situations in which:

- students feel that they can ask questions without fear of ridicule
- students are required to ask a question.

Some suggestions can be found on page 218, with further ideas on page 188.

Phase four

" *Trying to learn without reviewing is like trying to fill the bath without putting the plug in.* "

Mike Hughes, *Closing the Learning Gap*

We have all taught lessons that overrun or, equally as bad, peter out. Yet people remember more from the beginning and end of a learning experience than they do from the middle. It means that the last ten minutes (the recency effect) and the first ten minutes (the primacy effect) of the lesson are prime learning time – see page 181.

The last ten minutes of the lesson provide us with an opportunity to do four things:

1   Recap and summarize the lesson – referring to the learning outcomes outlined in phase one.
2   Ensure students know what they know – the learning activities during phase three should have allowed the students to demonstrate their understanding. This should be emphasized during the summary of the lesson.
3   Encourage students to reflect upon their personal targets for the lesson. We are trying to create a sense of success and achievement. Remember, success creates success.
4   Cement learning and understanding and ensure that it is remembered.

The brain is not designed to remember large amounts of content: information, even when it has been understood, will quickly be forgotten. The graph opposite, known as the 'Ebbinghaus curve of forgetting', illustrates how we forget at the end of a learning experience. Three things are apparent.

1   Recall peaks a few minutes after the learning experience ends. This is the time taken by the brain to subconsciously file and sort the information.
2   Up to 40% of the material is forgotten within five minutes! (That's right – by the time they get to the dinner queue, they have forgotten nearly half of your lesson!)
3   Up to 80% of the material is forgotten within 24 hours! (It explains why the teacher's opening question of, 'Who can remember what we did last lesson? – Oh come on, it was only yesterday!' is so often greeted with silence.)

From the a teacher's perspective, it is rather distressing to think that so much of our carefully prepared lessons will be forgotten so quickly. The good news is that there are two things that we can do to counter the Ebbinghaus curve of forgetting.

If review is so important – why don't we have a whole-school approach to it?

- Devote ten minutes a day to reviewing yesterday's key points.

- Provide students with crayons to shade in their key words – see page 225.

- Encourage students to verbalize the key points from yesterday's lessons. Use prompts – *'tell me three things that you learned in science yesterday'.*

- Encourage students to review and describe their learning maps.

- Ask students to transform their notes – for example if they recorded their key points as words, ask them to change them into the form of a diagram.

- *Make your lessons memorable* by employing the memory strategies outlined in Section Five. When material is seen to have a personal relevance; when it is unusual, dramatic and exaggerated and when we apply a simple mnemonic to it, significantly more material will be remembered.

- *Review the material.* When material is reviewed at key, strategic moments, memory is significantly enhanced. Indeed many experts claim up to a 400% improvement in memory when review techniques are employed.

Review is a key to memory. While it should not be confined to the end of the lesson – information should be constantly reviewed and reinforced *during the course of the lesson* – it does provide us with the focus for the fourth and final phase of the lesson. Reviewing material need not be particularly time-consuming – the trick is to review the information systematically, at specific key moments: five–ten minutes after the learning experience, 24 hours later, one week later, one month later and, finally, three months later.

Step-by-step guide to review

1   Stop learning new material 15 minutes before the end of the lesson (assuming a one hour lesson).

2   Spend five minutes clearing away resources, tidying up, and so on This may be a good time to collect in homework from the previous session or set this week's task. This is the five minutes 'down time' that the brain needs to subconsciously process information.

3   There is now ten minutes of the lesson left to review. This is the ideal time for the first review as it corresponds with the point of maximum recall.

4   Make sure that the students are relaxed and focused. Possibly play some gentle background music.

5   You are now ready to review. It is only necessary to review the key learning points of the lesson (between two and six depending upon the age and ability of the students). The process is more powerful if individual learners identify the key points, the teacher's job being to guide and prompt. It is sufficient to ask the students to identify the three most important (variations include significant or interesting) things that they have learned this lesson. An alternative is to challenge students to identify three questions that they can now answer but couldn't have done at the beginning of the lesson.

Although it is important for the learners to identify their own key points, the most important thing is that they think that they have picked out the key issues on their own! It is possible to cheat a bit here and, as you stroll around the class, say things like, '*You may of course be thinking that the most important thing that you learned today was X, or you may think that Y was more important…*'

A variation that is always popular with younger children – imagine that when you are asleep tonight, an alien spacecraft will be hovering above your house. The aliens have sophisticated equipment that can probe your mind and read your innermost thoughts. Unfortunately, when you wake up, your memory of today's lesson will have been completely wiped. Luckily, the aliens allow you to remember just one piece of information from today's lesson – which bit do you choose to remember?

Phase four

- How much time do you spend in phase four?

- What do you normally do in the last ten minutes of a lesson?

- Do your lessons ever peter out or overrun?

- Do you systematically review information?

- Do you link this review with the learning objectives outlined during the beginning of the lesson?

- How do you ensure that students leave your room knowing what they know?

- Do students review what they have learned, how they have learned, or both?

Award yourself a mark out of ten (ten being the highest) for phase four of one of your typical lessons. Identify one thing that you could do differently that would enable you to increase this score by one mark.

For older students try the following prompt: *'If you could take a postcard into the exam with you, summarizing today's lesson, what would you write?'*

In both cases, the principle is the same – students are *choosing* to remember.

As part of the review, reference should be made to the learning objectives of the lesson. For example, if the aim of the lesson was to make sure that before students left the room, they all knew the difference between an atom and an element, one of the questions that everyone should now be able to answer is, what is the difference between an atom and an element?

Students write down their three key points. Some will wish to express them in diagrammatic form while others will wish to add them to their learning map. Remember to use different colours for the keywords – this will engage both hemispheres of the neo-cortex (see page 152). Writing the points down ensures that conscious attention is paid to the key points of the lesson for a little longer. (Lack of conscious attention is one of the key reasons for forgetting.)

Depending on time, it can be helpful – particularly for auditory learners – to share their key points with the person sitting next to them. This activity will force students to organize their thoughts in order to verbalize them and will so develop understanding and cement memory. It can also be useful to discuss the reasons for any differences in the choice of key points in order to force students to think a little more carefully about the lesson that has just passed.

Kinesthetic learners will benefit from moving around the room to talk to other students: *'You have three minutes to move around the room and tell three different people the three things that you consider to be the most important from today's lesson'*

6   Although the next important time for review is 24 hours later, it can be helpful to include an extra review at the end of the day. This can be as simple as students explaining what they have learned during the day to their parents when they return home. They do not need to talk to another person – although there is the potential for interaction when talking to an adult – a pet or poster will do. The act of explaining demands an internal sorting and organizing of ideas that has a beneficial effect upon understanding, while going over the material once again will enhance memory.

7   The next review – 24 hours after the learning experience – is arguably the most significant, yet the most difficult to control. Whereas the teacher has total control over what happens during the last ten minutes of their lesson and what happens a week later, they have little control (unless they happen to be teaching the class again the following day) over what happens the day after the initial lesson. There is no problem with motivated learners (they can be trusted to review independently) but a little cunning is required for the majority of secondary school students.

The review need only last between three and five minutes. Simply try to recall your three key points again, *before* looking at your notes. Consciously use a variety of strategies during the various reviews. For example, if you wrote down your key points during the first review, verbalize them or convert them into a diagram during the second.

To ensure that reluctant learners spend some time reviewing their work 24 hours after a lesson, try the following technique. During the first review, make sure that students write down their key points in a different colour. Then 24 hours later, they must shade a box around each key word in a second colour. To ensure that they do this on the correct day, do not announce which colour they should use for the shading until 24 hours after the lesson. For example, if the initial lesson was on a Monday, leave a note in the register for their tutor to announce, *'Attention Miss Smith's history class. Today's colour is orange and your books are due in by the end of the day'*. It may also be a good way to get the tutor interested in the technique of

Summary - structure

- Learning is enhanced when lessons are structured to reflect the distinct phases of the learning process.

- Lessons should include:

  an overview of what is to be learned
  new information
  an opportunity to make sense of that information
  a review of what has been learned and how it has been learned.

- Lessons need a balance between teacher input and opportunities for students to make sense of, and understand, new information.

- When phase three (processing) is neglected, lessons are reduced to little more than the transfer of information and it is unlikely that students will understand the material they have encountered.

- Although the four-phase model provides an effective structure, it is the strategies that are employed in each of the phases that will have a major bearing upon the extent to which students learn.

- Strategies in phase three must be consciously designed to engage students and extend their thinking so that:

  they are more likely to understand information
  teachers are able to assess the extent of their understanding.

- The detailed interpretation of the four-phase lesson structure may vary considerably between subjects. However, it is a model that generates a common language within a school and can provide the focus for any improvement programme.

- It is not restrictive, nor prescriptive; it is simply a framework for reflection, planning, observation, monitoring and development.

review! Alternatively, post a notice outside your room.

8   The next review should take place one week after the learning experience, which for many teachers, will coincide with another lesson. The review need only take about three–five minutes and can take a variety of forms. It may be appropriate to begin a lesson by asking students to recall the three most important things they learned last week or to change the way in which the key points had been recorded – for example organize key words into a learning map.

It is always helpful for students to try and recall the information prior to looking at their notes and to consciously use a variety of strategies at each review. To cement the memory, carry out a further review at one month and again at three months after the initial learning experience.

This technique has a dramatic effect upon the Ebbinghaus curve of forgetting, as illustrated on page 220. Each time the brain begins to forget information, the memory is 'topped up', significantly increasing the amount of information that can be recalled. It is a technique that learners of any age would do well to master.

My thanks to Jane Steer of Deer Park School, Cirencester for the brilliantly simple idea of using crayons in the review process.

Smile!

Lessons should end where they began – with a smile. The message – verbal and non-verbal – must be, *'I enjoyed that, it was fun, I'm looking forward to teaching you again'*. Words can of course convey those sentiments but nowhere near as effectively or unambiguously as a warm, genuine smile.

Reflecting on *how* you have learned

Encouraging students to reflect upon *how* they have learned at the end of a lesson, is equally as important as reflecting upon *what* they have learned. It is also essential if we are to address seriously the key skill of *'improving own learning and performance'*, now embedded in the National Curriculum.

It needn't be time-consuming and can be achieved by inviting students to reflect – individually or in pairs – on the following prompt questions.

- How did you tackle the problem/go about the task?
- What were the advantages of working in this way?
- Were there any drawbacks with the way in which you chose to work?
- What would have been an alternative way of approaching the exercise?
- What would have been the advantages/disadvantages of working in this way?
- If you had to do the same or a similar task again, how would you approach it?
- If you had to give one piece of advice to someone tackling the same exercise tomorrow, what would it be?
- What did we do today that you found most helpful when you were learning?
- What did we do today that you found less helpful?

This exercise can be extended by encouraging students to keep a simple Learning Log, either by providing time at the end of a lesson or inviting them to fill them in at home.

Lesson planning/observation pro forma

	PHASE/FOCUS	STRATEGIES
1	**OVERVIEW** Link the lesson Provide overview Describe outcomes Stimulate curiosity Set the challenge Set individual targets	
2	**INPUT (new information)** Visual Auditory Kinaesthetic	
3	**PROCESS** Developing understanding Demonstrate understanding Assessing understanding	
4	**REVIEW** Reflect on *what* has been learned Reflect on *how* it has been learned Know what you know	

This form can be completed by the teacher as a planning sheet and/or by
an observer as the basis for providing feedback

Strategies for Closing the Learning Gap

Using the four-phase lesson structure

The four-phase lesson structure is intended as no more than a loose framework and it is acknowledged that it will be interpreted and implemented in significantly different ways in various curriculum areas. Nevertheless, it offers a generic framework and generates a common language within a school that can provide both clarity and impetus to any improvement programme.

The four-phase lesson structure can be used by teachers, departments and schools for:

- identifying which specific aspects of lessons would benefit from a 'tweak'
- planning
- monitoring, observation and self-evaluation.

Planning

By adopting a common four-phase lesson planning proforma such as that opposite, we constantly draw teachers' attention to the fact that lessons should be structured in order to guide students through the key stages of the learning process.

The emphasis here is on *strategies* and it will force teachers to consider *how* they are going to help students learn, rather then what they are going to teach.

A worthwhile extension – even occasionally – is to complete the sheet in different colours to represent opportunities for different types of learner to learn in their preferred style. That is, opportunities for visual learners are written in blue, auditory learners in red and kinaesthetic learners in green. It is then possible to tell at a glance if any students are being disadvantaged by a mismatch between the way in which they prefer to learn and the way that they are being taught. The message is particularly powerful when a trend appears over the course of a few lessons.

The main benefit of using such a planning form is to focus the teacher's attention on what they are doing and how their practice compares to a nominal ideal lesson structure. The pace of life in schools is so fast that teachers can easily go from term to term on auto-pilot, teaching in largely the same way, day in, day out. Opportunities to reflect upon and evaluate practice are, sadly, few and far between. Anything that requires teachers to stop and consider what they are doing and why is therefore beneficial.

The ease with which they complete the four sections and the detail that they are able to include in the various phases, will provide them with important clues as to *precisely* which bit of their lessons could be tweaked to bring about improvements in learning.

Monitoring, observation and self-evaluation

Monitoring the quality of teaching and learning in the form of lesson observation is becoming a common activity in schools. When done well, increasing the opportunities for teachers to observe colleagues in action and to receive feedback upon their classroom performance, can be an effective strategy for improving the quality of teaching and learning in a school.

However, without a specific focus, there is a danger that observation and the subsequent feedback becomes rather too general and the impact of the strategy is significantly diluted. Telling someone that a lesson was *satisfactory* or *good* will do little to help them improve.

Identifying the bit to tweak

This can be done individually or collectively.

Reflect upon each of the four phases

- Award yourself a mark out of ten for how effectively you teach each phase.

- Which phase do you teach relatively most effectively?

- Which phase would most benefit from a tweak?

- Identify one strategy in each phase that you could introduce into your lessons that would enable you to improve your mark out of ten for that phase by one point.

Phase	Mark out of ten	Strategy to be introduced
One		
Two		
Three		
Four		

The purpose of feeding back is to help colleagues identify the 'bits that need tweaking', so that they may move forward and develop. This demands feedback that is *precise* and *specific*. Teachers need to know *precisely* which parts of the lesson worked particularly well and which *specific* strategies proved effective. Equally, they need to know *precisely* which aspects of their teaching would benefit from a 'tweak'.

The four-phase lesson structure offers such a focus and can form an appropriate framework for both monitoring and self-reflection. It works equally well at an individual or whole school/department level.

Self-evaluation

Reflect for a moment on the evaluation prompts on pages 190, 192, 216 and 224.

- Which phases of the lesson do you consider yourself to be particularly strong in?
- Which particular phase of the lesson do you feel that you need to develop?
- Which of the strategies outlined in this book will help you develop in this area?

School/departmental monitoring

Focus upon the four phases of the lesson during your observation/monitoring programme.

- Which strategies are being used by teachers in each section of the lesson?
- Which parts of the lesson are consistently being delivered effectively?

Reflect upon the lessons that you have observed. As a department or management team, award each of the four phases a mark out of ten (ten being the highest) that best sums up the quality and effectiveness of that particular section of the lesson.

What does this exercise tell you? Where are your relative strengths? Which parts of lessons do you teach relatively well? Which part of lessons do you particularly need to develop?

Peer observation

> *The biggest and most underused resource teachers have is each other.*
>
> Scottish Consultative Council on the Curriculum

All schools have excellent teachers. More specifically, all schools have teachers who are wonderful exponents of particular aspects of the job. Giving teachers the opportunity to observe colleagues who are proficient at specific phases of a lesson can lead to significant improvements.

It is a particularly effective strategy when the relative strengths and development needs of teachers are matched during the observation programme. For example, a teacher who has identified phase four as an area for development is given the opportunity to observe a colleague who is particularly effective at recapping and reviewing the lesson.

We know that:

- we remember more from the beginning and end of an experience than we do from the middle;

- unusual, dramatic and exaggerated things are more likely to be remembered;

- we remember anything that has a strong emotion attached to it;

- imagination and association play an important role in memory;

- memory is enhanced when we are relaxed;

- information is best remembered when it is 'chunked' into small pieces;

- taking frequent breaks during studying enhances memory;

- we are more likely to remember something when we are in the same state as we were when we first encountered it;

- something is more likely to be remembered if it is regularly reviewed;

- simple memory strategies or mnemonics can significantly enhance memory.

Strategies for Closing the Learning Gap

Section Five: Memory

" There is no learning without memory. "

Colin Rose

There are many people who find the whole topic of memory fascinating – how memories are formed, how they are stored and how they are retrieved. However, from the teacher's perspective, what really concerns us is not so much how the memory works, but how to make our lessons memorable. This is just as well for, despite the fact that our understanding of the memory has come a long way since Plato postulated in the fourth century that the memory was akin to a wax tablet, each event leaving an imprint that would gradually fade with time, much of the precise detail of the how the memory actually works remains something of a mystery. Fortunately, we do have extensive knowledge of what the brain is likely to remember and therefore how to increase the likelihood of something being remembered.

We know that:

- we remember more from the beginning and end of an experience than we do from the middle;
- unusual, dramatic and exaggerated things are more likely to be remembered;
- we remember anything that has a strong emotion attached to it;
- imagination and association play an important role in memory;
- memory is enhanced when we are relaxed;
- information is best remembered when it is 'chunked' into small pieces;
- taking frequent breaks during studying enhances memory;
- we are more likely to remember something when we are in the same state as we were when we first encountered it;
- something is more likely to be remembered if it is regularly reviewed;
- mnemonics (simple memory strategies) can significantly enhance memory;
- memory is an integral component of learning; how strange therefore that professional educators are not trained in the use of memory techniques. Equally absurd is the lack of memory training for school children.

For further information see:

- *Learn to Remember* by Dominic O'Brien (Duncan Baird, 2000)
- *The Great Memory Book* by Karen Markowitz and Eric Jensen (The Brain Store, 1999)
- *Use your Memory* by Tony Buzan (BBC Books, New Edition 2000)
- *Accelerated Learning for the 21st Century* by Colin Rose (Dell, 1997)

Imagination

Imagination, according to Einstein, is more important than knowledge and, if Napoleon is to be believed, rules the world. Imagination also plays a key role in memory. It lies at the heart of all memory strategies and has done since the days of the ancient Greeks. Quite simply, the more you are prepared to use your imagination to make things unusual, exaggerated, and absurd, the more your memory will improve.

> **In this section we will look at the three key principles which underpin any attempt to enhance the memory of our students.**
>
> ➡ **Teach students memory strategies. Encourage them to apply them as and when appropriate.**
> ➡ **Make your lessons memorable!**
> ➡ **Introduce the question, 'How will you remember this forever?' into your teaching.**

Teach students memory strategies

" *Asking students to learn and memorize material without providing them with the skills to do it is rude, unprofessional and unrealistic.* "

Eric Jenson

We all use them; consider the question, '*How many days are there in August?*' and you will almost certainly use a memory strategy. People who appear to have better memories than the rest of us have not been blessed with any great gift – they have the same basic equipment as everyone else – they are, consciously or otherwise, employing relatively simple memory techniques. Memory strategies are used frequently in schools:

- *i before e except after c* is one of many spelling 'rules'
- *Richard Of York Gave Battle In Vain* helps us remember that **R**ed **O**range **Y**ellow **G**reen **B**lue **I**ndigo **V**iolet are the colours of the spectrum.

Although the majority of students believe that reciting the rhyme '*Richard Of York Gave Battle In Vain*' is the way in which they can remember the colours of the spectrum, few see beyond this and recognize that taking the first letter of each word and creating an acrostic poem is a technique that can be employed to remember anything.

When teachers say, '*Mother Very Eagerly Makes Jam Sandwiches Under No Protest – this is the way in which we remember the order of the planets from the Sun*' (**M**ercury, **V**enus, **E**arth, **M**ars, **J**upiter, **S**aturn, **U**ranus, **N**eptune, **P**luto), students will remember the order of the planets from the Sun.

It requires only a slight change in emphasis to consciously and systematically teach a range of memory strategies, using the subject content to illustrate a particular technique. For example:

'*Today we are going to learn about a simple technique that you could use to help you remember information. We are also going to learn about where the planets are in relation to the Sun and each other.*'

or

'*By the end of today's lesson you will all be able to remember the order in which the planets are from the Sun. You will also be able to use a simple technique called 'acrostics' to help you remember anything you want.*'

Mnemonics

- acronyms
- acrostics
- rhymes
- words to remember numbers
- Roman room system
- journey method
- number – shape system
- link systems or memory chains

Students have now been equipped with a memory strategy that they themselves can employ whenever appropriate, *and* they will remember the order of the planets from the Sun!

Teach students memory strategies and encourage them to employ these as and when appropriate. It is a subtle change of emphasis that can bring about significant improvements in memory. Teaching them that this is 'how you remember' a particular piece of content is limiting: students will remain dependent upon the teacher and when faced with a large amount of information to remember many will inevitably struggle. When we encourage students to develop their own approaches to remembering, we empower them.

Mnemonics

Memory strategies, or as they are correctly known, mnemonics, are not new – they were used extensively by the ancient Greeks and Romans – nor are they particularly difficult to master. There are many variations on the mnemonic theme, but all are based upon two key principles: *imagination* and *association*.

Memory expert Tony Buzan claims that in order to remember something, we have to associate or link it with some known or fixed item. We use our imagination to make the link: the more absurd, exaggerated and dramatic the link, the greater chance that it will be recalled. Incredibly, this simple formula that forms the basis of the memory strategies used by the memory experts around the world today is exactly the same as the techniques used by the Greeks and the Romans so many years ago!

Different mnemonics are appropriate for different memory challenges and most people are more comfortable with some techniques than others. A detailed description of how to use the various strategies can be found in the texts recommended on page 282. Try them and see which ones work for you. The memory is like a muscle – the more you use it the stronger it gets. Neglect it, however, and it will begin to deteriorate. Next time you go to the supermarket, abandon your list and rely instead on a mnemonic. The more you use them, the better you will get.

Popular mnemonics

> *Most people do not know that memory can be extended by techniques anyone can master.*
>
> Dominic O'Brien, six times world memory champion

Acronyms
An *acronym* is a word (often nonsensical) made up of the initial letters of the words you are trying to remember. For example, the Great Lakes of North America are often remembered by the mnemonic *HOMES* (**H**uron, **O**ntario, **M**ichigan, **E**rie and **S**uperior).

Acrostics
An acrostic is similar to an acronym but does not always result in a single word abbreviation. For example, '*Every Good Boy Does Fine*' to remember the notes EGBDF on the treble clef or '*Mother Very Eagerly Makes Jam Sandwiches Under No Protest*' to remember the order of the planets from the Sun.

The fact that dreams (that is, visual stories) appear to be a natural way to remember things, accounts for the fact that a very good memory device is to make up an easy-to-visualize story.

Colin Rose

Rhymes

For example, '*In fourteen hundred and ninety two, Columbus sailed the ocean blue*' reminds us that Columbus discovered America in 1492 while the rhyme '*Divorced, Beheaded, Died – Divorced, Beheaded, Survived*' is often used to recall how the six marriages of Henry VIII ended.

Words to remember numbers

Dominic O'Brien in *Learn to Remember* gives the example of using words containing the corresponding number of letters to remember the first five decimal places of pi. Pi = 3.14159 which means that we need a word of one letter, followed by a word of four letters and so on. He suggests, '*I have a super technique (to help me remember pi)*'.

The Roman room system and the journey method

These systems are similar to each other and depend upon 'fixed pegs' upon which we hang each new memory using our imagination. In the room system, which the Romans used to remember lengthy speeches, various items that are always in the same place around the room are selected to be the pegs. For example, if you stand in the doorway of your living room and look around in a clockwise direction, you may see the settee, followed by the television, followed by a large painting and so on. As long as these items are fixed and you can recall them, they are suitable pegs.

In the journey method, you select a known journey and identify a series of landmarks as your pegs: the more 'memorable' the landmark, the better. For example, if your chosen journey is from home to work and you always pass a fire station followed by a church, these would be two of your pegs.

The pegs are fixed items. Choose a room that you know well or a journey that is very familiar to you as it is vital that you can recall your 'pegs' with ease. The next step is to link the new item – the thing that has to be remembered – to your peg. For example, if you want to remember to buy a newspaper, a pint of milk and some eggs when you visit the shop, you must use your imagination to associate these items with the pegs. The association will be stronger and easier to remember if it is ridiculous and exaggerated. It will also help to concentrate on what you hear, feel, smell and taste.

If you are using the Roman room system, try imagining that you come home to find your *settee*, including the cushions, completely covered in *newspaper*. Look around the room and notice that your *television* is sitting in a giant bowl of *milk* and the milk is spilling out over the top of the bowl on to the carpet. (You may be able to smell spilt milk at this point.) You then notice that someone has thrown *eggs* all over your favourite *painting*. Watch in horror as the eggs slide down the canvas and fall to the floor. If you were using the journey method, you would use a similar procedure to link the newspaper, milk and eggs to the landmarks along the way.

When you get to the shop, think of your pegs in turn and, if you have made strong association, you will have little difficulty recalling that the settee was covered in *newspaper*, the television was sitting in *milk* and there were *eggs* on the painting. Shopping lists can be a thing of the past!

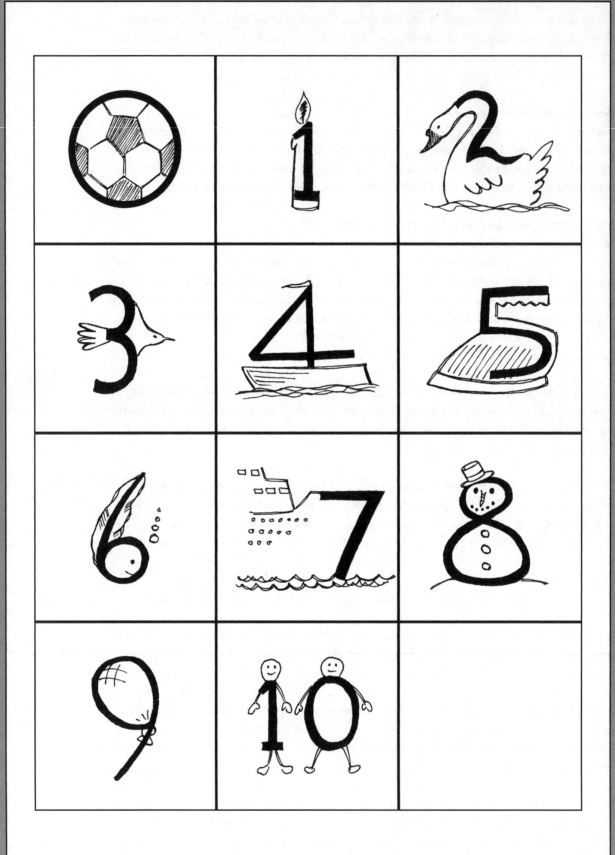

Strategies for Closing the Learning Gap

Number–shape system

This is my personal favourite and involves creating fixed pegs out of numbers by imagining that each number is an object. The technique is probably easiest to illustrate with the number 8. What does the shape remind you of? For many people it is a snowman although some people see a toy racing track and a few people see an hourglass. Now personalize your object, making it as ridiculous as possible. For example make your snowman bright orange and make him 30 feet tall – the tallest, brightest snowman in the world!

Follow the same procedure for the numbers 0–10. (If you are struggling to see an image, try drawing the number and looking at it through half-closed eyes.) This technique is more powerful if you identify your own objects; the following are no more than suggestions.

0   wedding ring, football, inflatable ring

1   candle, telegraph pole, rocket

2   swan, ear (Mr Spock!) coat-hanger

3   Macdonald's sign blown on its side, seagull, puckered lips

4   yacht, picnic table, fish, bow-tie

5   teletubby, rocking chair, iron, Gendarme

6   tadpole, golf club, pregnant woman

7   the bow of a boat (usually the Titanic!), shark, boomerang

8   snowman, hourglass, racing track

9   netball hoop, musical note, balloon on a stick

10 thin and fat man (Laurel and Hardy) ball hitting a bat, plate with a knife and no fork

These are the known pegs. Fix them in your mind, making them as absurd and memorable as you can. All that you now have to do is to associate the new item to be remembered with your memory peg, in much the same way as for the Roman room system. For example, if you need to remember to hand in your homework to Mrs Smith, pay the deposit for the ski trip and take your boots to school for football practice, you might imagine Mrs Smith blowing out a candle on her birthday cake, a swan skiing across a lake and a seagull wearing a pair of football boots.

The number–shape system is particularly useful for remembering phone numbers and PIN numbers: *'It is a dark night and a swan is swimming across a lake with a candle under one wing (to light up the way) and a rubber ring under the other. It is swimming across to rescue a snowman who has fallen into the water and cannot swim.'* This simple story, which can be turned into a graphic and absurd visualization, will always remind that your PIN number is 2108 (swan, candle, rubber ring, snowman).

By making some subtle changes to the pegs, it is possible to remember more than ten items. For example, you can imagine the same images but this time encased in huge blocks of ice for the numbers 11–20. Turn your images into jet-black objects for the numbers 21–30 and so on. Under normal circumstances, your memory would be limited to holding around seven items of information. The number-shape system will enable you to remember well into double figures. In fact, experts claim that if you can remember nine out of ten on a simple memory test, you will be able to remember 90 out of 100 items using this technique!

Strategies for Closing the Learning Gap

The link system or memory chain

This system is unlike the Roman room, journey and number–shape systems as it does not involve the use of fixed memory pegs. Instead each item to be remembered is associated with, and therefore linked, to the previous item in the list. In effect, we are creating a story in our own minds and the fact that stories are memorable in their own right is one of the reasons why this technique is so effective.

For example, if you wanted to remember to buy a packet of biscuits, some sausages, some orange squash and a camera (which I have got to do tomorrow!), you imagine the following story. The more vivid, absurd and multisensory it is in your mind, the more likely that it will be remembered.

> '*I am sitting in the living room eating a packet of my favourite biscuits when there is a knock on the front door. I answer the door and, to my surprise, I am confronted by a giant sausage, who is well over six feet tall. He is wearing a fluorescent yellow T-shirt with a red letter S on it and is holding a smaller sausage in his hand. For some reason, the sausage is very angry and begins to attack me, beating me incessantly over the head with the smaller sausage. I yell out loud and run into the kitchen looking for something to defend myself with. All I can find is a bottle of orange squash, and I throw the juice at the sausage, catching him in the eyes. He stumbles back and at that exact moment, the door is thrown open and a news reporter bursts in. He is carrying a camera with the biggest round flash gun that I have ever seen. "Smile please", he says in a broad American accent, "I've just got to get a shot of this!"'*

Using mnemonics in schools

There will no doubt be teachers who are sceptical about the benefits of using such strategies in schools and who will struggle to see the practical applications of the techniques in the classroom. After all, we are not required (although you never know what the next initiative will be!) to teach GCSE shopping lists. There will also be those who are concerned that we risk trivializing learning, reducing it to no more than a superficial memory quiz.

I share those concerns, and do not suggest for one moment that memory strategies can or should be a substitute for developing understanding. Ensuring that students fully understand whatever it is they are learning will always remain our prime objective. However, it is important that what is understood is remembered and memory techniques such as the ones outlined above, can, in the right circumstances, play a part. We are also working in a context in which the success of students, teachers and schools is judged largely, arguably solely, upon examination performance and, sadly, examinations are still heavily dependent upon memory. If we test it, should we not also teach and develop it?

Let us keep in mind that remembering something does not mean that we have learned it. Memory is just one component of learning (learning = understanding + memory) and is only of real value when it accompanies and complements understanding. If we accept this, and use these strategies as and when they are appropriate, mnemonics do have a place in schools.

Make your lessons memorable

- Ensure students are in the right 'state'.
- Exploit the BEM principle.
- Multisensory learning experiences.
- Reduce to keywords.
- Write keywords in a different colour.
- Trigger a memory.
- Display the keywords.
- Put the keywords to music.
- Make your lessons dramatic and unusual.
- Do something!
- Teach something.
- Chunk it.
- Provide the brain with 'down time'.
- Structure the lesson to enhance memory.
- Picture it!
- Use learning maps.
- Review.

Strategies for Closing the Learning Gap

As we consider the use of mnemonics in schools, we should bear in mind the following.

- The more we use and extend our memory, the better it gets.
- It is important to demonstrate to students that memory is not fixed – everyone can improve their memory.
- We are simply extending and formalizing something that we do already.
- Students should be aware of the vast range of memory strategies that anyone can use to remember anything they want.
- Mnemonics will be appropriate, even essential, when students are required to learn a list of facts, spellings or vocabulary.
- Students will be able to adapt and personalize the techniques outlined above. For example, the strategy to remember different types of vaccines described on page 251 is a combination of an acrostic and the kind of visualization used in the peg systems.

Opening up students' minds to the possibilities is, in my view, the real value of mnemonics. When this awareness is accompanied by opportunities to use them and the question, *'How will you remember this forever?'* (see page 271), we have something really powerful.

What to do if you can't remember

If we are to introduce students to strategies to improve their memory, it seems logical that we should also equip them to deal with occasions when they are struggling to remember. We have all experienced moments when we know that we know something but we just can't quite recall it, no matter how hard we try. It is no coincidence that these *'on the tip of my tongue'* moments occur when we are under pressure such as during an exam.

Having a strategy to call upon during such moments is a great comfort and will actually reduce the likelihood of us forgetting! The next time you just can't quite remember something try the following.

1   Do not try to remember. The harder you try, the less likely it will be that you remember!

2   Relax! Breath deeply and smile. (Try the blowing up your balloon exercise on page 247.)

3   Think around the thing that you are trying to remember. Bring to mind anything that is associated with the missing information and allow the power of association trigger your memory.

Make your lessons memorable

> *Lessons should be hard to forget.*
>
> Year 8 boy in response to the question, 'What makes a good lesson?'

Memory will improve if students are in an appropriate 'state'

Students need to be in the correct state to learn effectively. The optimum state for learning is often referred to by accelerated learning experts as one of 'relaxed – alert' and is achieved when the brain slows down and operates within the alpha wave band of between 8–12 cycles per second. (See page 49 for more information on brain waves.)

Even if your brain were fed ten items of data every second for 100 years, it would still have used less than one-tenth of its storage capacity.

Tony and Barry Buzan

Dominic O'Brien, the six times world memory champion, goes a stage further, claiming that:

> 'In order to optimize our ability to memorize, retain and recall information, we need to make the most of our brain when it is highly suggestive – that is, when it is emitting theta rhythms (preferably combined with alpha rhythms).'

Theta rhythms are slower than alpha rhythms and are the brain waves associated with the drowsy state between sleeping and waking. They are also the brain waves associated with dreaming, which, many experts believe, plays an important role in the memory process. This presents teachers with a practical difficulty: sending students to sleep is not something we normally do. Certainly not intentionally! According to O'Brien, the way around this is to consciously relax.

Relaxation techniques are not part of the national curriculum, nor are they normally taught in schools. However, they are simple to introduce and research has shown significantly greater recall – some studies have suggested figures as high as 25 per cent – when they have been employed.

One of the easiest ways to relax is to focus on breathing. My personal favourite technique, which is easy to use in the classroom, is to blow up an imaginary balloon.

1   Get the students to shut their eyes and ask them to relax.
2   Tell them that they each have a balloon in their stomach that they need to blow up. (Ask them later what colour their balloon is and many will instantly tell you!)
3   As they draw in a deep breath, tell them to imagine the balloon slowly inflating (expanding) until it is full inflated.
4   As they slowly breathe out, (breathe out for a little longer than the in-breath) they imagine the balloon slowly deflating.
5   Repeat three or four times.

It is a technique that is particularly useful for students sitting exams and can be used before or even during the examination to calm the nerves. Laura sat her GCSE exams this year. Four weeks before they were due to begin, she was a nervous wreck and so I suggested she might like to 'blow up a balloon' before the start of every revision session. By the time the exams started, she had grown into a confident young lady ready to do justice to her ability. She told me afterwards that she had felt fine in all of her exams with the exception, for some inexplicable reason, of one science paper. She added, 'but I just shut my eyes, blew up my balloon and I was fine!'

Exploit the BEM principle

Students will remember more from the beginning and end of a learning experience than they will from the middle (see page 182).

Therefore, it is important to:

● Make a crisp start to lessons. Do not waste prime learning time by collecting in homework or routine administrative tasks. Rather, exploit the students' increased attention and curiosity by addressing the *key learning point* of the lesson in the first few minutes.

The neo-cortex itself is divided into specialist parts (lobes) for speech, hearing, vision and touch. This means we store sensory memories in different places. If we want to create a strong memory we store the information using all of the senses.

Colin Rose, in *Accelerated Learning for the 21st Century*

- Create a number of beginnings in your lessons. By including two or three different activities in the lesson, you create a number of beginnings and the associated heightened concentration. By limiting activities to no more than 20 minutes you will ensure that the task does not outlast the students' natural concentration span. (Concentration span is approximately chronological age plus two minutes – see page 183.) Longer activities can be broken up with 'state breaks' or 'time-outs' (see page 41).
- Consciously exploit the 'recency effect' by recapping and reviewing the lesson in the last ten minutes (see page 223).

Multisensory learning experiences

Make sure that students encounter new information through more than one sense. If possible, aim to engage three of the five senses every lesson. Not only are we increasing the chances of students being able to learn in their own preferred style (see Section Three), we are increasing the likelihood of information being remembered, by activating their *multiple memory systems*.

Consciously give students opportunities to:

- see information – read about it; study pictures, diagrams and so on
- visualize information – create pictures in the mind
- hear information – summarize in their own words; explain to a neighbour, ask questions about the material
- 'feel' the information – touch something, act it out; arrange something, write notes on postcards and physically sort them.

Put simply, the more ways in which students encounter information, the more likely it is that it will be remembered.

Reduce to keywords

Reduction is a strategy that ensures that students are required to cognitively manipulate and think about information (see page 199). It is also a useful strategy for helping students remember. Consider the following example taken from a Year 10 science lesson.

Students are required to remember the five different ways in which vaccines can be made and an example of a disease that different vaccines immunize against. When presented with the text below and asked to remember it, students will invariably find the task daunting.

A vaccine contains antigens derived from a pathogenic organism, which on administration will protect against infection by that organism. There are five common ways of producing a vaccine:

1 Using the killed virulent organism; for example, whooping cough

2 Using a live, non-virulent strain of the organism; for example, tuberculosis, rubella; this is usually derived from many generations of selective sub-culturing in the laboratory

3 Chemically modifying a toxin molecule so that it is no longer toxic but still resembles the toxin antigenically; for example, diphtheria, tetanus

4 Separating antigens from the microbe and using them as a vaccine; for example, influenza

5 Using genetically engineered bacteria to mass-produce the relevant antigen; for example, hepatitis B virus

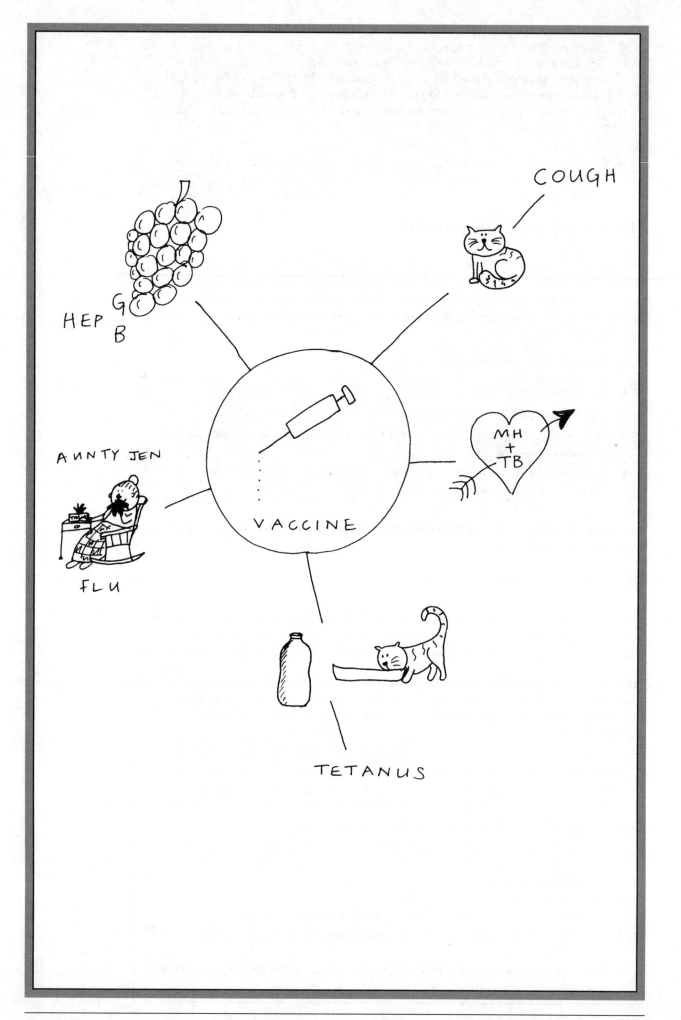

Strategies for Closing the Learning Gap

Step one

Reduce the section to the keywords and we are faced with an altogether more manageable challenge.

A vaccine contains antigens derived from a pathogenic organism, which on administration will protect against infection by that organism. There are five common ways of producing a vaccine:

1 Using the **killed** virulent organism, for example whooping **cough.**

2 Using a **live,** non-virulent strain of the organism, for example **tuberculosis,** rubella; this is usually derived from many generations of selective sub-culturing in the laboratory.

3 Chemically **modifying** a toxin molecule so that it is no longer toxic but still resembles the toxin antigenically, for example diphtheria, **tetanus.**

4 Separating **antigens** from the microbe and using them as a vaccine, for example **influenza.**

5 Using **genetically** engineered bacteria to mass-produce the relevant antigen, for example, **hepatitis B** virus.

Step two

Now, we have to remember five words:

killed   live   modifying   antigens   genetically

Let us attempt to do that by employing one of the memory techniques outlined on page 237.

Take the first letter of each word – k l m a g – and turn them in to an *acrostic poem*:

kittens love milk and grapes

Step three

Now employ a visualization exercise in order to link the vaccine with the disease. Remember, the more absurd, exaggerated and detailed it is, the better.

Shut your eyes and relax (you may like to play some quiet, relaxing music in the background – see page 53). Imagine a kitten. See the colour of the kitten – make it something ridiculous such as shocking pink – feel what it is like to stroke the kitten – hear the kitten mew. Make your kitten unusual in some way – imagine it is ten feet tall. Now picture it coughing. Not just a little cough; a violent, persistent cough. See the kitten cough, hear it cough, feel the effects of the coughing – that's right, the more disgusting your picture, the greater chance you will have of remembering it!

The next time that you think of 'your' kitten, you will automatically think of it coughing. You have linked the kitten with the cough and by remembering one, you will recall the other.

Do the same exercise for the words *love, milk* and *grapes*. Link them in some way to the appropriate disease. Remember to make them dramatic, vivid and ridiculous.

Oh the thinks you can think up if only you try!

Dr Seuss

Engage a range of senses in order to lock the images in your memory. Describe them to a friend or draw them on a sheet of paper. The pictures on page 250 were drawn by a Year 10 student as part of this exercise.

All you now have to do to recall the information about vaccines, is to remember that *'kittens love milk and grapes'*. Picture your kitten. How big was it? What colour was it? What was it doing? Now make the links:

kitten → k → killed – cough

'A vaccine made from the killed virulent organism is used to vaccinate against whooping cough.'

This technique was outlined to a Year 10 science group. Six weeks later, 28 students out of a class of 30 scored a perfect 10/10 when asked, without prior warning, to name five different types of vaccine with an example of an illness that it is used to immunize against.

Write key words in a different colour

This is a very simple and yet very effective technique. Not only will recall be greater and revision more effective, marking is easier! The key benefits of the strategy are:

- Students have to identify which are the keywords. This means that they are forced to think carefully about the information that they have written. Their choice of keywords also gives the teacher an indication of their level of understanding.

- By pausing to change pens, conscious attention is paid to the keywords for a few seconds longer.

- Writing the key words in a different colour engages both hemispheres of the neo-cortex (see page 163). Although both sides of the brain are involved in all activities to a certain extent, the two hemispheres process information very differently; the left hemisphere processing the symbols of the words while the right hemisphere processes the pattern of the colour. Engaging the 'whole brain' in this way, is a key characteristic of accelerated learning strategies.

Trigger a memory

Music is a powerful memory jogger with particular pieces of music triggering vivid and emotional memories for most people. There are particular songs and tunes – and they are specific to each individual – that are guaranteed to bring a wistful look to the face as memories of falling in love, the birth of our first child or that special holiday come flooding back. We are powerless to resist as the music, even if only for a few seconds, influences our mind and our mood.

Exploit this in the classroom by playing a piece of music while students are studying a particular topic and then playing the same music as they try and recall it. Memory is enhanced as we recreate the same conditions to retrieve information that existed when it was originally received.

You are more likely to recall something if you are in the same state as when you first encountered it.

Holding revision sessions in the exam hall, particularly when students are encouraged to 'hang' key information on different features in the room and 'post' important words and diagrams on different parts of the wall, can significantly enhance recall during examinations.

This strategy can be used to enhance recall during examinations:

- Arrange to hold your last revision session (more if possible) in the room where the examination is due to take place. Make sure that the room is arranged exactly as it will be for the exam and ensure that students are sitting in the seats that they will occupy on the day.

- As the students enter the room have some music playing in the background. Choose some gentle baroque music, making sure that it is audible but not intrusive. *Keep the music playing during the entire revision session.*

- Encourage the students to relax. If they are used to deep breathing exercises or other relaxation techniques, spend a few minutes going through their normal routine. Encourage students to have a good look around so that they become familiar and comfortable with the environment and surroundings.

- Allow students to review their learning maps (see page 267) or their notes. Use the information on the learning maps to attempt some exam-style questions or some past papers. (Challenging students to select the key information or learning maps that they think will best help them tackle some past papers is a useful sorting and revision exercise in its own right.)

- Display large learning maps and other visual information such as keywords, diagrams, or information in bullet points, around the room. Remember to use a variety of colours.

- On the day of the exam, the students will automatically feel more relaxed as they know exactly where they will be sitting and precisely what to expect. Play the same music again as the students congregate before the exam and as they enter the exam room in order to relax them further and help them recall the key information that they will need during the examination. Essentially we are returning students to the state that they were in when they received the information in order to make it more likely that they will be able to recall the material. This so-called, state-dependent memory is a technique often used by the police in order to help witnesses remember the details of an incident.

Do not be surprised if the students look up and glance around during the exam; they are subconsciously looking for the visual information that had been displayed around the room during the final revision session.

Display the key words

Have you ever seen a pupil pause during an exam, look up and then continue to write? They are simply 'looking' for the information that had been displayed on the wall of the classroom they had sat in for so many lessons prior to the exam, even though they are not aware of what they are doing!

Many researchers claim that a large amount of learning (as much as 99 per cent) takes place subconsciously. Capitalize on this by displaying keywords and information around your room. Use different colours and display the information just above eye level when pupils are sitting. There is no need to draw attention to the information as the brain will find it quite naturally. Change the material on a regular basis and ensure that it is relevant to the current unit of work.

Display key vocabulary around the French room – label key features appropriately (for example, *'fenêtre'*, *'porte'* and so on). Make sure that key dates are prominent in the history room, key formulae in the maths room, and so on.

CHANSON – 'Mots de link' (Song – 'Linking Words')

Je me suis levé ce matin
    (I got up this morning)

Je suis tombé du lit
    (I fell out of bed)

En bref, j'ai mal aux jambes
    (In short my legs hurt)

Où est mon cahier de Français?
    Where is my French book?

J'ai besoin de 'mots de link'
    (I need my linking words)

Le Français me manque
    (I am missing French)

Aujourd'hui c'est un désastre
    (Today is a disaster)

C'est un blague
    (It is a joke)

C'est un grand désastre
    (It is one big disaster)

À mon avis
    (In my opinion)

Je n'ai pas de chance
    (I have no luck)

Quoi qu'on dise
    (Whatever you say)

C'est vachement vrai
    (It is really true)

Il pleut comme des cordes
    (It is raining hard)

De tout façons
    (In any case)

Je vais aller dans
    (I'm going to go in)

Dans le 'Sixth Form'
    (In the 'Sixth Form'

Ce sera un grand désastre
    (It will be a big disaster)

from Clayton Hughes, Denbigh School, Milton Keynes

This is a strategy that will benefit all students as attaching a rhythm to words is an effective memory aid. Students with a strong musical intelligence will particularly benefit as they are able to learn a language through their dominant intelligence.

Put the key words to music

Ever wondered why teenage students are able to repeat the words from popular songs with apparently little effort? Partly of course, it is because they want to and can see a personal relevance, but partly it is because they are once again engaging their whole brain in the learning process. (In simple terms, the left hemisphere processes the words, while the right hemisphere processes the rhythm.)

Capitalize upon this in the classroom by getting students to put the key words from any topic to a well-known tune. Different tunes will lend themselves to various subject content, 'Happy Birthday' and 'One man went to mow' being two of my personal favourites. Even if the finished product lacks some polish, the process of grappling with the key words, making sense of them, making connections between them and paying conscious attention to them will help develop understanding. By setting it as a homework task, we ensure that material is reviewed quickly after it has been encountered (see page 221).

Anything can be put to music: quadratic equations to the tune of... now, there's a thought! The same beneficial effect upon memory occurs when keywords are converted into a poem or song (see 'Jimmy the raindrop' on page 200).

Make your lessons dramatic and unusual

The brain best remembers things that are unusual, unexpected and dramatic. It will also remember anything that is exaggerated or absurd. For example, you would always remember an INSET day if the trainer appeared dressed in a pink rabbit suit! You would certainly not be expecting it and the impact that such an event would create would be very easy for you to remember.

The fact that people remember anything that is outstanding (known as the 'Von Restorff effect') can be exploited to our advantage in the classroom. Make a conscious effort to cover the key points of a lesson or unit of work in a way in which students would not be expecting. Share with your colleagues ideas on how particularly important facts or concepts can be delivered in a novel and unusual way so as to significantly increase the chances that they will be remembered.

Who can forget pulling the teacher's car in order to calculate force/weight ratio or throwing buckets of water against the window to simulate wave erosion?

Who can remember writing about it!?

Do something!

We remember very little of what we read and hear (some research suggests it is as low as 10 per cent), but significantly more of what we do.

Colin Rose in *Accelerated Learning* quotes extensive research demonstrating that: the more active the involvement in the learning process, the greater the recall and the deeper the learning. In one study, three groups were asked to learn new nouns. The first group simply read the words aloud, the second group were instructed to sort the words by the type of word, while the third group were required to form one sentence that contained all of the new words. Retention of the third group was a staggering 250 per cent better!

Chunk it!

A widely used rule of thumb, based upon the research of George Miller, is that the brain is limited to holding about seven pieces of information in the short-term memory at any given time.

Students are therefore more likely to remember information when it is broken down into small, easily digestible, 'chunks'.

What would you remember the most?

- being told about the working of the lungs
- writing about them
- seeing a diagram
- actually inflating a lung

Learning is done *by* people; it is not done *to* them. The more that students are required to do in the classroom, the more involved they are in their learning and the more they will remember. For example:

- *mime* a quadratic equation
- *role play* a conversation in French
- turn a diagram of a waterfall into a *model* (just using everyday classroom items – chairs, desks, bits of your uniform, bags, diaries, books and so on – don't forget to use yourselves!)
- summarize *Romeo and Juliet* into six key events. Represent each event as a *'frieze'*
- *re-enact* the trial of Charles I.

Teach something

The same research that suggests that so little of what we read and hear is remembered, also tells us that we remember around 90 per cent of what we teach. This should come as no surprise because in order to teach others, we first have to make personal sense of the topic to be taught and organize our own thoughts.

Involving learners in a teaching role will force students to organize and make sense of their own thoughts, develop understanding and significantly increase the probability of material being recalled.

A range of strategies that place the student in the role of the teacher can be found on page 203.

Chunk it

How do you eat an elephant?
A piece at a time!

It is often said that the largest number of pieces of information that the brain can cope with at any one time is seven (plus or minus two) and, although the original research in this area by George Miller was done with nonsense syllables (the brain will retain more information if there is a personal relevance), the general rule that the brain has a limited capacity to absorb the sort of information encountered in classrooms, holds true.

Information is therefore more likely to be remembered if it is broken down into more manageable chunks. For example, it would be more effective to break down a page of text into sections or paragraphs, pausing at the end of each section to reflect upon and make sense of the information, than it would be to study the whole page in its entirety.

Breaking the learning up into easily digestible pieces can also have a beneficial psychological effect and reduce the stress created by the perception of more information than can be handled. Too much information, or too many tasks presented simultaneously can overwhelm even the most gifted learner.

Structure the lesson to enhance memory

1 Break the lesson up into a series of short (20-minute) tasks. This is compatible with the average concentration span of the brain. It also creates a number of beginnings in the lesson, thus maximizing the 'primacy effect'. Do not be afraid to interrupt activities that take longer than 20 minutes – this will actually enhance recall.

2 Chunk information around these 20-minute slots into easily digested pieces.

3 At the end of each slot, make sure that information is reviewed. In this way review is woven throughout the lesson, in addition to having the major review at the end (see page 221).

4 Provide a five-minute break at regular intervals. As a general rule, try to avoid working for longer than 30 minutes without a break.

5 Allow students to stand and move around during the 'time-outs', to allow more oxygen to get to the brain. All students will benefit from this, but kinesthetic learners will particularly appreciate the opportunity to stretch and move around.

6 Review during and at the end of each lesson.

As adults and successful learners we tend to chunk quite naturally; indeed the ability to break down a complex problem or task into a series of logical steps is a sign of learner maturity. However, we should not lose sight of the fact that many of the students that we teach do not yet have the ability to chunk for themselves. It is therefore our responsibility to ensure that the information that students encounter is in small enough pieces for them to absorb and remember.

Provide the brain with 'down time'

The brain cannot take in new information continually (in a classroom environment) without a break. Many experts suggest that the average concentration span of the brain is equivalent to the person's chronological age plus one or two minutes. Taking a break from focused cognitive activity will actually improve memory because it provides the brain with a rest from new information and an opportunity to subconsciously process and sort the material that it has just encountered.

Memory is actually at its peak a few minutes after we stop learning. This effect, known as 'reminiscence', is believed to be the result of the memory traces in the brain strengthening. By taking frequent breaks during learning, we are simply increasing the number of reminiscence periods, thus enhancing memory. Breaks need not be long; five minutes away from the task is sufficient to prepare the brain to receive more new information, and should be taken every 30 minutes or so. Use the time to organize or tidy resources or as an opportunity for students to move around and get some oxygen to the brain (see 'time-outs' on page 43).

Lessons can be structured in such a way as to provide natural breaks between activities. Do not worry, however, if you have to interrupt a task in order to provide the brain with some down time; the 'Zeigarnik effect', named after the researcher of the same name, shows that interrupting a task can actually improve memory.

Picture it!

> *Visual images are remembered far better than words.*

Colin Rose

Help your students to create 'pictures' in their mind by encouraging them to visualize a scene or a story. This strategy is actually more than just visualization because it can, and should, involve all five senses. It will significantly enhance memory as vivid pictures in the mind will be far easier to recall than information in written form. In order to make the image as real, and therefore, as memorable as possible, encourage students to concentrate not only on what they see, but also what they hear, feel, smell and even taste.

The mind is a powerful and creative tool and does not know the difference between reality and fantasy. Prove it to yourself by allowing your mind to transport you to another time and place. Relax and shut your eyes. (You may need someone to read this out to you!) It is Christmas morning and you are a young child. Where are you? What can you see? Who is there with you? Concentrate on every little detail of the room you are in and the people that you are with. What can you *hear*? Laughter? Carols on the radio? Christmas morning television? The sound of wrapping paper being torn off presents? Shrieks of delight? Pick up a present. What does it *feel* like? Heavy? Soft?

National Parks

Relax. Play some gentle background music and clear your mind. You may find it easier to ask someone to read this to you so that you can close your eyes.

Create a picture in your mind. Concentrate upon every little detail and make the image as vivid as possible. Involve all of your senses. What do you see, hear, feel, smell and taste?

You are in the countryside walking across a sloping field. The field is bordered by dry stone walls and is full of sheep who grow ever more excited as you approach. You stand in the middle of the field and survey the scene; to your left there is a large forest of coniferous trees. It looks dark and uninviting and the regimented rows of trees remind you of soldiers on parade. To your right is a large lake and the gentle breeze is whipping the surface of the lake into small waves which lap gently against the shore. You think to yourself how refreshing it would be to sit on one of the big boulders at the edge of the lake and bathe your aching feet in the cool water.

You begin to walk towards the top of the field, climbing gently. As the hill begins to get steeper you begin to gasp for breath and are just about to stop when you become aware of a noise – like a humming – towards the top of the field. The noise grows louder and louder as you get nearer. It is now a deafening roar, so loud that you cannot hear yourself talk. As you walk over the brow of the hill you discover where the noise is coming from as a huge waterfall comes into view. You walk up to the waterfall - the noise which had been deafening is even louder now - and you can feel the spray from the water on your face as you slip along the rocks by the river. The water is crashing down on huge boulders and your attention is drawn to a peculiarly shaped boulder directly beneath the waterfall. As you peer through the spray you realise that it is not a boulder after all but as giant pot of honey with giant bees swarming around it, their buzzing being drowned by the crashing of the water. You lick you lips as you 'taste' the honey but hurry away, scared of the giant bees.

You quickly retreat down the hill, the noise from the waterfall fading away into the distance until it is no more than a quiet hum. You appreciate the quiet of the countryside, but not for long! The roar of the waterfall is quickly replaced by another, strangely familiar noise. As you run down the hill, the noise grows louder and you realize that what you can hear is the sound of traffic on the road at the bottom of the field. You look over the wall and survey the scene. There is a huge traffic jam; engines are overheating and drivers and passengers are looking tired, frustrated and bored. There is a procession of vehicles; a white car, a blue car, a red car, a white car, a blue car, a caravan, a white car, a blue car, a coach, a white car, a blue car, a tank. The tank driver, his head sticking out of the turret, is coughing and spluttering, engulfed in a black cloud of fumes from the car in front.

There is a family in the first car; Gerald is driving and Wendy is sitting in the passenger seat. Both are looking hot and bothered and you notice that Gerald, who is driving one handed with the window down, has cut his elbow; the dripping blood showing up clearly against the white door. In the back, the boys, Bill and Ben, are squabbling over the last bar of chocolate. Ben snatches the chocolate triumphantly from his brother, stuffs it into his mouth and throws the wrapper, without looking, out of the window.

Strategies for Closing the Learning Gap

Guess what it is. Were you right? *Smell* the smells of Christmas morning: turkey roasting in the oven, stuffing being prepared and sherry being poured. What can you *taste*? Can you taste your Christmas dinner? (If I am relaxed enough, I can always 'taste' the bacon wrapped around the cocktail sausages – my mouth is watering as I type!)

Pictures in the mind are easy to create and the fact that they seem so 'real' makes them very easy to recall. It is almost as if you have actually seen it! Almost anything can be turned into a mind picture and as students become more comfortable and competent working in this way they will be able to create pictures in the mind quite independently of the teacher. It is also possible for the teacher to guide a student or a whole class as they create an image. In this way the teacher can ensure that the detail and information that needs to be remembered is included in the picture.

Step-by-step guide to creating 'mind pictures'

- Get the students into the right state. Make sure they are relaxed and focused. It is often appropriate to play some gentle background music while doing this exercise (it will help recall if the same music is playing when the students are trying to re-create their images later on) and allow students, if they wish, to close their eyes.

- Describe the picture out loud and ask the students to create the scene in their own mind. As you are describing the general 'picture', encourage students to personalize it and add detail. Make your description as vivid and detailed as possible and encourage students to do the same. Continually remind students to focus upon every aspect of the scene; ask them *precisely* what they can see, hear and so on at every stage of the 'story'. Ask students to concentrate on where in the picture they see particular images (top left, bottom right and so on) and how big things are. Give objects a colour; give people a name and a personality. Constantly remind students that they need to 'look' and 'listen' very carefully while you are describing the 'picture'.

- Employ all of the memory strategies and principles that you can. Make the 'picture' absurd, exaggerated and unusual. Encourage students to do the same. Remember, the more ridiculous the better! (In the 'picture' opposite, for example, Laura saw a sheep driving the tank!)

- Some students may become totally immersed in their picture, as if they have entered a different world. Give them a few seconds warning before you finish talking and allow them a few seconds to readjust when they 'come back' to the classroom.

- In order to ensure that the picture is remembered, it is important to review it at key, strategic moments (see page 221). After you have described your picture, allow students an opportunity to describe their pictures to each other. This will help cement the memory. Build some review opportunities into the next ten minutes by asking them questions that will require them to recall their picture. For example, ask them what colour or how big something was. Encourage students to tell somebody – a parent, pet or poster – at the end of the day.

- Remember that all students will have different preferred learning styles and not all will find visualization easy. To help compensate for this, give students an opportunity to follow up the exercise 'in the mind' with something more tangible. Some students may wish to physically draw their picture, while some will be happy to simply describe their picture out loud. Kinesthetic learners may wish to move to the corresponding place in the room as they focus upon each piece of the picture in turn. Alternatively, they may wish to reproduce the components of their picture on post-it notes and physically arrange them into the completed image. All of these activities will help cement the memory.

National Parks (cont)

An old lady dressed in a pink overall with rollers in her hair stands at the end of her drive and surveys the scene. She is not at all happy; her frowning face, shaking head and the position of her hands on her hips indicate how cross she is. As you listen carefully, you can hear her sigh with exasperation.

Across the other side of the road, anorak man is setting out for a walk. He is dressed for walking in the hills; his trousers tucked untidily into his thick woolly socks and his big heavy boots clumping along the road. He is wearing a bright orange anorak which clashes sharply with his pink woolly bobble hat and a huge map case dangling around his neck sways violently as he marches briskly along. He tries to climb the dry stone wall but as he does so dislodges a stone that drops to the floor and lands with a loud plop in the mud on the other side. The noise alerts the farmer who is returning from a shooting trip. He is angry with anorak man and, brandishing his shotgun, bellows, 'be off with you, you little rascal!'

This 'picture' was first created with a group of Year 11 students who were studying National Parks in preparation for GCSE geography at Foundation level. The image is designed to trigger their memory and highlight some of the issues that they had identified as the key points of the module.

Key points included in the picture

- Land use in National Parks: farming (extensive sheep grazing), forestry, water, storage, HEP, tourism, military use.
- Beauty spots in National Parks are 'honey pots' and attract large numbers of tourists.
- Conflict in National Parks: volume of traffic which leads to congestion. This is exacerbated by narrow roads (this is how Gerald cut his elbow!) and by large vehicles such as caravans.
- There is often conflict in National Parks between hikers and farmers. The picture went on to describe how the countryside had been spoiled by footpath erosion etc.
- Military use of National Parks can cause conflict with locals, farmers and visitors.

The group then went on to create a second 'picture'. This image, of a later time, included all the measures that have been taken to manage the large number of visitors in National Parks.

For example: as anorak man climbs over a stile, he hits his head on the footpath sign that is designed to ensure that walkers are 'channelled' along identified routes in a bid to manage footpath erosion. As he climbs over the stile, the farmer smiles, waves and shouts, *'Good morning!'* He drops to the other side of the wall and the plop that was heard when the stone fell in the mud, is replaced by a thud as he lands on a hard core path – another measure designed to reduce footpath erosion.

Remember that the picture is in *your* mind and that, rather like a television set, you are in control of the settings. Try it now: you can alter the brightness of your picture; you can change the size of your picture; you can even turn it into black and white. Practise pushing the picture away from you and making it smaller and then gradually bringing it back. These different 'settings' are known as 'submodalities' in NLP (see below) and the more that you experiment with them, the more you realize just how powerful your mind is.

It is helpful to know precisely where in your mind you store your visual images so you can encourage your students to concentrate on where, in their minds, they actually see their picture. This will improve your memory, as it will be easier to recall your image if you are looking for it in the right place. It is relatively easy to check out where people store their pictures by asking them questions that require them to find a visual image in their memory (such as, *'What colour were your bedroom walls when you were a child?'* or *'What shape is North America'*) and watching where their eyes go. The majority of people will look upwards if they want to 'see' something in their mind and so it will be easier for most people to recall a picture if they are looking up.

Getting started

These strategies are very different from the normal classroom experiences of most students and teachers. Consequently they need some practice and it may take two or three attempts before you find them particularly effective. Try a few, such as the one on page 262, by yourself or with a friend before you try them in the classroom.

When you do feel comfortable enough to introduce them to students, consider carefully which group would be most likely to be receptive to the approach. It may be beneficial to start with a small group of students, possibly an out-of-hours revision group, rather than try the technique for the first time with a whole class. When you do start using the strategy with students, keep it short and simple and gradually build up to more elaborate visualizations when you feel more confident and the students are familiar with the approach.

Many of the visualization techniques suggested here have been influenced by the discipline known as Neuro-Linguistic Programming or NLP for short. Anyone who wishes to explore these strategies in more depth should refer to one of the many general NLP texts available from the Anglo American Book Company (see page 283).

Two texts that may be particularly useful are:

- *NLP for Lazy Learning* by Diana Beaver (Element Books, 1994)
- *In your Hands – NLP in ELT* by Jane Revell and Susan Norman (Saffire Press, 1997)

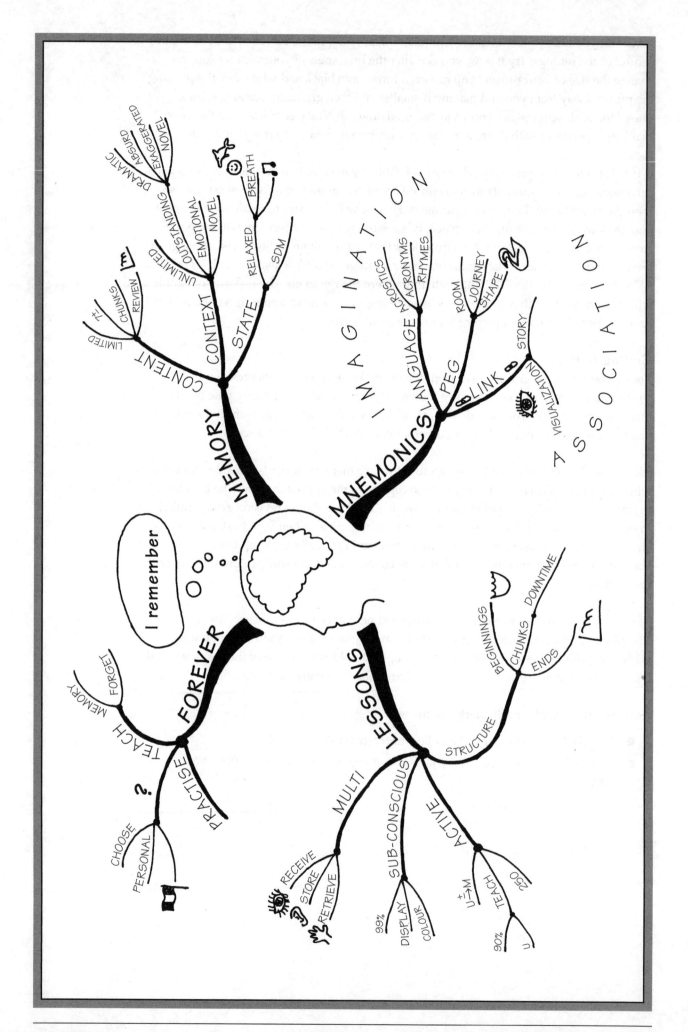

Strategies for Closing the Learning Gap

Use learning maps

Most people forget what they note because they use only a tiny fraction of the brain in the note-taking process.

Tony Buzan

Learning maps were invented and developed by Tony Buzan (who refers to them as Mind Maps) and are being increasingly used in schools. Described by Dominic O'Brien as *'a physical representation of information to be held in the memory'*, they use a combination of key words, colour and visual images to capture everything to be remembered about a particular topic, on a single sheet of paper.

They have a considerable advantage over traditional linear notes in that they are compatible with the way in which the brain thinks and operates. The brain operates through billions of tiny neurons (brain cells) connecting with each other via an electrical and chemical process. As the neurons communicate, complex neural networks are formed. These networks are based upon association and fan out or, to use Tony Buzan's word, radiate, from an initial stimulus. Learning maps mirror this process, providing the capacity to accommodate a complex network of associated ideas flowing from a central concept expressed as an image. Essentially, ideas are written down in the same way in which they are thought.

Learning maps offer some considerable benefits:

- They give the opportunity to see the Big Picture and the component parts simultaneously.
- They help the learner make sense and meaning out of something. Making meaning of something lies at the very heart of the learning process.
- All of the key words are on the same page – in linear notes they are often spread out over a number of pages.
- The links and associations between the component parts of the topic are clearly visible. (Association plays a key role in the memory.)
- They require active involvement in the process of making notes. Tony Buzan argues we are note-making as opposed to note-taking when we construct this kind of diagram. He claims that *'note-making means organizing your own thoughts, often in a creative, innovative way. Note-taking means summarizing someone else's thoughts.'*
- Learning maps are more than memory aids. The act of constructing a learning map requires the learner to arrange information and organize their thoughts. This helps develop understanding.
- Oliver Caviglioli and Ian Harris claim that learning maps actually reveal how the learner is learning by making thinking visible.
- Learning maps engage the whole brain. (Tony Buzan claims that traditional note-taking uses less than half of the capacity of the cerebral cortex). The use of colour and visual images ensures that more of the brain is involved in the learning process. (The left hemisphere will decode the words while the right hemisphere will process the pattern of the different colours: the hemispheres are connected and learning is enhanced.)
- Learning maps appeal to people with different learning styles. Kinesthetic learners are able to note down their initial thoughts on post-it notes and physically rearrange them before completing a neat version of their map.

Constructing a learning map

1   Write down all your thoughts in the form of keywords and phrases about a particular topic. Simply let your brain spill out on to the paper. (Some people find it helpful to do this exercise on post-it notes.)

2   Organise your thinking. Categorize your thoughts by association. This will leave you with groups of associated words. Think of these groups like chapters in a book. Give each group of words a keyword heading. This is the chapter heading. (For example, if you were thinking about *memory* you may have grouped acronym, acrostic, peg system and memory chain under the heading *mnemonics*.)

3   Use a large (preferably A3) sheet of blank paper for your map. Make sure that you have variety of coloured pens.

4   Start with an image in the centre of the page that crystallizes the topic that your are trying to study. Make frequent use of visual images as they are more easily remembered than words.

5   Draw a curved, coloured line from the central image upwards and to the right. (approximately 2 o'clock). This line is like a large bough in a tree. Write down your first key word - a chapter heading - in block capitals along the line.

6   Draw curved branches off the main bough using the same colour. On each branch write down a key word associated with the main chapter heading. Write these words slightly smaller than the main word. Remember that visual images can be substituted for keywords.

7   You can now subdivide again. Draw thinner lines off the branches (twigs if you like) to record any key idea that you associate with the trigger word on the branch. You can continue subdividing as many times as you wish, depending upon the amount of detail you want to include on your map. As you move further away from the centre, the ideas become less important (central) to the theme of the map. This is reflected by decreasing the size of the words and images as you move away from the centre.

8   Repeat this process with the other groups of words. Work your way around the page in a clockwise direction, using a different colour for each 'chapter.'

9   Although the active involvement and process of constructing your learning map will help you remember the information, it is important to review your creation at regular intervals, in order to maximize your recall (see page 223).

- The process of constructing a learning map will enhance memory. It is also easier to review a summary of all the information associated with a particular topic on one piece of paper than it is to reread pages of notes.

Practical application of learning maps

For the teacher:

- planning schemes and units of work
- giant learning maps hang on the wall to provide students with an overview of a module of work or a GCSE course
- department and school development plans can be constructed in the form of a learning map.

For the student:

- as a homework exercise
- as a note-making device
- as a summary of a unit of work
- as a revision tool.

Getting started

- Do not try to teach your students to create learning maps until you are comfortable and confident using them yourself. If you have never used the technique before, it may take you between ten and 20 attempts before you are using them naturally.
- Find out more about them. As they were invented by Tony Buzan it would make sense to read a book written by him. *The Mind Map Book* is an excellent place to start. *Mapwise* by Oliver Caviglioli and Ian Harris is another comprehensive text and well worth a read.
- Practise using them. Write out your next shopping list in map form. Or create a learning map about *memory* after you have finished reading this section!

Recommended further reading:

- *The Mind Map Book* by Tony Buzan (BBC Books, 2000)
- *Mapwise* by Oliver Caviglioli and Ian Harris (Network Educational Press, 1999)

Review

If information is not reviewed, it will be quickly forgotten. However, reviewing material, even for a few moments, can dramatically halt the natural process of forgetting and significantly boost memory and recall.

For a detailed explanation of how to review, see pages 223 to 227.

Summary - memory

- Memory plays a key role in learning.

- The more we practise using memory techniques and the more we use our memory, the better it gets.

- Teaching students simple mnemonics and encouraging them to use them as appropriate can dramatically improve recall.

- Teaching students basic relaxation techniques, and what to do when they forget, can enhance recall during examinations.

- We have a comprehensive understanding of what people find memorable. Information is more likely to be remembered if we consciously base our lessons around these principles.

- Asking students, 'How will you remember this forever?' is a simple but highly effective strategy for improving recall.

- Reviewing and remembering information is a whole-school issue that demands a whole-school approach.

How will you remember this forever?

It is often said that the simple strategies are the best and this one is no exception! Instead of asking students the answer to a particular question, ask them how they will remember it forever.

For example, a young girl recently asked me if she could go to the library as she didn't know what the French flag looked like and needed to know in order to complete her work.

At this point it is interesting to note that when I asked the girl (who claimed that she didn't know what colour the French flag was) what she did know about it, she was able to tell me that it was red, white and blue; that the strips were vertical and that white was in the middle! (page 79) It makes you wonder just how much students who claim that they don't know, actually do know! *'Well, tell me what you do know'*, may be an appropriate response to those claiming no knowledge. It is also important to note that there is no need to waste time and effort trying to remember something that is already understood.

I gave her permission to go to the library with the instruction to return and tell me how she would remember the colours of the French flag forever. She returned a few moments later with a smile on her face. *'Easy'*, she said, *'**B** comes before **R** in the alphabet. It's **Blue, White, Red**'*. Not only had the question, *'How will you remember this forever?'* forced her to pay *conscious attention* to the matter in hand, she had *personalized* the French flag and thereby significantly enhanced her chances of remembering it.

Is it Carri**bb**ean or Cari**bb**ean? The answer is Cari**bb**ean, but how will you remember the correct spelling forever? *'Easy'*, replied a boy in Year 7 (who had previously been introduced to a range of memory techniques). *'Picture the Caribbean Sir. What do you see? What do you hear? What do you taste? Do you see white sand, cloudless skies, palm trees, deep blue ocean? Do you hear the sound of calypso and the beat of a steel band? Do you taste coconut? Look closer. Can you see people on the beach? Can you see the beautiful **babes**?! There are beautiful **babes** in the Cari**bb**ean. That's how I will remember to spell Caribbean forever, Sir – and so will you!'*

It is a simple strategy and requires only a slight and subtle change in emphasis. However, it is incredibly effective and is particularly powerful when the students have previously been introduced to a range of memory strategies. Indeed, of all the strategies in this book, consistently asking the question, *'How will you remember this forever?'* is the one that will arguably bring the most noticeable gains.

The way forward

At the start of this book, you were encouraged to award yourself a mark out of ten for the quality of your teaching. Unless you do something differently, you will remain on this score tomorrow.

What are you going to do differently, in order to raise your score by one mark?

From tomorrow, I will...

1

2

3

4

5

How will you know when you've improved your score by one mark? What will you see, hear and feel that will indicate that an improvement has taken place?

The Way Forward

The fact that this sentiment is expressed so frequently, in no way invalidates it; in order to improve the quality of our teaching, we have to do something different. This is often easier said than done. People, never mind teachers, are often cautious of change, as change involves an element of risk – however small – and departure from the comfort zone.

It is no more possible to make teachers change their practice, than it is to make children learn. All that we can do is strive to create the conditions that make it more likely that people will want to, or least be prepared to, tread into unknown territory.

If the three keys to effective learning are:

- state
- style
- structure

then the four keys to improving the quality of learning are:

- specific
- support
- strategy
- steps.

Specific

This book is based upon the premise that the key to sustainable school improvement is improving the quality of learning in the classroom while simultaneously acknowledging that the majority of teachers are doing a good job with most of the students most of the time.

We are therefore seeking to make the relatively minor adjustments to our teaching that can have a dramatic impact upon the way in which students – at least some of them – learn. In short, we are looking to tweak and apply some polish rather than instigate a major overhaul.

This situation demands that any attempt to improve classroom practice is precise and highly specific. The general nature of an attempt to *improve teaching and learning,* will, almost inevitably, have limited impact. However, an initiative to *implement a greater range of strategies to appeal to Adam, Kieran and other underachieving kinesthetic learners by systematically writing these opportunities into schemes of work* will have a significantly greater chance of success.

Many schools devote INSET days to the broad theme of learning and improving the quality of learning in the classroom. Yet how many schools devote INSET sessions to *specific aspects* of learning such as memory strategies, lesson endings and beginnings, and positive and stress-free language patterns?

Shut your eyes. Picture a lesson that you normally teach – concentrate upon as many details as you can.
What are you doing? What are you saying? What are the students doing? What is Adam doing?

Now picture a lesson that you would like to teach. What are you doing? What are you saying? What are the students doing? What is Adam doing?

Write down as many differences as you can. Choose one. What could you do differently tomorrow to move closer to your ideal lesson?

However, the only way that new ideas will find their way into the classroom (no matter how entertaining and informing the INSET) is to devote sufficient time to particular and specific issues so that:

- they can be explored in depth
- there is time to identify the strategies, produce the necessary resources and write the agreed strategies into the appropriate schemes of work.

The chances of new ideas being consistently and universally adopted by teachers are greatly enhanced when:

1   Training and improvement projects are specific and tightly focused.

2   The appropriate *bits to tweak* – that is, the aspects of classroom practice that need to be modified in order to improve the quality of learning – have been accurately and precisely identified by a combination of self-reflection and external observation/monitoring.

3   There is a focus upon the *strategies* that teachers can employ in order to address the issue of concern. In other words, there is an emphasis not only upon which bits need tweaking, but also on *how* they can be tweaked.

4   Training time is matched by planning time. There is little point to providing teachers with high-quality training if nothing happens as a result because there is no time for them to produce the necessary resources and lesson plans. Take INSET days in pairs; one day for the training, with a follow-up day for the planning and preparation. Replace departmental meetings with departmental planning time.

5   You do not move on to a fresh initiative until strategies have become embedded in daily classroom practice. This could well mean that there is just one focus for improvement per academic year.

6   All of your training, monitoring, peer observation and planning time for this period is based around one specific issue

Support

Leaving the comfort zone to try something new carries, in the minds of many people, an element of doubt that the new technique will fail to work and they will end up losing control of the class. The prospect of being supported in the classroom by a senior colleague for the first few lessons can provide the reassurance necessary for teachers to stop thinking about trying something different and to actually do it.

Senior staff and Heads of Department – offer your support. Be proactive. Be specific. A general offer of support – *'I'm available anytime, just give me a shout'* is less likely to produce results than a specific, targeted offer, such as:

> *'I'm free next Tuesday when you are teaching top set Year 8. That would be an ideal opportunity for us to try out that strategy that we were discussing at last night's meeting. Do you want to plan it now, or shall we arrange to meet later?'*

Teachers, be proactive. Approach senior colleagues with specific requests for support. Ask in a way that makes it hard for them to say no!

> *'I'm planning to get my Year 10 set to role play the movement of molecules in solids, liquids and gases. I'd very much like you to come in and support me – that's OK isn't it?'*

The strategies in this book have proved to be effective in a wide range of schools. They even work in O.U.R. High School.

That's right, they'll even work with 'our kids'!

Trying something new, however carefully it is planned, involves an element of risk. Teachers have to be convinced that it is safe to take that risk and that they will not end up with rapped knuckles if things do not go as well as hoped. Teachers will make a judgement – consciously or subconsciously – about the extent to which it is safe for them to experiment with a new strategy and take a risk. It is a judgement that will have a significant bearing upon the likelihood of new approaches to teaching and learning being adopted in the classroom.

A key influence upon this judgement will be the ethos of the school and the subtle messages that emanate from middle managers and senior staff. Are development projects, experiments, action research (there are many labels):

a   frowned upon and discouraged

b   tolerated

c   actively encouraged and supported?

Unless the answer is **c**, it is highly unlikely that any lasting and substantial developments will take place.

Strategies

Placing the focus firmly upon strategies has two key benefits.

1   Teachers are becoming increasingly aware of *what* needs to be done – provide more opportunities for kinesthetic learners – and *why* a particular issue is significant – kinesthetic learners are often disadvantaged in schools by having fewer opportunities to work in their preferred style. What they are less sure about however, is *how* to address the issue. Identifying practical strategies that are grounded in research and will work in the classroom is a key challenge for the profession. Providing teachers with an extensive range of strategies through training or in the form of a school or departmental handbook makes it more likely that they will try them out. All schools have teachers who have come up with a great idea that works in the classroom – what a pity that there are so few opportunities to share this expertise!

2   Focusing upon strategies – particularly when they have been identified collaboratively – depersonalizes the issue and reduces the feeling of personal threat that often accompanies developments in this area.

> *'I'll come in and see if that **strategy** that **we** identified works as well as **we** had hoped.'*
> *'That **strategy** was brilliant.'*
> *'That **strategy** didn't seem to go as well as **we** hoped it would.'*

are very different messages to:

> *'I'll come in to see how well **you** teach.'*
> *'**You**/she/he were/was brilliant.'* (even a positive judgement on your teaching is a judgement – it carries the risk that next time it might not be so favourable!)
> *'**Your** lesson didn't go well.'*

The secret of getting ahead is getting started. The secret of getting started is breaking your complex overwhelming tasks into smaller manageable tasks, and then starting on the first one.

Mark Twain

Steps

Making progress gradually, through small steps, makes it *more likely* that that any developments you make will become embedded in your teaching. Walking, or even crawling, before you can run is excellent advice when developing your teaching repertoire.

- Identify the group that you enjoy the best relationship with. Try any new techniques with them before you use them with the rest of your classes.

- Introduce one strategy at a time. Become comfortable with it before you try something else.

- Go one step at a time. If you walk in tomorrow to the strains of Mozart and ask your bottom set Year 11 to imagine that they have a balloon in their stomach while rubbing their key acupressure points, three things are likely:

  1 Someone will say, *'Have you been on a course?'*

  2 The approaches will be so different from the usual experiences of the students, they will be highly unlikely to work.

  3 You will go away convinced that the strategies don't work and will unlikely to try them again.

As ever, the *first step* is highly significant. Consider the first thing that you will do differently in order to improve the quality of learning in your classroom. It is important to note that your first step will not necessarily involve doing anything in the classroom! Here are some suggested first steps:

1 Reflect on the questions posed on pages 112, 178 and 224.

2 Complete the exercise on page 272.

3 Write a list of useful phrases and stick it to your desk (see page 70).

4 Identify the students who are surly and unco-operative in your classroom. Make an effort to find out what they are good at/interested in and use it to your advantage in the classroom.

5 Install a self-esteem wall in the staffroom.

6 Do a VAK and/or multiple intelligences summary sheet for your next unit of work.

7 Keep a VAK tally chart (page 121) on your desk for the next fortnight.

8 Identify students who are underachieving in your lessons. Compare their preferred learning style with your usual teaching approach.

9 Write a list of all the strategies that you could use for kinesthetic learners and stick it to your desk.

10 Arrange to observe a lesson in a different curriculum area – for example observe a technology or PE lesson. Notice the behaviour/attitude/motivation of students that you normally have problems with.

11 Reflect on pages 190, 192, 216 and 224. Which part(s) of the lesson do you teach particularly well? Which parts of the lesson could you tweak?

12 Identify one strategy that you could implement to improve the beginning and end of your lesson.

13 Keep a piece of paper on your desk for a fortnight and record how much time you spend on phase two and phase three activities.

14 Write a list of all the strategies you could use in phase three. Do this collaboratively if possible. Stick it to your desk and include at least one in every lesson.

Once upon a time a young man decided that he wanted to be wise. His mother, pleased with her son's ambition, told him of a wise man who lived far away (on the other side of the Earth) by a large mountain. Confident that the wise man would be able to grant him the wisdom that he sought, the young man set out on a journey to find him.

Surprisingly quickly, and with very little trouble, the young man arrived at the foot of the mountain where he met an old man. Assuming him to be the wise man he sought, he asked the old man to share with him the secret of wisdom.

The man, surprisingly unhappy for one so wise, replied that the secret of wisdom was responding to every suggestion with the reply, 'You can't do that – that will never work'. The man went on to explain that everything had already been tried and had failed and that is why we do things the way we do.

Years passed and the young man grew increasingly troubled. He had found wisdom yet still he felt unhappy and dissatisfied. One night he had a dream and in the dream he learned that the old man he had listened to years before was not in fact a wise man at all. The real wise man lived at the top of the mountain.

Once more the young man set out on a journey to discover wisdom. When he arrived at the foot of the mountain he met the same man who he had met all those years ago. When he explained that he was climbing the mountain, the man tried to block his path. 'You can't go up there,' he said, 'It's too high.' The young man looked up. He was filled with doubt. It did look like a long way up. He was just about to turn around when a strange feeling of strength came over him. Ignoring the older man's pleas to abandon his futile trek, he began to climb the mountain.

It was a long hard climb. The winds raged and the rain lashed down. The path was steep and treacherous. Many times he felt like turning back, but each time a powerful inner voice persuaded him to continue. One by one the young man overcame the obstacles. The crevasses, the overhangs and the precipices conquered, he approached the summit.

Peering through the mist the young man spotted a hunched figure, sitting on a large boulder. It was a wrinkled old man with a grey beard. He instinctively knew that this was the real wise man. 'Tell me the secrets of wisdom,' said the young man when he finally reached the place where the old man was sitting.

The wise man smiled down at his younger friend knowing the sacrifices he had made to reach that place. 'There is no great secret to wisdom,' he said softly, 'wisdom is simply about saying, "Wow, that's an interesting idea – let me go away and think about it."'

IF YOU DO WHAT YOU'VE ALWAYS DONE, YOU'LL GET WHAT YOU ALWAYS GET.

Strategies for Closing the Learning Gap

Strategies for Closing the Learning Gap – Summary

- State, style and structure are the keys to effective learning.

- People learn best when they are in an appropriate physical and emotional state. Learning is optimized when the brain is nourished and students are relaxed, confident and motivated.

- Although we do not control the physical state of students, we do have an influence and must use every opportunity to make a positive impact, however small. We are more likely to be effective if we do so consciously, consistently and congruently.

- People learn best when they are given frequent opportunities to learn in their preferred style. The key to providing for students with different learning styles is variety and choice, but variety and choice do not just happen, they have to be planned for.

- Lessons should be structured to reflect the distinct phases of the learning process. Gaining a balance between input from the teacher and time for students to internally process information is crucial if learning is to be effective.

- Learning involves making personal sense of something. Learning activities must therefore be consciously designed to help students understand material and to enable the teacher to assess the extent of that understanding.

- There are no guarantees or magic wands. However, there are strategies that we can adopt in the classroom that will make it more likely that students will understand and be able to remember information that they encounter during a lesson.

- In order to improve the quality of learning that is taking place within our classroom, we have to do something different. We are not seeking dramatic changes; just a tweak here and there to develop and extend existing good practice.

Further Reading

By these authors

Closing the Learning Gap, Mike Hughes (Network Educational Press, 1999)
ISBN 1 85539 051 5
Lessons are for Learning, Mike Hughes (Network Educational Press, 1997)
ISBN 1 85539 038 8
Tweak to Transform, Mike Hughes with David Potter (Network Educational Press, 2002)
ISBN 185539 140 6
Confident Classroom Leadership, Peter Hook & Andy Vass (David Fulton, 2000)
ISBN 1 85346 686 7
Creating Winning Classrooms, Peter Hook & Andy Vass (David Fulton, 2000)
ISBN 1 85346 691 3

General

The New Learning Revolution, Gordon Dryden and Jeanette Vos (Network Educational Press, 2005) ISBN 1 85539 183 X
The Inner Game of Tennis, W. Timothy Gallwey (Pan, 1986)
ISBN 0 330 29513 6
The Learning Adventure, Eva Hoffman and Zdzistaw Bartkowicz (Learn to Learn, 1999)
ISBN 0 535387 0 2
SuperTeaching, Eric Jensen (Turning Point Publishing USA, 1994)
ISBN 0 9637832 0 3
Completing the Puzzle, Eric Jensen (The Brain Store Inc, 1996)
ISBN 0 9637832 5 4
Accelerated Learning, Colin Rose (Accelerated Learning Systems Ltd, 1985)
ISBN 0 905553 128
Accelerated Learning for the 21st Century, Colin Rose & Malcolm Nicholl (Dell Publishing, 1997) ISBN 0 440 50779 0
Superlearning 2000, Sheila Ostrander and Lynn Schroeder (Dell Publishing, 1996)
ISBN 0 440 50714 6
Accelerated Learning in Practice, Alistair Smith (Network Educational Press, 1998)
ISBN 1 85539 048 5
Accelerated Learning: A User's Guide, Alistair Smith (Network Educational Press, 2003)
ISBN 1 85539 150 3
Beyond Teaching and Learning, Win Wenger (Project Renaissance, 1992)
ISBN 981 00 400032
The Einstein Factor, Win Wenger & Richard Poe (Prima Publishing, 1994)
ISBN 0 7615 0186 x

Memory

Learn to Remember, Dominic O'Brien (Duncan Baird, 2000)
ISBN 1 900131 93 5
Use your Memory, Tony Buzan (BBC Books, new edition 2000)
ISBN 0 563 37102 1
The Great Memory Book, Karen Markowitz and Eric Jensen (The Brain Store, Inc, 1999)
ISBN 1 890460 04 4

Educational kinesiology (Brain Gym)

Brain Gym – Teacher's edition, Paul and Gail Dennison (Edu-Kinesthetics, Inc. 1989)
ISBN 0 942143 02 7
Edu-K for kids, Paul and Gail Dennison (Edu-Kinesthetics, Inc. 1987)
ISBN 0 942143 01 9
Smart Moves, Carla Hannaford (Great Ocean, 1997)
ISBN 0 915556 26
Making the Brain/Body Connection, Sharon Promislow (General Distributing, Canada, 1998)
ISBN 190 9681066 3

NLP

NLP for Lazy Learning, Diana Beaver (Element Books, 1994)
ISBN 1 86204 412 0
Introducing NLP, Joseph O'Connor & John Seymour (Mandala, 1990)
ISBN 1 85538 344 6
In Your Hands – NLP in ELT, Jane Revell & Susan Norman (Saffire Press, 1997)
ISBN 1 901564 00 2

Learning styles

The Dominance Factor, Carla Hannaford (Great Ocean, 1997)
ISBN 0 915556 31 6
Righting the Educational Conveyor Belt, Michael Grinder (Metamorphous Press, 1991)
ISBN 1 55552 036 7
The Power of Diversity, Barbara Prashnig (Network Educational Press, 2004)
ISBN 185539 118 X

Learning maps

The Mind Map Book, Tony and Barry Buzan (Revised edition, BBC Books, 2000)
ISBN 0 56353 732 9
MapWise, Oliver Caviglioli and Ian Harris (Network Educational Press, 2000)
ISBN 1 855 39 0590
Think it – Map it!, Ian Harris and Oliver Caviglioli (Network Educational Press, 2003)
ISBN 185539 139 2

Music in learning

Learn with the Classics, Ole Anderson, Marcy Marsh & Arthur Harvey (LIND Institute, 1999)
ISBN 1 883095 01 8
Tune your Brain, Elizabeth Miles (Berkley, 1997)
ISBN 0 425 16017 3 3

As a rule of thumb, any Baroque music is suitable as general background music. If you are just starting to use music in the classroom, it may be helpful to use CDs that have been specifically produced for this purpose. These can be obtained from:

Mark McKergow Associates, 26 Christchurch Road, Cheltenham, GL50 2PL (Tel: 01242 511441)

Useful contacts

Network Educational Press, PO Box 635, Stafford, ST16 1BF (Tel: 01785 225515)
(for any book published or course provided by NEP) www.networkpress.co.uk

Anglo American Book Company, Crown Buildings, Bancyfelin, Camarthen, SA33 5ND
(Tel: 01267 211880) *(for books on accelerated learning, NLP etc)*

Educational Kinesiology (UK) Foundation, 12 Golders Rise, Hendon, London NW4 2HR
(Tel. 0208 202 9747)

Society for Effective Affective Learning (SEAL), PO Box 2246, Bath BA1 2YR

Association for Neuro-Linguistic Programming, PO Box 78, Stourbridge, West Mids.
DY8 2YT

INDEX

Network Educational Press – much more than publishing...

NEP Conferences – Invigorate your teaching

Each term NEP runs a wide range of conferences on cutting edge issues in teaching and learning at venues around the UK. The emphasis is always highly practical. Regular presenters include some of our top-selling authors such as Sue Palmer, Mike Hughes and Steve Bowkett. Dates and venues for our current programme of conferences can be found on our website www.networkpress.co.uk.

NEP online Learning Style Analysis – Find out how your students prefer to learn

Discovering what makes your students tick is the key to personalizing learning. NEP's Learning Style Analysis is a 50-question online evaluation that can give an immediate and thorough learning profile for every student in your class. It reveals how, when and where they learn best, whether they are right brain or left brain dominant, analytic or holistic, whether they are strongly auditory, visual, kinesthetic or tactile ... and a great deal more. And for teachers who'd like to take the next step, LSA enables you to create a whole-class profile for precision lesson planning.

Developed by The Creative Learning Company in New Zealand and based on the work of Learning Styles expert Barbara Prashnig, this powerful tool allows you to analyse your own and your students' learning preferences in a more detailed way than any other product we have ever seen. To find out more about Learning Style Analysis or to order profiles visit www.networkpress.co.uk/lsa.

Also available: *Teaching Style Analysis* and *Working Style Analysis.*

NEP's Critical Skills Programme – Teach your students skills for lifelong learning

The Critical Skills Programme puts pupils at the heart of learning, by providing the skills required to be successful in school and life. Classrooms are developed into effective learning environments, where pupils work collaboratively and feel safe enough to take 'learning risks'. Pupils have more ownership of their learning across the whole curriculum and are encouraged to develop not only subject knowledge but the fundamental skills of:

- problem solving
- creative thinking
- decision making
- communication
- management
- organization

- leadership
- self-direction
- quality working
- collaboration
- enterprise
- community involvement

"The Critical Skills Programme... energizes students to think in an enterprising way. CSP gets students to think for themselves, solve problems in teams, think outside the box, to work in a structured manner. CSP is the ideal way to forge an enterprising student culture."

Rick Lee, Deputy Director, Barrow Community Learning Partnership

To find out more about CSP training visit the Critical Skills Programme website at www.criticalskills.co.uk